Local Heroes

*

Local Heroes

THE POLITICAL ECONOMY OF
RUSSIAN REGIONAL GOVERNANCE

*

KATHRYN STONER-WEISS

PRINCETON UNVERSITY PRESS

PRINCETON, NEW JERSEY

Library of Congress Cataloging-in-Publication Data
Stoner-Weiss, Kathryn, 1965–
Local heroes : the political economy of Russian regional
governance / Kathryn Stoner-Weiss.
p.   cm.
Includes bibliographical references and index.
ISBN 0-691-01195-8 (cl : alk. paper)
1. Local government—Russia (Federation)   2. Representative
government and representation—Russia (Federation)   3. Regional
planning—Russia (Federation)   4. Russia (Federation)—Economic
policy—1991–   I. Title.
JS6117.3.A3S76   1997
351.47—dc21   97-7355   CIP

This book has been composed in Sabon

Princeton University Press books are
printed on acid-free paper, and meet the guidelines
for permanence and durability of the Committee
on Production Guidelines for Book Longevity
of the Council on Library Resources

Printed in the United States of America by
Princeton Academic Press

1   3   5   7   9   10   8   6   4   2

To Eric

*

✷ Contents ✷

∗ List of Tables and Figures ∗

TABLES

FIGURES

* Preface *

THIS BOOK is a study of a key aspect of one of the great dramas of modern times—the reconstitution of the Russian polity and economy after more than seventy years of communist rule. As Russia endured the early phases of its transition to democracy and a market economy, newly democratic regional governments within the renewed Russian Federation faced fresh challenges and responsibilities. Capitalizing on a natural experiment, I hold institutional design constant in an effort to explain why some of the new democratic institutions in the Russian provinces weathered the monumental changes of the early 1990s better than others.

Drawing on the comparative politics literature on institutional performance, I develop a performance index that reveals significant variation among four sample regional governments. The remainder of the study is devoted to explaining variations in institutional performance—or why "local heroes" (higher-performing regional governments) existed in some places but not others. Using newly available economic, sociological, and political data, I probe the comparative politics literature on democratization for plausible explanations of performance variations. However, the best explanation for the variance in the performance of the new Russian representative institutions challenges those theories that rely on political culture, social structure, or wealth.

The theory here blends aspects of the political economy literature of the late 1970s and early 1980s on corporatist democracies with the newer comparative and international political economy literature. My empirical findings indicate that the legacy of the former economic system influenced the operation of new political institutions in important and often unexpected ways. I argue that in transitional situations the formation of coalitions between economic and political elites can have a positive effect on governmental performance. Past institutional structures, specifically the concentration of the regional economy (in terms of sector, labor, assets, and productive output), promoted the formation of political and economic coalitions within a new proto-democratic institutional framework. In sum, the more concentrated the regional economy, the higher was regional government performance.

These findings, however, will be somewhat troubling to students of democratic and market transitions. Although in the short term cooperation between key political and economic figures may promote stability within a transitional framework, in the longer term too much collaboration among a small set of actors may endanger the further growth of political pluralism. This collusive activity may also jeopardize the growth of market relations as regional governments may choose to artificially support and protect inefficient enterprises that market forces might otherwise force into bankruptcy.

A primary lesson of my argument, then, is that democracy's short-term development might be quite different from what sustains it in the longer term. The "local heroes" of today must therefore take care not to become the nemeses of the further growth of democracy and the market in the future.

Throughout this project I have had the good fortune to have been challenged and encouraged by many friends and colleagues. While I cannot begin to repay their kindness, I want to acknowledge their assistance.

I had the excellent fortune to be a graduate student in the Department of Government at Harvard University where this project began as a Ph.D. dissertation. Many thanks go to my teachers there and especially to my dissertation committee. I am particularly grateful to my supervisor and friend, Timothy Colton, for his ceaseless support and encouragement from my earliest interest in Russia as an undergraduate at the University of Toronto, through the completion of the dissertation phase of this project under his careful guidance at Harvard. He has also volunteered to read successive drafts of the manuscript as it moved toward final publication. Special thanks also go to Robert Putnam for taking such an interest in my work, giving so generously of his time, and for pressing me from start to finish to think like a political scientist. I hope that this book in some way reflects his commitment to outstanding scholarship. Celeste Wallander patiently coached my field work as well as critically read successive drafts of this project. Finally, although not officially a member of my dissertation committee, Peter Hall took time to read several draft chapters and made valuable suggestions for improvement.

Next, this project benefited immeasurably from the kind assistance and encouragement of Jeffrey Hahn, Jerry Hough, and Blair Ruble, who, with Timothy Colton, were the sources of my initial interest in the Russian provinces. Conversations I have had with Blair Ruble while I revised the manuscript also proved invaluable. Thanks also go to my many colleagues and friends in Russia, but most of all to the late Georgii Barabashev, Aleksandr Gasperishvili, Sergei Markov, Nikolai Petrov, Sergei Tumanov, Sergei Vaskov, and Vsevolod Vasil'ev. Countless government officials in the Russian provinces gave willingly of their time; although there are too many to mention individually, I want to acknowledge especially the unceasing efforts of Evgenii Gorkov, Evgenii Krestianinov, Dimitri Kibirskii, Vladimir Oseichuk, and Tatiana Rumiantseva. Todd Weinberg and Katherine Moore provided friendship and sometimes a place to stay in Moscow.

Back in the United States many friends and colleagues, including Josephine Andrews, Beth Mitchnek, Nicolai Petro, Peter Rutland, Randall Stone, Steven Solnick, John F. Young, and Kimberly Zisk cheerfully read drafts of this manuscript. I am indebted to them for their many thoughtful comments, criticisms, and suggestions for improvement. Thanks also go to David Laitin for reading a draft of chapter 2 and making many useful suggestions for revision at a Wilder House seminar at the University of Chicago. Extremely helpful comments were also provided by Philip Roeder and an anonymous reviewer.

I am also grateful to my colleagues at Princeton—particularly Kathleen McNamara, Atul Kohli, Sheri Berman, and Jeffrey Herbst for their careful and critical readings of the manuscript and for the many helpful conversations we have had about this project. Thanks also go to Stephen Kotkin for his wonderful sense of humor and his encouragement to give this project more than I thought I had to give. Michael Wachtel generously checked all the Russian transliterations. Thanks also go to Malcolm Litchfield of Princeton University Press for believing in this project and moving it smoothly through the review process and into publication.

Without the constant encouragement and support of my husband, Eric Weiss, this book might never have come to fruition. The final product would have suffered greatly had it not been for his critical eye, sharp wit, and seemingly endless patience. Finally, a special thank you to Samson Weiss who slept beneath my desk for a good part of this project. He provided me with welcome company during the many otherwise lonely hours that I spent at my computer.

The Woodrow Wilson School of Public and International Affairs and Princeton's Center of International Studies provided both summer support and an excellent environment in which to complete this book. Support for this study at the dissertation stage was provided by the Andrew Mellon Foundation, Harvard University's Davis Center for Russian Research, and the Social Sciences and Humanities Research Council of Canada. This book was also prepared in part under a grant from the Kennan Institute for Advanced Russian Studies of the Woodrow Wilson International Center for Scholars, Washington, D.C. The statements and views expressed herein are those of the author and not necessarily those of the Woodrow Wilson Center.

Alas, while I have been greatly assisted by friends, colleagues, and various institutions along the way, I alone am responsible for any mistakes and misunderstandings in what follows.

∗ *Note on Transliteration* ∗

THROUGHOUT this volume I use the Library of Congress system of Russian transliteration. Some words, however, appear in their commonly accepted English language spellings rather than what the transliteration system would otherwise require (thus Yeltsin rather than El'tsin and Yaroslavl' rather than Iaroslavl'). Unless otherwise indicated, the Russian translations are my own.

Local Heroes

*

Introduction

THIS STUDY addresses one of the most enduring problems of comparative politics: What are the necessary conditions for the creation of effective and responsive representative government? With the sudden rush to recast polities in the former Soviet Union and Eastern Europe in the shape of liberal democracies, the issue of good government—an ancient theme of political philosophy—has gained new relevance. The collapse of the communist systems and their command administrations necessitated the creation of new public and economic institutions in both the center and the periphery. This rapid regime change provides social scientists with the still relatively rare opportunity to observe the birth of political institutions and to reexamine the effect of formal institutional change on political behavior.

The political and economic reform effort in the former Soviet Union, and Russia in particular, has been carried out according to the seemingly reasonable premise that changing institutions—or merely transplanting democratic and market institutions—will bring about (more or less) corresponding changes in political and economic practice. My argument demonstrates that although, to a certain degree, this premise is correct, reality is always much more complicated. The performance of new political institutions anywhere depends on the ground in which these institutions are planted. The message here, then, is simple: context matters. The more interesting questions, however, are how, why, and what aspects of context are most important?

In contrast to studies of institutional performance that have been conducted in established democracies, as for example Robert Putnam's recent study of Italian regional government, this study focuses on a country in political, economic, and social turmoil.[1] Where the democracies of Western Europe benefited from the social, political, and economic effects of the Renaissance, the Industrial Revolution, and the Enlightenment, Russia remained largely insulated from these crucial historical turning points. Russian representative government institutions were constructed

---

[1] Robert D. Putnam, with Robert Leonardi and Raffaella Nanetti, *Making Democracy Work: Civic Traditions in Modern Italy* (Princeton, N.J.: Princeton University Press, 1993).

in the virtual absence of any democratic tradition. Whereas the key to "making democracy work" in Putnam's high-performance Italian regional governments was the presence of a civic community, Russia is a country recovering from more than seventy years of near-totalitarian rule and centuries of autocratic rule before that. As a result, Russian civil society is still stunted. Further, where other studies of democracy have noted the importance of markets to the quality of democratic governance, Russia in the 1990s was in the midst of constructing markets concurrently with the building of proto-democratic institutions—a dual transition, doubly difficult.

In the face of the challenges presented by Russia's transition, I draw on the first experiment ever with representative government in the Russian provinces. In using transitional Russia as a case study, therefore, this book aims to further our understanding of institutional performance and, to a lesser degree, institutional development. Despite the rapidity and scope of Russia's attempt to build democratic institutions from scratch, the factors that influence the performance of these new institutions should be of interest beyond the post-Soviet world. In short, what makes democracy work in provincial Russia should have implications for the building and functioning of representative government anywhere.

TRANSITIONAL RUSSIA

The post-Soviet world in the 1990s is in the throes of a massive economic and political transition. It is therefore fertile ground indeed for studies of institutional design and development. The first freely contested elections to national and regional legislatures took place in Russia in March 1990. In the Russian provinces, representative governments replaced the local Communist Party organs that Jerry Hough once called "a textbook example of the classic prefect in a modern setting."[2] Whereas regional Communist Party leaders, as the effective heads of local government, had at most "a modest impact on policy,"[3] after the 1990 elections the con-

---

[2] Jerry Hough, *The Soviet Prefects: The Local Party Organs in Industrial Decision-Making* (Cambridge, Mass.: Harvard University Press, 1969), p. 303.

[3] Howard Biddulph, "Local Interest Articulation at CPSU Congresses," *World Politics* 36, no. 1 (1983): 48.

tinued entropy of the Russian state forced the new Russian regional governments to take on fresh responsibilities and to face new challenges.[4]

In the face of the dramatic political, economic, and social changes in the early 1990s, however, many new governments in the Russian provinces appeared to be capable of little more than reacting to crisis after crisis. Others, though, were actually able to pursue policy objectives systematically and obtained higher degrees of constituent satisfaction for their efforts. When similar stimuli lead to different outcomes, the task of the social scientist is to understand why.[5] This study is therefore concerned with explaining why some regional governments were seemingly better able to cope in the immediate aftermath of the volatile postcommunist environment.

This project examines a crucial phase in Russia's political development— what I will refer to as the First Republic.[6] I consider the First Russian Republic to have existed from March 1990, with the multicandidate, competitive elections (at the national and local levels), until October 1993, when President Boris Yeltsin disbanded the Russian parliament and dissolved the local soviets. The Second Russian Republic began with the acceptance of the new constitution in December 1993 and the election of the reformed Russian parliament. Elections to smaller regional soviets, generally called dumas, began in December 1993 in Moscow and continued in the provinces throughout 1994.

The First Republic is a critical stage in Russia's political development because it was Russia's first real experience with representative government at the national and provincial levels. Further, in this brief time span, the elected local soviets grew from subservience to central authorities

---

[4] See, for example, Natalia Gorodetskaia, "Irkutsk Refuses to Pay Taxes into the Federal Budget," *Nezavisimaia gazeta*, May 22, 1992, p. 2; "Siberians Push for Economic Autonomy," *Current Digest of the Post-Soviet Press* 14, no. 13 (1992); and interview with R. Abdulatipov, Chairman of the Council of Nationalities of the Supreme Soviet of Russia, "Kuda nesiesh'sia Rus'?" *Pravda*, February 19, 1992, p. 1.

[5] Peter Gourevitch makes a similar point in "International Trade, Domestic Coalitions, and Liberty: Comparative Responses to the Crisis of 1873–1896," *Journal of Interdisciplinary History* 8, no. 2 (1977): 281.

[6] Several other authors have similarly conceptualized Russia's political development as akin to the evolution of the French Republics. Robert Sharlet, for example, provides a slightly different temporal classification of the Republics in "Russian Constitutional Crisis: Law and Politics under Yeltsin," *Post-Soviet Affairs* 9, no. 4 (October–December 1993): 314–336.

into increasingly powerful forces in Russian politics such that Yeltsin was sufficiently threatened by their growing authority to demand their dissolution and reelection. Finally, the patterns of institutional behavior established by these initial democratic experiments have set the course of future political and economic performance in the Russian provinces.

One cannot understate the importance of studying these first elected regional governments. Writing about pre-Revolutionary Russia, Frederick Starr noted, "The attitudes and institutions that define local government constitute a unique index to the mind and structure of the state as a whole."[7] This is no less true in the post-Soviet era. From 1990, power continued to devolve out to Russia's provinces. The collapse of the powerful Soviet central ministries, and the passing of various pieces of enabling legislation, greatly increased the sphere of regional government activity from what it was under the old command administration system. Moreover, as a variety of Russian publications have pointed out, "the weakening of presidential and executive structures [at the center] did not mean that power flowed to the Russian legislature, but to the heads of the republics, oblasts, and krais."[8] As any Russian citizen knows, but Western scholars are only just discovering, "Moscow isn't Russia." If reform is ever to take a firm hold, it must catch on in the heartland.

Although the first regional government elections took place in Russia in March 1990, we still know very little about what regional governments actually did and even less about why some did (and continue to do) "better" than others. Aside from short policy studies in a single oblast, like Blair Ruble's recent examination of housing policy in Yaroslavl',[9] other studies of the regional governments have mostly examined who won the 1990 (and to a lesser extent the 1993–94) provincial elections.[10] Many of these analyses relied primarily on information regard-

---

[7] S. Frederick Starr, *Decentralization and Self-Government in Russia, 1830–1870* (Princeton, N.J.: Princeton University Press, 1972), p. x.

[8] *Novoe vremia*, no. 12 (March 1992): 12.

[9] Blair A. Ruble, *Money Sings: The Changing Politics of Urban Space in Post-Soviet Yaroslavl'*, (Washington, D.C.: Cambridge University Press and Woodrow Wilson Center Press, 1995).

[10] See especially Jeffrey W. Hahn, "Local Politics and Political Power in Russia: The Case of Yaroslavl'," *Soviet Economy* 7, no. 4 (1991): 322–341; Gavin Helf and Jeffrey W. Hahn, "Old Dogs and New Tricks: Party Elites in the Russian Regional Elections of 1990," *Slavic Review* 51, no. 3 (Fall 1992): 511–530; Timothy Colton, "The Politics of Democratization: The Moscow Election of 1990," *Soviet Economy* 6, no. 4 (October–December 1990): 285–344; Mary McAuley "Politics, Economics, and Elite Realignment in Russia: A Regional Perspective," *Soviet Economy* 8, no. 1 (January–March 1992): 46–88. More in-

ing the new legislators' attitudes and individual personal and professional backgrounds in order to arrive at a classification of the political complexions of regional soviets. From this, scholars attempted to infer the *likely* behavior of these governments—either pro-reform or anti-reform, "liberal" or "conservative."

Although this work is important, it is only a beginning. Simply examining the backgrounds and views of regional legislators can lead to flawed explanations and predictions of who actually governed the Russian provinces. This is not only because of the significant changes in the structure of regional governments from 1990 (including the 1991 presidential appointment of heads of executives) but also because political complexion derived from the adage "where you sit determines where you stand" does not always provide an accurate guide to what governments actually do. Indeed, a great deal of evidence from other contexts indicates that performance is not necessarily determined entirely by partisanship or political complexion.[11]

This study therefore advances Western scholarship on post-Soviet Russia to the next and more important question regarding *what* actions the newly elected oblast governments actually took. It asks: Given that all oblast soviets and administrations had essentially the same capabilities on paper, what accounts for rather significant differences in their performance? Why were some regional governments more capable than others of making sense out of the chaos that prevailed in the wake of the Soviet Union's immediate collapse? In short, the study asks not only who governed these provinces in the first few years of representative political institutions, but also who governed them *well* and *why*.

This book is a testament to the diversity of provincial Russia. It is a journey through the Russian hinterland and offers a glimpse into the lives of people undergoing tumultuous change and into the institutions that govern them. Although this study does not travel to all eighty-nine terri-

---

depth analyses, but still limited to one or two regions, include Joel C. Moses, "Saratov and Volgograd, 1990–1992: A Tale of Two Russian Provinces"; and John F. Young, "Institutions, Elites, and Local Politics in Russia: The Case of Omsk," both in Jeffrey W. Hahn and Theodore Friedgut, eds., *Local Power and Post-Soviet Politics* (Armonk, N.Y.: M. E. Sharpe, 1994), pp. 96–137 and 138–161, respectively.

[11] Putnam, *Making Democracy Work*, p. 142; see also Robert D. Putnam, Robert Leonardi, Raffaella Nanetti, and Franco Pavoncello, "Explaining Institutional Success: The Case of Italian Regional Government," *American Political Science Review* 77 (March 1983): 72.

torial units of the Russian Federation, it stops in four provinces (or *oblasti*—generally referred to as *oblasts* in English) that are representative of "types" of Russian territories. The four regions are Nizhnii Novgorod, Tiumen', Yaroslavl', and Saratov. These four oblasts vary historically, geographically, economically, and politically. Although the performance of the new government institutions also varied considerably, regional government structures were identical.

Drawing from the comparative politics literature on institutional performance, the study employs a total of twelve indicators to compare the policy processes, policy output and implementation, and responsiveness to its constituents of each oblast government. These indicators form an aggregate performance index which demonstrates that some regional governments were clearly more responsive and effective than others.

EVALUATING INSTITUTIONAL PERFORMANCE

Chapter 4 provides more detail regarding specific performance measures and comparisons between regions, but a few words should be said here about evaluating the performance of political institutions. First, the enterprise is not particularly new. Plato and Aristotle were among the first to consider the advantages and capabilities of particular kinds of political institutions and political systems.[12] Much later, Alexis de Toqueville described and evaluated American political institutions and tried to explain their relative advantages over those of the Europe of his day.[13]

Second, whereas these early analysts of institutional behavior focused on the legitimacy of certain political institutions, one may conceptualize institutional performance in several other ways. The first is a concern with institutional design: Why are some institutional frameworks more capable of achieving certain tasks than others? Juan Linz, for example, has devoted considerable time and energy to outlining the relative advantages of parliamentary systems over presidential systems from the point of view of political stability.[14] Second, a considerable literature is concerned with proportional representation electoral systems versus single

[12] Aristotle, *The Politics*, ed. and trans. Edward Barker (New York: Oxford University Press, 1981); and Plato, *The Republic*, trans. G.M.A. Grube (Indianapolis: Hackett, 1974).

[13] Alexis de Toqueville, *Democracy in America*, vols. 1–2 (New York: Shocken, 1961).

[14] Juan Linz, "The Perils of Presidentialism," *Journal of Democracy* 1 (Winter 1990): 108–126.

mandate systems with respect to stable electoral outcomes.[15] Along these lines, R. Kent Weaver and Bert Rockman compare political systems (parliamentary versus separation of powers systems and variations within these system types) to discover what sorts of institutions are most advantageous for achieving policy-making effectiveness.[16]

This study of Russian regional government employs an alternative approach such that institutional capability—or efficacy—is measured as institutional design is held constant. By controlling for institutional design, while allowing institutional context to vary, the analyst can better examine the effects of context on differences in institutional capabilities.

Examining institutional capabilities is particularly appropriate in the 1990s. We are living in a decade where citizens everywhere appear increasingly disillusioned with government. North Americans, Europeans, and Russians want more government output, including more schools and higher standards of living, while handing over fewer resources to the state. Constituents want representative political actors to *act* rather than simply sit in national, state, and provincial capitals wrangling endlessly over policy decisions and accomplishing little.

The focus on relative government efficacy is also particularly appropriate for the post-Soviet context. Indeed, the aim of the reconstitution of the political and economic systems in Russia was to succeed where the old system had failed—that is, to increase the effectiveness of the distribution of goods and services, and to pass public policy directed at improving the lives of average people. But how do we know when a government is performing well?

As both Robert Putnam and Harry Eckstein have demonstrated, governments can be shown to be "good" positivistically.[17] Eckstein notes the following, however:

---

[15] See, for example, Arend Lijphart and Bernard Grofman, "Choosing an Electoral System," in Arend Lijphart and Bernard Grofman, eds., *Choosing an Electoral System: Issues and Alternatives* (New York: Praeger, 1984), pp. 3–12.

[16] R. Kent Weaver and Bert A. Rockman, "Assessing the Effects of Institutions," in R. Kent Weaver and Bert A. Rockman, eds., *Do Institutions Matter? Government Capabilities in the United States and Abroad* (Washington, D.C.: Brookings Institution, 1993), pp. 1–41.

[17] Harry Eckstein, "The Evaluation of Political Performance: Problems and Dimensions," *Sage Professional Papers in Comparative Politics* 2, no. 1-17 (1971); Putnam, *Making Democracy Work*, p. 6. See also Ted Robert Gurr and M. McClelland, "Political Performance: A Twelve Nation Study," *Sage Professional Papers in Comparative Politics* 2, no. 1-18 (1971).

A polity that performs well is not necessarily a good polity. That obviously depends on how one regards the goals a polity pursues and its structures and processes. Evaluation which does not simply take goals as found has an important place in positivist political study, but normative judgment remains distinct from it—except in these senses: polities can hardly be more than abstractly good unless they perform well and bad polities are only made more objectionable by efficient performance.[18]

With this in mind, this study considers a "good" democratic political institution to be one that is *responsive* to the demands placed on it and *effective* in making and implementing decisions. Responsiveness is the ability to provide solutions to demands. As Eckstein explains, "Efficacy denotes the extent to which polities make and carry out prompt and relevant decisions in response to political challenges. The greater is efficacy, the higher is performance."[19] Moreover, efficacy is "what regimes do and how intrinsically well they do it."[20]

Following Eckstein, "in any given case, over any given period, efficacy might be very economically measured by concentrating on a few of the more severe sets of pressures—as few or as many as resources permit."[21] Chapter 4 puts these comparative theoretical concerns into operation and produces a performance ranking such that Nizhnii Novgorod ranks highest followed by Tiumen', whereas Yaroslavl' and Saratov perform comparatively poorly.

Why the "local heroes"—higher-performance governments—existed is the other primary concern of this book. Other studies of democratization and variations in institutional performance have relied primarily on socioeconomic or cultural explanations.[22] This study explores, but ultimately dismisses, these explanations. The well-governed oblast was neither more economically developed nor were its citizens more civic-minded or "democratically" inclined. Residents of higher-performance

[18] Eckstein, "The Evaluation of Political Performance," p. 80.

[19] Ibid., p. 65.

[20] Ibid.

[21] Ibid., p. 72.

[22] See, for example, Robert A. Dahl, *Polyarchy: Participation and Opposition* (New Haven, Conn.: Yale University Press, 1971); Seymour Martin Lipset, *Political Man: The Social Bases of Politics* (New York: Doubleday, 1950; reprinted 1963); Gabriel A. Almond and Sidney Verba, *The Civic Culture: Political Attitudes and Democracy in Five Nations* (Princeton, N.J.: Princeton University Press, 1963); and Putnam, *Making Democracy Work*.

oblasts were not even necessarily more likely to participate in political life.

Instead, this study employs the tools of "modern" political economy to determine how, given the massive political and economic changes under way in Russia, key economic interests interacted with regional governments. Jeffry Frieden argues that modern political economy, as a direct descendant of the classical political economy approaches of Adam Smith, John Stuart Mill, and Karl Marx, is enhanced by recent developments in social science. Frieden explains that "modern political economy, simply put, studies how rational self-interested actors combine within or outside existing institutional settings to affect social outcomes." Modern political economy has four components that constitute a relatively clear mode of analysis: (1) defining the actors and their goals; (2) specifying actors' political preferences; (3) determining how (and whether) actors group themselves; and (4) following actors' interactions with other social institutions.[23]

This study identifies regional economic actors—enterprise directors—as key interests in the post-socialist context. The collapse of the Soviet system and the resulting economic and political chaos created opportunities and posed difficulties for regional economic actors. This study demonstrates that not all economic interests had the same concerns; it argues that in regions where labor, assets, and productive output were concentrated in a particular sector, or among a few large enterprises, competition between economic actors for access to political resources was reduced. Economic concentration therefore enabled political and economic actors to overcome two collective action dilemmas: (1) the formation of economic interest groups; and (2) cooperation between these key economic interests and regional governments for the benefit of both.[24] Economic concentration also promoted interdependency between economic and political actors such that commitments were rendered more credible.

Cooperation between economic and political actors fostered higher levels of institutional performance by enabling the state to employ the authority of key groups of economic actors in return for granting them systematic access to state resources. The result, at least in the short term,

[23] Jeffry Frieden, *Debt, Development, and Democracy: Modern Political Economy and Latin America, 1965–1985* (Princeton, N.J.: Princeton University Press, 1991), p. 16.

[24] Mancur Olson, *The Logic of Collective Action: Public Goods and the Theory of Groups* (Cambridge, Mass.: Harvard University Press, 1965; reprinted 1971).

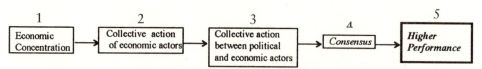

Figure 1.1. The Political Economy of Higher Regional Government Performance

was relative stability in an otherwise stormy political environment, and accompanying higher performance (see Figure 1.1).

Reduced to its simplest terms, this study argues that the concentration of the regional economy predisposed regional political and economic interests to cooperative arrangements. At the core of this cooperation was the institutionalization of regular negotiations between state and nonstate actors. This incorporation of economic interests into the political process established mutually agreeable boundaries and rules for the resolution of conflicts over political goals. The stability and consensus stemming from cooperative arrangements promoted higher levels of regional government performance.

Significantly, the findings here indicate that not all good things necessarily go together. Although regions with concentrated economies may have achieved more in the early stage of the transition to a market economy and democracy, in the longer term, and in the absence of mediating factors, strong coalitions between political and economic elites may ultimately have a negative effect on the relative performance of government in these regions. Over time, government responsiveness to emergent social interests may be sacrificed in favor of maintaining business and government cooperation.

METHOD OF INVESTIGATION

In differentiating between higher- and lower-performance governments, this project becomes the first major comparative study of the new Russian regional institutions.[25] The study itself begins in the spring of 1990 with the election of local soviets and ends with the demise of the First Russian Republic in the fall of 1993, although the reader will find occasional references to events taking place as late as 1996.

---

[25] The foremost study of local government under Communist Party rule was Hough, *The Soviet Prefects*.

Oblast-level governments were the logical subjects of this analysis because (at the time this research was conducted) they were home to more than 80 percent of the population of the Russian Federation, they had virtually the same potential power on paper, and, unlike the twenty-one republics of the Federation, oblasts were (and still are) predominantly ethnically Russian. Further, republic-level governments had different institutional designs and more powers than oblasts had within the Russian federal system. In not considering republic-level cases, therefore, this study purposely holds constant nationality factors and institutional design.

The four cases were selected such that they differed along economic, political, and geographical lines. Political performance, as a subset of political development, is often explained according to the relative wealth of polities and their apparent political complexions (partisanship). As a result, these oblasts represent different economic sectors (defense-oriented, agriculturally oriented, a mix of light and heavy industry, and rich in natural resources). They also vary according to the makeup of the soviets elected in 1990 (using the indicators shown in Table 1.2); their reaction to the August 1991 attempted coup (either for or against it); and their historical relationships with the central government in Moscow during the communist era as demonstrated by variation in central investment levels in the oblast. Finally, this sample of oblasts represents a certain amount of geographical diversity—Nizhnii Novgorod oblast lies in the heart of European Russia, Tiumen' lies over the Ural Mountains in Siberia, Yaroslavl' is located in the northern section of European Russia, and Saratov is in the south. A brief history and description of each of the four regions follows. Table 1.1 summarizes the most important characteristics of each region.

Nizhnii Novgorod Oblast

The center of Nizhnii Novgorod oblast lies 253 miles southeast of Moscow. The capital city of the oblast—also called Nizhnii Novgorod—is at the confluence of two great Russian rivers—the Volga and the Oka. The city was originally founded in the thirteenth century as a fortress defending Muscovy from the Mongol Horde. According to the 1989 Soviet census, the population of the province was about 3.7 million, and the city had approximately 1.5 million inhabitants. Residents often abbreviate the full name of the province to "Nizhnii."

At the time of this investigation, the oblast economy was largely industrial, although it had a modest agricultural sector. Approximately 23 percent of the oblast population lived in agricultural settlements. Oblast heavy industry was dominated by large defense factories making, among other things, nuclear-powered submarines, airplanes, and tanks. So strong was the military bent of the oblast's industrial sector that the area was completely closed to foreigners until the fall of 1991. There were also a variety of consumer goods factories and factories that had a dual defense/consumer production line, including GAZ (Gor'kovskii Avtomobil'nii Zavod), the largest automobile plant in Europe.

In 1934 Nizhnii Novgorod krai was renamed Gor'kii oblast after the socialist writer Maxim Gor'kii who was born in the region. In August 1990 (at the second session of the oblast soviet), as part of a growing regional self-consciousness, the original name was restored.[26] The capital city is still known for several features, not the least of which is that it was the home of the renowned human rights activist and dissident, Andrei Sakharov, during his forced exile from 1980 to 1986. (His former apartment is now a popular tourist attraction.) During the communist era, the oblast and city were training grounds for Communist Party leaders. Such big names in Soviet history as Kaganovich, Molotov, Mikoian, Zhdanov, Ignatov, and Katushev began their climbs to the upper echelons of Soviet power as local leaders in Nizhnii Novgorod oblast.[27]

Like Yaroslavl' to the north, the oblast was home to a small ecological movement opposing the construction of a nuclear power station in the late 1980s. However, whereas Yaroslavl' and many other provinces were relative hotbeds of liberal reform activity in 1988–89, Nizhnii Novgorod was not. In June 1991 more than 60 percent of the oblast's population voted for Boris Yeltsin as president, but in August 1991 the then chairman of the oblast soviet and the head of the *oblispolkom* (the executive arm of government) supported the putschists. As a result, many of the coup supporters were forced to resign in the fall of 1991. Following the August coup attempt, several personnel changes were made in Nizhnii Novgorod, including the appointment of the youngest governor in Russia, Boris E. Nemtsov, then thirty-three years old.

---

[26] Vladimir Ershov, *Ia vizhu tsel': Zapiski deputata* (GIPP Nizhpoligraf: Nizhnii Novgorod, 1992), p. 24.

[27] Ibid., p. 4. Interestingly, this tradition continues in the post-Soviet era. Governor Nemtsov was appointed first deputy prime minister of Russia in the spring of 1997.

Tiumen' Oblast

Tiumen' is the largest oblast in Russia, spanning 2,296 square miles—twice the size of Texas. Indeed, the distance between the southern and northern tips of the oblast is greater than that between the oblast's capital city and Moscow. The three other cases in this study are all located west of the Urals, but Tiumen' is situated farther east in Siberia. The capital city of Tiumen' was established initially as a city of the Golden Horde and was taken over by Russia in the late sixteenth century. Situated on the muddy banks of the Tura River, Tiumen' was reputed to be the first Russian city in Siberia.[28]

Compared to neighboring Sverdlovsk and Omsk, Tiumen's development was rather slow. In 1918 the location of the provincial administration was transferred from the city of Tobol'sk to Tiumen'. Although the territorial delineations of the new Soviet state shifted through the 1930s and 1940s, much of the present Tiumen' oblast was officially located within Omsk oblast. In August 1944 the current oblast borders were created.[29] The oblast continues to be home to two autonomous okrugs (ethnically based territories)—Khanty-Mansi and Yamal-Nenets—although the population of the oblast as a whole in 1989 was still about 75 percent Russian.[30] The city's population in 1989 was approximately 600,000, and the oblast population was about 3.1 million.

Until the discovery of oil and gas in the oblast in the 1950s and early 1960s, Tiumen was perhaps best known as the place that sheltered Lenin's body from 1941 to 1945 when it was evacuated from Moscow for safekeeping during the Nazi invasion of the Soviet Union. For most of the last thirty to forty years, however, Tiumen's name has been synonymous with oil and gas. In 1953 the first major gas discovery was made there, and the oblast experienced its "third birth."[31] Geological institutes were established in the city of Tiumen', and their researchers began hunting for more gas and for oil. In 1959 to 1960 the first significant oil discoveries were made in the north of the oblast. Tiumen' is currently by far the largest oil and gas producer in Russia. Most of the oil

[28] D. I. Kopiilov, V. Y. Kniazev, V. F. Retunskii, *Goroda nashego kraia: Tiumen'* (Sverdlovsk: Sredne-ural'skoe knizhnoe izdatel'stvo, 1986), p. 1.

[29] Ibid., p. 6.

[30] *The First Book of Demographics for the Republics of the Former Soviet Union: 1951–1990* (Shady Side, Md.: New World Demographics, 1992), p. D-5.

[31] Kopiilov et al., *Goroda nashego kraia*, p. 234.

and gas reserves are in the north of this huge oblast, and at the time this investigation was completed some light industry and agriculture had developed in the south. The city of Tiumen' continues to house the infrastructure for the province's oil and gas industry.

In 1991, 56 percent of Tiumen's voters supported Yeltsin's presidency. The oblast leadership stood by Yeltsin during the attempted coup in August 1991. The first head of the oblast administration (governor), Iurii Shafranik, was appointed the oil and gas minister of Russia in January 1993 (and remained in that position until August 1996 when a new national cabinet was appointed following Yeltsin's reelection as president). Tiumen's oblast soviet had the most progressive potential of the four cases.

Yaroslavl' Oblast

The capital of Yaroslavl' oblast (the city of Yaroslavl') is located in north/central European Russia, 157 miles northeast of Moscow. A traveler can easily take the train from Moscow to Yaroslavl' in the morning and be back in Moscow the same evening. It is the smallest region in this study, with approximately 1.5 million people in 1989, and covers approximately the same territory as the states of Connecticut and Massachusetts combined. The city that gives the oblast its name had a population of about 650,000 according to the 1989 census and is located on the northerly section of the Volga River. Yaroslavl', founded in the eleventh century before the establishment of Muscovy, is the oldest of the four provinces in this study.

Before the industrialization drive of the 1930s, the oblast economy was largely agricultural—devoted to flax cultivation and dairy products. More recently, the oblast economy has been devoted to a mix of light and heavy industry and the production of consumer goods. In the years covered by this study, the oblast had a relatively small agricultural sector; about 19 percent of the population lived in agricultural settlements, whereas 96 percent of the oblast's economic output at the time of this study was industrial.[32]

In the late 1980s and early 1990s Yaroslavl' was generally considered to lie in the center politically. Gavin Helf and Jeffrey Hahn note that Yaroslavl' was actually among the first cities in central Russia to cultivate

---

[32] Iurii Shumakhanov, deputy of the Yaroslavl' oblast soviet, in an interview with the author, April 1993. Chapters 4 and 5 contain more detailed information regarding the economic profiles of each of the four oblasts.

a rather active popular front movement in 1988.[33] It also was home to an active ecological movement, "Green Twig" (*Zelenaia vetka*), formed in opposition to the construction of a nuclear plant in the oblast. In the 1991 presidential elections, the oblast voted 54 percent in favor of Yeltsin. Further, oblast leaders supported Boris Yeltsin during the attempted conservative coup in August 1991.

Saratov Oblast

The capital of Saratov oblast is approximately 452 miles almost due south of Moscow. The oblast's northern border meets the fertile Black Earth zone of European Russia, and it shares a southern border with the republic of Kazakhstan. Saratov's capital was founded as a fortress defending the southern borders of Russia in the sixteenth century, somewhat later than either Nizhnii Novgorod or Yaroslavl'.[34] It is at the crossroads of historical trade routes connecting central Russia to the Urals and to Central Asia in the South (the Silk Road). Saratov oblast is cut into two roughly equal halves by the Volga River, and the city of Saratov sits on the western bank.

The oblast had a population of approximately 2.7 million in 1989, a third of which lived in the capital. Although the region's economy at the time of this investigation was industrial and the oblast was home to a few large defense factories (it was also off limits to foreigners until early 1992), Saratov's agricultural sector was considerably stronger than those of the other three oblasts in this study. Saratov has long been famous for its high-quality wheat, the basis of its agricultural sector. It was also a producer of consumer goods and had a relatively small oil industry. Thus, at the time of this study, Saratov's economy was far more diverse than those of Nizhnii Novgorod, Tiumen', or Yaroslavl'.

More than 55 percent of Saratov's residents voted in support of Yeltsin's presidency in 1991, although, like Nizhnii Novgorod in particular, the oblast leadership supported the putschists in August 1991. On the whole, Western observers generally considered the oblast soviet to be rather conservative.[35]

---

[33] Helf and Hahn, "Old Dogs and New Tricks," p. 515.

[34] For additional historical background on Saratov, see Donald J. Raleigh, *Revolution on the Volga: 1917 in Saratov* (Ithaca, N.Y.: Cornell University Press, 1986).

[35] Jeffrey W. Hahn, "Counter-Reformation in the Provinces: How Monolithic?" (paper prepared for the Annual Meeting of the American Association for the Advancement of Slavic Studies, Phoenix Arizona, November 19–22, 1992).

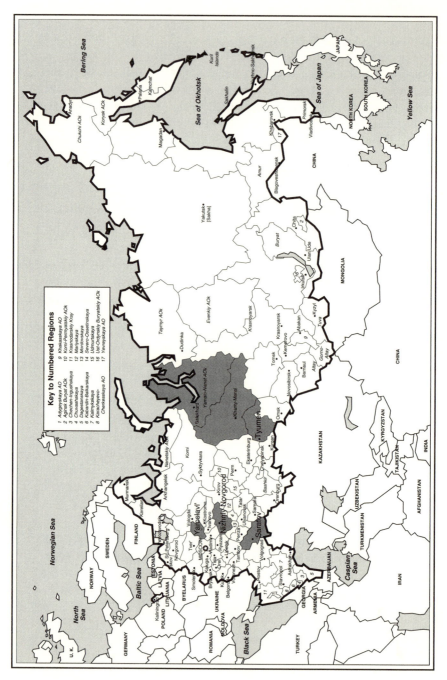

Figure 1.2. Map of the Russian Federation Highlighting the Four Regions under Analysis

Key to Numbered Regions

1 Adygeyskaya AO
2 Aginsk Buryat AOk
3 Chechen–Ingushskaya
4 Chuvashskaya
5 Dagestanskaya
6 Kabardin–Balkarskaya
7 Kalmykskaya
8 Karacheyevo–
   Cherkesskaya AO
9 Khakasskaya AO
10 Komi–Permyatskiy AOk
11 Krasnodarskiy Kray
12 Mariyskaya
13 Mordovskaya
14 Severo–Osetinskaya
15 Udmurtskaya
16 Ust–Ordynskiy Buryatskiy AOk
17 Yevreyskaya AO

Figure 1.2 locates each of the four oblasts geographically in the Russian Federation. Some salient characteristics of the four oblasts are summarized in Table 1.1.

PRELIMINARY POLITICAL COMPARISONS
BETWEEN THE FOUR OBLASTS

Residents of Nizhnii Novgorod, Tiumen', Yaroslavl', and Saratov oblasts elected somewhat similar regional soviets in the spring 1990 elections (Table 1.2). In all four cases, a high percentage of the first ever popularly elected deputies were members or candidate members of the Communist Party of the Soviet Union (CPSU). Indeed, in Nizhnii Novgorod, the oblast soviet mandate commission reported that the number of deputies from the CPSU that were elected to the soviet in 1990 was 30 percent higher than in the previous soviet where deputies were not popularly elected.[36] Given that Party membership is sometimes associated with conservatism or backwardness, the fact that the incumbency rate in Nizhnii Novgorod was so high is significant especially in light of the fact that Nizhnii Novgorod was the highest scorer on most measures of performance. The policy process in Nizhnii Novgorod reached a degree of professionalism not present in the other oblasts under consideration; the regional government created mechanisms for implementing its policy outputs; and it consistently provided the most innovative solutions to the various policy challenges all the oblasts faced. Not surprisingly, therefore, the regional government in Nizhnii Novgorod earned the highest degree of constituent satisfaction of these four oblasts.

On the face of things, however, Nizhnii Novgorod, in comparison with other oblasts in 1990, looked like it might be voted "the oblast least likely to succeed." The traditional measures that Western scholars use, in the absence of strong political party affiliations, to classify and describe political complexion in Russia appear in Table 1.2. Of the four oblast soviets, Nizhnii Novgorod's appeared to be slightly more dominated by Communists and apparatchiki. According to these parameters, the Nizhnii Novgorod oblast soviet ranked no lower than first or second along all but one of these traditional measures of "conservativeness." Of the four oblasts, the Nizhnii Novgorod oblast soviet had the second highest rate of incumbency (that is, deputies that sat in the previously non-

---

[36] See *Gor'kovskaia pravda*, March 20, 1990.

TABLE 1.1
Characteristics of Four Oblasts in 1990

	Nizhnii Novgorod	Tiumen'	Yaroslavl'	Saratov
Population of Oblast (millions)	3.7	3.1	1.4	2.7
% Urban Population	77	76	81	74
% Rural Population	23	24	19	26
Distance and Direction of Capital from Moscow[a]	253 miles east	1,066 miles east	157 miles northeast	452 miles south
Supported Attempted Coup	Yes	No	No	Yes
Political Complexion in 1990 (according to measures in Table 1.2)	Traditional	Progressive	Progressive	Traditional
Central Capital Investment per Capita, 1981–85 (millions of rubles)[b]	2,487	20,659	3,012	3,158
Central Capital Investment per Capita, 1986–89 (millions of rubles)	2,557	21,801	2,855	2,966
Relative Concentration of Economy (labor, economic sector, and industrial assets and output)[c]	Highly concentrated	Concentrated	Dispersed	Highly dispersed

Source: Demographic information is from Narodnoe khoziaistvo RSFSR 1989 (Goskomstat).
[a]The First Book of Demographics, p. A-3.
[b]All investment data were collected in Moscow and have been kindly provided by Professor Ronald Leibowitz, Department of Geography, Middlebury College. Units are the average value of the ruble from 1981 through 1985 and from 1986 through 1989.
[c]See Table 6.1.

TABLE 1.2
Backgrounds of Deputies in Oblast Soviets, 1990

	Nizhnii Novgorod	Tiumen'	Yaroslavl'	Saratov
Average Age of Deputies	46	41	47	48
Rate of Incumbency (%)[a]	16.1	6.1	11.9	19.8
CPSU Membership (%)	88.0	78.0	81.9	84.5
Industrial Managers (%)	29.0	12.0	33.7	23.0
Employed in Agricultural Sector (%)[b]	7.0	3.9	4.2	4.3
Higher Schooling (%)	88.7	83.0	89.7	76.6
Formerly Worked in Soviet or in Party Organs[c]	18.0	21.8	15.0	24.0

Source: Information comes from a combination of sources. These include local newspapers (Yaroslavl'—*Zolotoe kol'tso*; Nizhnii Novgorod—*Gor'kovskaia pravda*; Saratov—*Kommunist*; and Tiumen'—*Tiumenskaia pravda*) that published reports of oblast soviet mandate commissions during their first sessions in April and May 1990. Further, the protocol departments in each of the oblast soviets themselves provided the author with lists of deputies by profession. Deputy professions not listed here include primarily doctors, teachers, journalists, blue-collar workers, and jurists.

[a]Deputies previously sitting in non-popularly elected soviets.

[b]Includes sovkhoz and kolkhoz directors.

[c]Includes deputies who listed themselves as first party secretaries of county, raion, city, oblast, or autonomous okrug committees as well as those listed as full-time employees in other local party organs or local soviet organs.

democratically elected soviet)—only slightly lower than that of Saratov but higher than that of Yaroslavl' and Tiumen'; the highest percentage of deputies claiming CPSU membership; the second highest percentage of deputies who were enterprise managers; the highest percentage of deputies employed in the agricultural sector; and a high percentage of deputies who were previously employed in either the apparatus of the CPSU or the previous generation of non-democratically elected soviets—the "apparatchiki." Although Saratov distinguished itself by having a higher number of apparatchiki and a significantly lower number of deputies with higher education, on balance, of the four cases, Nizhnii Novgorod appeared to have the slightly more traditional deputy corps.

In contrast, Tiumen' appeared to have a more potentially progressive oblast soviet. It had the youngest deputy corps, a strikingly low rate of incumbency, comparatively few industrial managers who were deputies, and even fewer deputies who worked in the agricultural sector. Although potential explanations of performance differences are systematically tested later in this study, the contrasts between the apparent political complexions of the Tiumen' and Nizhnii Novgorod oblast soviets suggest initially that these measures are rather unreliable indicators of how effective and responsive oblast governments were likely to be. For despite the "conservative" surface complexion of the Nizhnii Novgorod oblast legislature and the "liberal" complexion of Tiumen's, a comparative analysis of regional government performance in all four oblasts demonstrates that Nizhnii Novgorod consistently ranked higher than Tiumen' oblast. Tiumen's performance was consistently better than Yaroslavl's, and Saratov was a consistent laggard.

In part, differences in performance between regions after the August coup of 1991 may have been a result of personnel changes in some places. In Nizhnii Novgorod and Saratov oblasts, for example, where legislative leaders of the oblasts more or less supported the August 1991 putsch, new individuals were elected as chairmen of the oblast soviets and heads of the *ispolkomy* (executive committees) until new heads of administrations (executives), or *glava administratsii*, were appointed everywhere. Although this undoubtedly had an impact on policy output after the fall of 1991, the composition of the oblast soviets remained the same as in 1990 and legislation on the local level still had to be approved by those same deputies originally elected in 1990.

Further, in Nizhnii Novgorod oblast, evidence suggests that some policy outputs of the pre-putsch oblast government were not all that "backward" despite the fact that the previous chairman of the oblast soviet was also the obkom first Party secretary. The previous leadership had, for example, already begun to reconstruct the oblast's economic potential, including reviving the once famous Nizhnii Novgorod Iarmarka (Fair) (housing trade shows displaying products from Nizhnii Novgorod and throughout Russia), and in May 1991 Nizhnii Novgorod was among the first few regions to establish a privatization committee. Thus apparent political complexion alone is at best an inconclusive indicator of government performance.

Chapter 5 extensively reviews other theories that are similarly incapable of explaining performance differences. These include both socio-economic, cultural, and social-structural hypotheses. Capitalizing on the variation between cases, I probe hypotheses regarding the possible effects on performance of differences in wealth, variations in relationships with the central government in Moscow, levels of social conflict, and attitudes toward democracy and the market. Significantly, whereas in Robert Putnam's Italy, social context mattered most in accounting for variations in regional government performance, in post-Soviet Russia, where there was virtually no civil society nor a tradition of civicness and where a simultaneous change in economic institutions was (and is still) under way, social context did not yet appear to matter much. Instead, in the Russian case, performance was most influenced by the residue of former economic institutions which affected relationships between key economic and political actors in new political institutions.

METHODOLOGY AND PLAN OF THE STUDY

This study benefited greatly from both improved access to information in post-Soviet Russia as well as recently available access to provincial cities long closed to foreigners. I am thus able to employ a wide variety of social science research tools—both quantitative and interpretive. Regional government officials were, in general, quite willing to be interviewed and provided policy information, budgets, and statistical materials in each oblast. I was also able to use survey data on oblast deputies,[37] as well as executing my own survey of approximately eight hundred to one thousand residents in each of the four oblasts.[38] Where

[37] Professor Jeffrey Hahn, Villanova University, kindly made data available on the Yaroslavl' and Saratov legislatures.

[38] The questionnaire for this survey was written jointly by the author and Professor Josephine Andrews, University of California, Davis. The survey itself was conducted with the assistance of the Moscow State University Opinion Research Center under the able management of Dr. Sergei Tumanov and Dr. Aleksandr Gasperishvili. Professor Donna Bahry, Department of Political Science, Vanderbilt University; Professor Robert Putnam, Department of Government, Harvard University; and Professor Ellen Mickiewicz, Duke University, provided helpful advice in compiling the questionnaire. Professor James Alt, Department of Government, Harvard University, advised on sampling techniques. The survey covers 3,774 respondents: 1,002 in Yaroslavl' oblast, 998 in Nizhnii Novgorod oblast,

possible, I employ material from other oblasts for a broader national perspective. These harder social science measures were supplemented by immersion in the local ambiance of each case ("soaking and poking") through extended trips to each oblast.

The book is organized as follows. Chapter 2 presents a theory of why some of the new Russian provincial governments were local heroes (high performers) while others were not. Chapter 3 provides a description of the politics of regional government structural reform. The chapter examines the gradual increase in regional autonomy in the late 1980s and early 1990s and the effect that institutional change had on the behavior of provincial politicians. In reviewing the relevant legislation and describing the structure of oblast institutions, this section demonstrates how power and influence were redistributed in comparison with the Soviet period.

Chapter 4 demonstrates that although the new political institutions may have been structurally identical and similarly reformed (as shown in chapter 3), what the four regional governments in this study were able to accomplish varied considerably. To demonstrate this, chapter 4 provides a comparative framework for measuring and comparing relative oblast government performance. Through an analysis of oblast decision-making processes, policy output and implementation, as well as responsiveness, we ask the following questions: Which cases had the smoothest policy processes? Which governments had the most coherent and effective solutions to policy dilemmas faced by all four regions? Which governments were most responsive? This chapter demonstrates that clear and significant differences existed in the level of regional government performance. Through twelve indicators, a clear performance ranking emerges among these four oblasts, with Nizhnii Novgorod oblast at the top, Tiumen' and Yaroslavl' following, and Saratov consistently ranking lowest. These performance differences become the dependent variable to be explained in the second half of the study.

Chapters 5 and 6 test hypotheses that might explain variations in performance. Using newly available primary source materials, chapter 5 tests some of the dominant hypotheses of the comparative politics literature. These hypotheses include the possible effect of variations in levels of economic modernity and wealth; the influence of variations in levels of social conflict; and the possible effect of cultural and social-structural variables on regional government performance. This chapter also evalu-

---

1,000 in Saratov oblast, and 774 in Tiumen' oblast. Because of rough terrain, we were forced to draw a smaller sample in Tiumen' oblast than in the other three cases.

ates what influence previous center-periphery relationships might have had on post-Soviet oblast political performance. These hypotheses, however, do not provide a convincing and coherent explanation of the regional government performance variations documented in chapter 4.

As a result, chapter 6 presents a fresh approach to explaining differences in political performance and empirically tests the theory presented in chapter 2. Chapter 6 demonstrates that in regions where economies were concentrated, as in Nizhnii Novgorod and Tiumen', cooperative relations were established between organized economic interests and political actors. The embeddedness of social interactions in regions that resembled "company towns" focused regional interests and heightened the interdependence of economic and political actors as the destabilizing transitions to the market and democracy transpired. The concentration of the regional economy also narrowed the pool from which political elites were drawn such that horizontal (preexisting) professional networks further helped to sustain credible commitments and collective action between political and economic actors.

The cooperation that arose from the concentration of the regional economy was such that the state included economic interests in the policy process, and economic interests gained material advantages from the state. In return, economic interests helped guarantee broad consensus on key issues and used their resources to promote government efficacy and legitimacy within civil society. These convergent interests therefore sustained consensus and higher government performance—at least in the short term.

Chapter 7 discusses the normative implications of the argument initially presented in chapter 2 and illustrated empirically in chapter 6. These include the obvious concern that high degrees of elite consensus and collective action could as easily lead to oligarchy as to higher regional government performance. Responsiveness to emergent groups could decrease as elite relationships freeze.

This, however, does not necessarily have to be the case. The incorporation of nonstate interests into state decision making promoted stability and encouraged consensus on political goals. In the context of volatile post-Soviet Russia, the stability that cooperative arrangements between business and government brought allowed governments to get things done. A record of achievement under the auspices of representative institutions may in fact build support for representative government rather than lead inevitably to authoritarianism and oligarchy.

Nonetheless, chapter 7 notes that the results here are more than a little unsettling. Although the concentration of the regional economy created elite relationships that enabled the new regional governments to accomplish goals in the short term, in the longer term these relationships may have a negative effect on the growth of a market economy and democracy in Russia. In some cases it may encourage support for what are often gigantic and inefficient enterprises rather than allow the market to determine which enterprises are fit to survive.

Mitigating factors do exist, however, that may enable some regions to overcome this problem. One of the lessons of this study for regions with dispersed economies is that the way in which demands on their government resources are packaged may enable them to accomplish more. In the long term, they may want to encourage the development of organized interest groups that might help to give rise to an environment of political inclusion.

The generalizable conclusion of this study is that under certain structural conditions, transitional or crisis situations can engender cooperative relationships between key political and economic actors. In the short term, cooperation between political and economic elites may promote governability under the auspices of proto-democratic and proto-market institutions. In the longer term, however, these relationships may in fact prove problematic for the further development of democracies and markets.

The Political Economy
of Government Performance

THIS STUDY makes two central arguments of importance to comparative politics. First, the empirical findings here highlight how the legacy of the past influences the operation of new institutions in the present in important and often unexpected ways. Second, and more centrally, this study argues that in transitional situations, the formation of coalitions between economic and political elites has a dramatic effect on government performance. In sum, past institutional structures promote the formation of political and economic coalitions within a new institutional framework. These coalitions, where possible, promote higher levels of institutional performance in the early stages of simultaneous political and economic transitions.

Despite an increased emphasis on institutional studies in the former Soviet Union, thus far few scholars have taken into account how old norms and institutions affect the interpretation of incentives provided by the new institutions.[1] As Martin Malia recently noted with regard to the first few years of Russia's transition, "Although the old regime had been decapitated with the dissolution of the central Communist Party apparatus and the Union in 1991, its detached limbs and sinews were everywhere."[2] Yet, in the Russian case at least, scholars to date have not done much to explore how precisely "shadows of the past"—or former institutions—influenced the operation of new proto-democratic and proto-market institutions. The experience of regional government performance in the First Russian Republic indicates that although changing institutions does indeed change political behavior, this change is not always in line with our expectations of how representative government

---

[1] Recent institutional studies dealing with (formerly) communist countries include Philip Roeder, *Red Sunset: The Failure of Soviet Politics* (Princeton, N.J.: Princeton University Press, 1993); Steven Solnick, "The Breakdown of Hierarchies in the Soviet Union and China: A Neo-Institutional Perspective," *World Politics* 48, no. 2 (January 1996): 209–238); and Randall Stone, *Satellites and Commissars: Strategy and Conflict in the Politics of Soviet-Bloc Trade* (Princeton, N.J.: Princeton University Press, 1996).

[2] Martin Malia, "Russia's Democratic Future: Hope against Hope," *Problems of Post-Communism* (Fall 1994): 34.

institutions should behave. Preexisting norms of behavior derived from the remnants of the former planned economy and command administration clearly influenced the behavior of actors within new institutions. In the words of economic historian, Douglass North:

> *Even discontinuous changes (such as revolution and conquest) are never completely discontinuous [as] a result of the imbeddedness of informal constraints in societies.* Although formal rules may change overnight as the result of political or judicial decisions, informal constraints embodied in customs, traditions and codes of conduct are much more impervious to deliberate policies. These cultural constraints not only connect the past with the present and future, but provide us with a key to explaining the path of historical change.[3]

Because context varies, the effects of the residue of old institutions on the behavior of new institutions were not uniform throughout First Republic Russia. What matters most in explaining variations in regional government performance were the relationships that different economic contexts fostered: *the more concentrated (by sector, assets and output, and employment) was the regional economy, the higher was regional government performance.* Where the economy was concentrated, competition for access to political resources was reduced and key groups of economic actors could collectively pursue inclusion in the governing process. Most significant, economic concentration also promoted interdependence and cooperation between economic and political actors.

The form of interest accommodation and collective action described here facilitated better government by enabling the state to employ the authority of key groups of economic actors while those economic actors, in turn, gained systematic access to state resources. The result, at least in the short term, was higher regional government performance—smooth policy processes, effective policy implementation, and a high degree of constituent approval. In the long term, however, the concluding chapter of this study argues that this relationship may also result in lower performance, and possibly oligarchy, as governments may be forced to sacrifice responsiveness to emerging actors.

The theoretical foundations of this argument are situated in both the political economy literature of the early 1980s, specifically studies of cor-

---

[3] Douglass C. North, *Institutions, Institutional Change, and Economic Performance* (New York: Cambridge University Press, 1990), p. 6; emphasis added.

poratist democracies,[4] and the more recent comparative and international political economy literature.[5] The latter stresses the influence of factor endowments on the formation of economic coalitions that support and oppose various political outcomes. My argument shares with these two general approaches a model for political action such that economic (and social) structure gives rise to certain forms of interest group political organization. This organization of interest group activity then determines political outcomes.

Corporatism, as classically defined, emphasizes the policy outcomes that arise from a tripartite relationship between the state, business, and labor within the countries of Western Europe in particular. The process of negotiated and consensual outcomes between business and government found in some of Russia's regions parallels the corporatist example. Further, just as much of the corporatist literature was intended to describe the governing arrangements that arose in times of crisis in post-World War II Europe, the negotiated and relatively consensual governing processes in higher-performance Russian regional governments also took place against the background of a more general economic crisis wrought by the collapse of an empire.

In addition, the corporatist literature, and the approach to coalitions and state capacity presented here, share the requirement that economic interests be relatively well organized. Some of the corporatist literature even stresses the importance of market structure in forming these key economic interest groups. Philippe Schmitter, for example, notes that numbers make a difference in determining initial associational expression:

> New interest organizations might be founded by some unrealistic entrepreneur or ideological zealot, but given the sheer numbers involved, the probable dispersion of preferences, and the ease with which any initial

---

[4] Peter J. Katzenstein, *Corporatism and Change: Austria, Switzerland, and the Politics of Industry* (Ithaca, N.Y.: Cornell University Press, 1984); Peter J. Katzenstein, *Small States in World Markets: Industrial Policy in Europe* (Ithaca, N.Y.: Cornell University Press, 1985); Philippe C. Schmitter, "Still the Century of Corporatism?" *The Review of Politics* 36 (1974): 85–131; Philippe C. Schmitter, "Interest Intermediation and Regime Governability in Contemporary Western Europe and North America," in Suzanne Berger, ed., *Organizing Interests in Western Europe* (New York: Cambridge University Press, 1981), pp. 285–327.

[5] For example, Ronald Rogowski, *Commerce and Coalitions* (Princeton, N.J.: Princeton University Press, 1989); and, in particular, Jeffry Frieden, *Debt Development and Democracy: Modern Political Economy and Latin America* (Princeton, N.J.: Princeton University Press, 1991).

success would attract competitors—not to mention selective incentives not to join or repression costs if one did—such organizations were unlikely to survive or prosper. Where the number of potentially interested actors was small or concentrated, an association might have been more likely to appear, because each participant would contribute measurably to its success.[6]

In his study of Japanese energy markets, Richard Samuels also notes the importance of economic concentration and, like Schmitter, adds that business and labor interests must hold a representational monopoly in political bargaining with government.[7] Finally, once groups are formed, both corporatism and the approach presented in this study of Russia stress the importance of the systematic inclusion in the governing process of these organized interests. But perhaps most significant for the current study, the corporatist literature emphasizes the consensus corporatist arrangements bring regarding political (and economic) goals, and the positive impact this has on regime governability and performance.

Much of the corporatist literature was written with an eye to explaining how Western governments could find their way out of the apparent crises of governability—an overload of societal demands relative to state resources—that they faced in the 1970s and 1980s. In describing a corporatist solution to the West European dilemma, Schmitter argued that the relative governability of states is "less a function of differences in aggregate overload, of 'imbalance' between the sum total of societal demands and state capabilities, than of the discrete processes that identify, package, promote, and implement potential interest claims and com-

---

[6] Schmitter, "Interest Intermediation," p. 290.

[7] Richard J. Samuels, *The Business of the Japanese State: Energy Markets in Comparative Historical Perspective* (Ithaca, N.Y.: Cornell University Press, 1987), p. 14. Samuels also emphasizes the importance of market structure—specifically sectoral concentration (the number of firms in a given sector). He concludes that the sector itself may be important in determining business group influence in politics. For example, concentrated oil producers are likely to have more political clout than coal producers because of the relative value of the commodity they produce. Further, sectoral decline may encourage economic actors to organize and seek accommodation from government. See also Michael Atkinson and William D. Coleman, "Strong States and Weak States: Sectoral Policy Networks in Advanced Capitalist Economies," *British Journal of Political Science* 19 (1989), where at page 53 they note "how business is organized at the sectoral level will help determine whether or in what way major socio-economic groups can make a contribution to policy development and implementation."

mands."[8] He argues that the demands facing various Western democracies in the 1970s were not that different and therefore could not account for differences in their capabilities. Instead, the differences between states that rode out the crisis and ones that did not were "the processes of political intermediation by which the potential volume of societal demands was captured and focused and through which the eventual pattern of public policies was evaluated and sifted."[9]

In explaining consensus and conflict in Italy and Britain, Mario Regini explores similar processes of interest group accommodation by the state.[10] Regini also emphasizes the importance of reciprocity in describing the concerted action of labor and government as "political exchange." Political exchange involves a trade-off of different types of political power:

> The state devolves portions of its decision-making authority to [economic interests] by allowing them to play a part in policy formation and implementation and thus to gain advantage from the material and symbolic resources which the state can distribute. In return for this, [economic interests] deliver their indirect political power to the state by guaranteeing consensus and by *drawing on their own resources to ensure the legitimacy, effectiveness and efficiency of state action.*[11]

In parallel fashion, Schmitter argues that where organizations formed that had broad representational coverage, dense memberships, and whose relations with the state were mediated through a societal corporatist structure, government should be more effective.

Similar to the West European situations described by Regini and Schmitter, provincial Russian governments following the collapse of the Soviet Union faced a "load" crisis—too many demands, too few resources, and, in many regions, very little societal organization (certainly less than a traditional corporatist solution would require). Yet, where most of the corporatist literature underplays its influence, the degree of economic concentration played an important role in Russia's regions in determining how these demands were presented to governments. The volatile and unpredictable post-Soviet environment pushed still weak re-

[8] Schmitter, "Interest Intermediation," p. 287.

[9] Ibid.

[10] Mario Regini, "The Conditions for Political Exchange: How Concertation Emerged and Collapsed in Italy and Great Britain," in John Goldethorpe, ed., *Order and Conflict in Contemporary Capitalism* (New York: Oxford University Press, 1984), pp. 124–142.

[11] Ibid., p. 128; emphasis added.

gional political institutions to the limit. Industrial output plummeted and wages remained insufficient relative to increases in inflation. At the same time, the federal government in Moscow divested itself of costly policy responsibilities (health, social welfare, and consistent support of the economy) and foisted these on newly established, and poorly financed, regional governments. In short, given Russia's steep economic decline, regional government responsibilities exceeded their abilities to meet these demands—resulting in government "overload" in many regions. Not unexpectedly, conflicts over the allocation of scarce regional government resources became especially sharp in many parts of provincial Russia.[12]

Where economies were diverse—spread into various sectors and among various small actors within the same sector—competition was intense for access to state resources for relief from economic woes. As explained in detail below, diverse economies inhibited collective action among societal (specifically, economic) actors. Therefore governments in regions with dispersed economies faced diverse and conflicting demands. Dispersed and unorganized economic power gave rise to a similarly uneven distribution of political power. This was reflected in conflict within government and among levels of government. Some regional governments were so overloaded that the best they could do was attempt to "stamp out fires"—reel from one crisis to the next. In short, while trying to simultaneously satisfy divergent, conflicting, and unorganized regional interests, these governments satisfied few, if any.

Conversely, the concentration of the regional economy had a significant focusing effect on a regional government's "load." As I explain more thoroughly in the second section of this chapter, and demonstrate empirically in chapter 6, the concentration of the regional economy promoted the organization of key economic interest groups. This focused societal demands and enabled regional governments to easily identify and include the major societal interests in the region in the governing process. Interestingly, where corporatist-like arrangements of interest group intermediation are thought to arise as a state moves economically from a purer form of capitalism toward socialism, in the post-Soviet case, business/government accommodation came about as the economy moved from highly regulated state socialism toward a freer market and capitalism.

[12] Anthony King makes the same point about British government overload in the 1970s. See Anthony King, "Overload: Problems of Governing in the 1970s," *Political Studies* 23, nos. 2–3 (September 1975): 289.

Moreover, although corporatist models do cast some light on regional government performance in Russia, there are several important omissions and weaknesses in corporatist analysis that make it a less-than-perfect fit for explaining performance variations. First among these is the role of labor. As noted above, a corporatist system is generally acknowledged to be one that includes a tripartite system of interest intermediation between the state, labor, and capital. Schmitter's classic reformulation of corporatism presents it more generally as,

> a system of interest representation in which the constituent units are organized into a limited number of singular, compulsory, non-competitive, hierarchically ordered and functionally differentiated categories recognized or licensed (if not created) by the state and granted a deliberate representational monopoly within their respective categories in exchange for observing certain controls on their selection of leaders and articulation of demands and supports.[13]

Although this definition appears to include any social groups, Schmitter's examples of corporatist arrangements involve the interaction of the state, capital, *and* labor. If corporatist interest intermediation does indeed require the participation of organized labor, there is good reason to avoid applying the concept to the post-Soviet Russian case. For as yet, it is still difficult to identify organized labor as a distinct social force given the traditional dependence of the Soviet worker on the state and enterprise management. Indeed, one of the great ironies revealed by the collapse of the "worker's" state, is that workers were politically disempowered in favor of managers.[14]

Further, and more problematic, is that much of the corporatist literature is largely descriptive. Although structure is clearly important in a corporatist polity, it is not always easy to explain situations where corpo-

---

[13] Schmitter, "Still the Century of Corporatism?" p. 93.

[14] A few attempts were made in the early 1980s to apply corporatism as a form of interest intermediation to the Brezhnev regime. See, for example, Valerie Bunce and John Echolls, "Soviet Politics in the Brezhnev Era: Pluralism or Corporatism?" in Donald R. Kelley, ed., *Soviet Politics in the Brezhnev Era* (New York: Viking, 1980), pp. 1–26; Valerie Bunce, "The Political Economy of the Brezhnev Era: The Rise and Fall of Corporatism," *British Journal of Political Science* 13 (1983): 129–158; and Blair A. Ruble, "The Applicability of Corporatist Models to the Study of Soviet Politics: The Case of the Trade Unions," *The Carl Beck Papers in Russian and East European Studies*, paper no. 303 (Pittsburgh: University of Pittsburgh, 1983). A careful reading of all three of these works reveals that corporatism was a rather poor fit with the Soviet system for it underplayed the power of the Soviet state.

ratist arrangements fail to come about even though the organizational context appears supportive. Peter Katzenstein's study of the smaller corporatist West European democracies indicates that the small size of a country is often thought to be an important component to encouraging corporatist arrangements, yet not all small states are corporatist. In the four Russian provinces under consideration here, there is not a great deal of difference in population size, yet two developed relatively cooperative state-business relationships and two did not. In sum, much of the corporatist literature frequently overlooks a fundamental dilemma of collective action—the case when the situation seems ripe for cooperation, yet none takes place. In this sense, the corporatist literature is not particularly rigorous in providing a causal logic to interest group cooperation with the state.

In contrast, the theory of state-business cooperation that I present here requires key supporting conditions that make cooperation a rational strategy in only some cases. These include the concentration of economic power among a few actors.

In making economic structure a central aspect in explaining business-government coalitions, and their influence on government performance in some of Russia's provinces, my argument not only fills some gaps in corporatist analysis but also owes some intellectual debts to recent comparative political economy. My argument parallels, in some respects, the example of Jeffrey Frieden and others in placing a similar emphasis on the structure of the economy and the resulting organization of economic interests in explaining particular political outcomes.

Like the argument presented here, Frieden posits that in five Latin American debtor nations from 1965 to 1985 economic structures and corresponding economic interests played an important role in determining political outcomes—specifically economic policy and the process of engaging in political activity by socioeconomic groups. Frieden argues that "government actions are the response of policymakers to sociopolitical pressures brought to bear upon them by interest groups."[15] In addition, he explores "why and how individuals and groups interact in the political arena, why and how existing coalitions or institutions persist or are changed, why and how political forms endure or deteriorate."[16] More simply, Frieden's argument is that "political outcomes are the result

[15] Frieden, *Debt, Development, and Democracy*, p. 6.
[16] Ibid.

34

of choices made by social groups . . . [, and] economic interests of social groups are central to their policy choices."[17]

Frieden also seeks to explain the links between economic interest, political behavior, and political outcomes. He argues that the patterns of socioeconomic interest group cohesion and conflict determine both economic policy as well as shifts to democracy or authoritarianism. Frieden posits that the groups having the most influence on government action were those that were highly organized. He identifies asset specificity and concentration as two key factors in explaining the abilities of economic groups to organize and exert pressure on government policy decisions. The policy stakes for an economic group were higher if the group's assets were specific for one particular use, making members of the group lobby harder for particular outcomes favorable to the preservation of the value of their assets. Further, as in Russia's regions, Frieden notes that sectoral concentration, because fewer economic agents are involved, makes political mobilization easier and therefore more likely.[18]

Frieden's focus on the interaction between coalitions of economic interests and state decision making, in some important ways, parallels my argument concerning the effect of economic concentration on interest group formation in higher-performance Russian provinces. However, we diverge in two significant respects. First, as noted earlier, my argument emphasizes the importance of past institutional structures and their influence on contemporary processes and outcomes. Second, where Frieden treats the state as being largely at the mercy of strong and well-organized economic interest groups in Latin America, my argument is that well-organized economic interests have a "shared project"[19] with the state during times of great economic (and political) change; that is, Frieden's and my perspectives on the role of the state are quite different. Where he, and others like Helen Milner and Ronald Rogowski, tend to view state actors as largely reactive to powerful economic interests, in higher-performance Russian regions economic interests and the state were far more mutually dependent.[20]

---

[17] Ibid., p. 7.

[18] Ibid., p. 8.

[19] This term comes from Peter Evans, *Embedded Autonomy: States and Industrial Transformation* (Princeton, N.J.: Princeton University Press, 1995).

[20] Helen V. Milner, *Resisting Protectionism: Global Industries and the Politics of International Trade* (Princeton, N.J.: Princeton University Press, 1988); Rogowski, *Commerce and Coalitions.*

These divergent perspectives on the relationship between political and economic actors may be a result of the fact that Frieden's dependent variables are economic policy change and regime change, whereas the focus of my study is on variations in government capacity. As a result, Frieden looks more at the "demand side"[21] of politics, presenting the state as reactive to interest group pressure. In contrast, I go beyond this to look at both interest group demands *and* state needs, and then examine what each was able to (and did) supply the other.

This emphasis on shared projects between the state and economic interest groups in my argument meshes well with recent descriptions of comparative economic development in other contemporary contexts, especially Asia.[22] Examining the relationship between the state and key business interests in newly industrializing countries, Peter Evans argues: "Both industrial elites and the state are interested in transformation, neither can implement this project on their own, and each brings something to the task."[23] Similarly, Alice Amsden and, to a lesser extent, Robert Wade, in examinations of South Korea and Taiwan, respectively, also emphasize the symbiotic relationship between growing industrial interest groups and the state in achieving developmental projects.

Clearly, then, in a comparative context, cooperation between economic elites and government can have an impact on public policy choices, economic development, and even regime type. I will argue throughout this book, however, that business-government cooperation also has a critical impact on what new representative governments can accomplish in times of sweeping political and economic change. But why should relationships between political and economic elite actors, instead of regional societal attributes like political culture and relative wealth, for example, be so important to regional government performance in transitional Russia? Despite their relative lack of clear authority in the early to mid-Soviet periods, in the Soviet Union's waning years, and in the first few years of Russia's transition to a market economy, the demands of change have stimulated economic interest groups to play especially important roles in post-Soviet Russian governance.

Since the late 1980s, and especially since 1990–91, Russia has, of

[21] Frieden, *Debt, Development, and Democracy*, p. 36.

[22] Evans, *Embedded Autonomy*; Alice Amsden, *Asia's Next Giant: South Korea and Late Industrialization* (New York: Oxford University Press, 1989); and Robert Wade, *Governing the Market: Economic Theory and the Role of Government in East Asian Industrialization* (Princeton, N.J.: Princeton University Press, 1990).

[23] Evans, *Embedded Autonomy*, p. 37.

course, undergone massive economic and political change. This has pre-cipitated remarkable societal, economic, and political dislocation. Rem-nants of the old economic order persisted, while new political institutions were still relatively weak. The importance of the workplace to the aver-age Soviet citizen, and the fact that the already enormous influence of enterprise directors over regional economies often increased, suggests the need to look at how (or whether) these economic interests were repre-sented and accommodated by new regional political institutions. The si-multaneous processes of democratization and marketization caused se-vere political and economic strain. This, coupled with the presence of politically influential enterprise directors and a weakly organized civil society, meant that political success (higher-regional government perfor-mance) depended on the incorporation of especially dominant economic interests into policy making.

Enterprise directors were often still relatively powerful, and regional political actors were dependent on gaining at least their tacit consent in order to keep government running well. Following the methodology of "modern political economy,"[24] in the remainder of this chapter I first identify enterprise directors as important players in the post-Soviet con-text. I then explain their rise as key economic and political players through the last years of Soviet Russia and the first three years of repre-sentative regional government, identifying their preferences and main in-terests. Finally, I examine how these increasingly powerful economic ac-tors interacted with regional government.

ENTERPRISE DIRECTORS AS POTENT POLITICAL FORCES

Key Actors in the Command Economy

Any reader with even a passing familiarity with the operations of the command economy is undoubtedly aware of how highly centralized it was. This was maintained through the dual subordination of enterprises to both mammoth central ministries located in Moscow (which main-tained branches in the localities) and the Communist Party as the leading force in all aspects of Soviet society. Under this system, planners intended for enterprise directors to have little independent hiring and firing au-thority (this was done with the approval of the enterprise's primary Party organization, or PPO), and they were obligated to meet plan targets es-

---

[24] Cf. chapter 1, page 11.

tablished by bureaucrats in Moscow. The PPO had *"pravo kontrolia,"* or the right to verify all manner of managerial decisions.[25]

Although managerial control over enterprises was promoted through the principle of *edinonachalie*—one man rule, in reality the city or oblast Party committees could tame an overly independent director. Writing in 1969, Jerry Hough explains, for example, that edinonachalie was actually quite a limited concept denoting merely a manager's ability to make routine (day-by-day) operating decisions independently. It also carried with it a managerial right to emphasize labor discipline. By no means, however, was edinonachalie to be understood as personal control or power (*lichnaia vlast'*) over an enterprise.[26] On the contrary, on any significant matter that could be interpreted as having policy implications, managers were required to discuss all possible options with Party officials and secure their approval.[27]

Local Party organs—specifically, oblast committees (*obkomy*)—were charged with the responsibility of overall political and economic oversight for their regions. Thus local Party secretaries were generally held responsible for enterprises in their oblast not meeting plan targets. This meant, at various times, that obkom first secretaries found themselves acting as regional coordinators, ensuring reliable delivery and distribution of raw materials to local factories. It was in this context that Hough described the role of first Party secretaries as modern prefects.[28]

Peter Rutland, however, writing on the role of Party organs in economic management in the 1970s and 1980s, argues that the coordinating function that Hough ascribes to Party secretaries diminished somewhat in the decades following Khrushchev's *sovnarkhoz* reform.[29] Oversight and directing functions reverted to the sixty-five powerful industrial ministries in Moscow and their branches (*otrasli*) at the local level. This was the essence of the vertical chain of economic command. Vladimir Andrle's analysis of managerial power in the 1970s confirms this assessment. He argues that personal relationships between plant directors and Party officials were still important for managerial success but that gradu-

---

[25] Jerry F. Hough, *The Soviet Prefects: The Local Party Organs in Industrial Decision-making* (Cambridge, Mass.: Harvard University Press, 1969), p. 87.

[26] Ibid., pp. 82–85.

[27] Ibid., p. 95.

[28] Ibid., p. 213.

[29] Peter Rutland, *The Politics of Economic Stagnation in the Soviet Union: The Role of Local Party Organs in Economic Management* (New York: Cambridge University Press, 1993). For Rutland's differences with Hough on the Party's role as regional economic coordinator, see especially chapter 4.

ally managers became more dependent on relations with ministerial superiors to achieve plan targets.[30] Andrle adds that the best way for an enterprise manager to gain increased independence was to consistently overfulfill plan targets. In this way, some managers were able to build their own "little empires."

With Mikhail Gorbachev's 1986 initiation of perestroika, this system began to decline. Although it took five years for the role of official Party involvement in the economy to disappear, Rutland notes the impact perestroika had on the ministerial bureaucracies in Moscow. Throughout the late 1980s their staffs were slashed, and they were subject to a series of ill-conceived reorganizations.[31] In 1988 plan targets were abolished and replaced with "state orders" (goszakazy) used primarily for defense-related production. Beyond this, firms were supposed to be fully economically accountable, according to the principle of khozraschet—cost accounting. They were also supposed to find their own suppliers and customers.[32]

With the final collapse of the Soviet Union in late 1991, the domineering central ministries fell into further disarray. Regional Party organizations were completely abolished. Their property was generally taken over by the local soviets, popularly elected a year earlier. Enterprise directors found themselves free from Party oversight and much of the domination of (and also assistance from) their respective ministries.[33] In short, the authority of enterprise directors, including directors of kolkhozy and sovkhozy (collective and state farms, respectively) increased considerably. They had established themselves as de facto owners.

Thus, as the state bureaucracies and the Party ceded control to enterprise directors, the role of directors as de facto owners emerged and persisted throughout the collapse of the Soviet Union and the first three years of the existence of representative government at the regional level.[34]

But what of the workers' role? Classic works on industrial administration in the Soviet Union describe the relationship between worker and

[30] Vladimir Andrle, *Managerial Power in the Soviet Union*, (Lexington, Mass.: Lexington Books, 1976), p. 141.

[31] Rutland, *Economic Stagnation*, p. 208.

[32] Ibid., p. 211

[33] I have qualified this statement because many formerly all-union ministries quickly found new homes in Russian federal ministries. Still, their abilities to instruct and assist managers were severely circumscribed.

[34] For further confirmation of this, see also Vitali Naishul, "Institutional Development in the USSR," *Cato Journal* 11, no. 3 (Winter 1992): 489–496.

director as one of dependence.[35] This dependency arose as a result of the institutional arrangements through which many social services were traditionally provided through the enterprise. This often included housing, health, kindergartens, exercise facilities, and, for particularly large enterprises, stores and enterprise farms. Thus a worker's entire life often revolved around the factory. Not surprisingly, the enterprise director had a broad responsibility as paternalistic provider. Of particular relevance to the argument expounded in this study, this dependency was often even more acute in areas that came to resemble company towns constructed before and after World War II.[36]

While the power of management increased, the role of trade unions in the Soviet system was limited in comparison with the West. Although they represented some worker interests to management, for the most part trade unions were another instrument of control over labor. Indeed managers, not trade unions, often played the role of representing worker interests to large bureaucracies in Moscow.[37]

The uncertainties wrought by perestroika deepened the dependency of worker on manager. Further, even after the creation of workers' councils in the 1988 law on enterprises that on paper were vested with the authority to remove directors, this rarely happened.[38] Thus, when the privatization drive rolled around in 1992, workers were rarely in a position to challenge directors' continued control of enterprises (and seldom did they have the inclination to do so).

Economic Reform 1991–1993: The Entrenchment of Managers as Owners

Concurrent with the establishment of representative governments at the regional level, Russia was, of course, enduring major economic change.

[35] See, for example, Joseph Berliner, *Factory and Manager in the USSR* (Cambridge, Mass.: Harvard University Press, 1957). More recent works on the position of enterprise managers include Sheila Puffer, ed., *The Russian Management Revolution* (Armonk, N.Y.: M. E. Sharpe, 1992).

[36] For example, Nizhnii Novgorod's submarine factory, Krasnoe Sormovo, had twenty-four day care centers and owned several cattle farms in addition to housing facilities for its 19,600 employees.

[37] See Janos Kornai, *The Socialist System: The Political Economy of Communism* (Princeton, N.J.: Princeton University Press, 1992), p. 470, for confirmation that this behavior persisted through the reform period. Mining unions that led strikes in the late 1980s and early 1990s are an exception.

[38] Michael McFaul, "Agency Problems in the Privatization of Large Enterprises in Russia," in McFaul and Perlmutter, *Privatization, Conversion*, p. 44.

Although this afforded managers increased opportunities to assert control over their enterprises, it also placed many enterprises under considerable strain. The pressures caused by the sudden liberalization of prices and the implementation of a crash program of privatization are detailed below. Further, although one of the goals of privatization was to limit directors' power over their enterprises, the effort failed to separate ownership from management, and directors remained potent economic and political forces.

PRICE LIBERALIZATION

Beginning in January 1992 most prices were freed from central government control except for energy and transportation prices. The sudden (250 percent) increase in prices within a few days led to an increase of currency in circulation. Wages, however, did not rise as quickly. Real wages in fact fell drastically, resulting in a drop in consumption. Concurrently, the Gaidar government attempted to cut budgetary expenditures including the once sacred cows of enterprise subsidies as well as military procurements.[39]

Initially, enterprises did not respond to drops in demand and continued to produce at their old rates.[40] This resulted in the accumulation of massive stocks. But as credit was cut, directors could no longer finance their stocks and they stopped paying their bills. As a result, inter-enterprise debt rose considerably, as did demands for increased credits. By April enterprises began to cut production, and by June 1992 industrial production was down 25 percent from what it had been in June 1991. For their part, regional governments had some discretion in determining the extent to which prices were liberalized in their regions as long as they provided any subsidies out of their own budgets and not from the central budget. Any tinkering they could do, however, was not enough to combat the high levels of inflation and the drops in production sweeping the country as a whole.

Following the April meeting of the Congress of People's Deputies in Moscow, rather striking concessions were made to industry in the form of credits. While this slowed, somewhat, the fall in industrial production, it produced intense inflationary pressure and inflation rose as high as 25 percent per month in the last half of 1992.[41]

---

[39] See Richard Layard, "Stabilization versus Reform? Russia's First Year," in Olivier Blanchard, Maxim Boycko, et al., eds., *Post-Communist Reform: Pain and Progress* (Cambridge, Mass.: MIT Press, 1993), pp. 15–36.

[40] Ibid., p. 19.

[41] Ibid., p. 20.

The cycle of credit emissions, alternating with attempts to reassert stricter monetary policies, continued throughout most of 1993. Inflation also rose fairly steadily from month to month. This was a result of both on-again, off-again credits from the central bank as well as the Russian aversion to enforce needed austerity, which may have resulted in some measure of higher unemployment but reduced inflation.

PRIVATIZATION

Shortly after prices were freed, in July 1991, the Russian Federation government initiated a sweeping privatization program. Because of the disruption of the August 1991 coup attempt, privatization did not begin in earnest until November 1991 with a final all-Russian plan submitted to the Russian parliament in March 1992 and approved that June.

Privatization was intended to transfer property rights from the state to private owners. In general, however, as noted above, privatization failed to separate ownership from management. This was because it was not entirely clear that shares of an enterprise were the state's to distribute. As Maxim Boycko and Andrei Shleiffer note, "Many 'stakeholders' had existing ownership rights, *in the sense of being able to effectively exercise control rights over assets*."[42] Chief among the "stakeholders" in privatization were the increasingly empowered enterprise directors.

More often than not privatization enabled enterprise directors to become de facto *and* de jure owners of enterprises. Given that managers, with few exceptions, maintained and even strengthened their positions as their enterprises were privatized, they remained a significant political force at the local level. They continued to wield considerable influence over their employees—who, after all, were regional voters—and they could affect the implementation of policy.

There is evidence, for example, from both the 1990 regional elections and the December 1993 national elections that these enterprise directors often decided which candidates they would allow to campaign on the factory floor.[43] Enterprise directors could choose which candidates to

---

[42] Andrei Shleifer and Maxim Boycko, "The Politics of Russian Privatization," in Blanchard, Boycko, et al., *Post-Communist Reform: Pain and Progress*, p. 38.

[43] Author's interview with deputies in Tiumen' oblast acknowledged that some of them had been elected with the assistance of enterprise directors. Further, in a personal correspondence Regina Smyth of Pennsylvania State University confirmed that in Saratov, during the December 1993 national elections, some candidates were certainly benefiting from favored access to enterprises.

sponsor (and in some cases finance) and thus could influence the composition of governments and regional government policy.

Further evidence of managerial influence over policy was that many of these enterprises were largely responsible for their workers' housing, education, and social services. Mary McAuley noted that in Perm and elsewhere, for example, it had been customary for enterprises to build housing with ministerial funds on land granted by the regional soviet. The enterprise would then give a portion of the completed housing to the local soviet for wider distribution. But when ministerial money dried up and enterprises found themselves paying for housing out of their "profits," they frequently balked at turning over apartments to the soviet. The consequence was a housing shortage for which constituents would hold their newly elected political representatives responsible.

Moreover, in the absence of the regional Party organization as a disciplining force, enterprises found little reason to consult with regional soviets regarding what they sold in the shops that they owned and at what prices.[44] This would make coordinating a regional economic policy difficult for regional soviets and have a negative impact on regional government performance.

Withholding tax revenues was a third significant sanction that enterprises could wield against regional governments. Just as under the planned economy, where enterprise directors underreported their production output in an effort to keep future output targets low, underreporting production volumes and product sales became a common practice in the 1990s to avoid having local governments tax the sales of their products. This practice enabled enterprises strapped for cash to sell these products covertly and pocket the proceeds.[45] Although regional governments were aware of the practice, they could do little to stop it.

A fourth source of continuing conflict in some regions concerned the right that oblasts gained in 1991 to sell 10 to 15 percent of the excess output of enterprises located on the oblast's territory.[46] Enterprise directors were protective of what they considered to be property at their disposal, and regional politicians often struggled to gain control of the output in order to trade with other regions. Again, to avoid turning over a percentage of their products, enterprises had another incentive to under-

[44] Mary McAuley, "Politics, Economics and Elite Realignment: A Regional Perspective," *Soviet Economy* 8, no. 1 (1992): 69–70.

[45] Interview with the head of the Finance Department, Saratov Oblast Administration, April 23, 1993.

[46] McAuley, "Politics, Economics, and Elite Realignment," p. 70.

report their production levels. If enterprises persistently withheld excess productive output, this would limit what regional governments could trade and use for barter with other oblasts to improve the flow of consumer products into their regions. Thus, without the cooperation of key groups of enterprise directors, the performance of a regional government could be significantly impaired.

However, just as it would be a mistake to conclude that capitalists or business interests in the West are a cohesive interest group, it would be an error to assume that enterprise directors, as the functional equivalent (and often the literal equivalent) of capital in post-communist Russia, formed a single lobby. The lack of support for Arkadi Volski's "Civic Union," a party specifically devoted to industrialists, in the December 1993 national elections is one indicator that enterprise directors did not all act together or think alike. If they did, Volski's group should have gotten a larger share of the vote than the 1.93 percent it received in December 1993.[47]

Further, a survey of enterprise directors in 1992 indicated that their attitudes were actually relatively diverse: "Although managers might be expected to exert united political influence as a powerful interest group, in fact their proxy preferences were ambiguous and diverse; different political forces could gain support from different parts of this group."[48]

The argument that follows demonstrates that managerial preferences were perhaps not as "ambiguous" as one might think. Instead, managers' behavior toward oblast governments, and the government's behavior toward them, was largely conditioned by the degree of dispersion or concentration of the regional economy among enterprises and sectors.

In lower-performance cases, the regional economy was relatively dispersed among competing actors. This created a high degree of competition for access to scarce political resources, and this competition was reflected in conflict among economic actors and among political actors in the regional government. This resulted in lower-performance governments.

Actors in regions with higher-performance governments therefore overcame two "collective action" problems—the first, a classic Olsonian cooperative dilemma, involved the cooperation of a powerful group of economic actors to collectively pursue systematic access to regional gov-

[47] Election results are from *Biulleten'* of the Central Election Commission of the Russian Federation, issue no. 12, March 1994.

[48] Irina Starodubrovskaia, "Attitudes of Enterprise Managers Toward Market Transitions," in McFaul and Perlmutter, *Privatization, Conversion*, p. 66. She also notes variation in the way enterprise directors reported that regional governments acted to further enterprise interests.

ernment; the second, slightly different collective action dilemma, involved the establishment of cooperation between this group and political actors in regional government. These two collective action problems were relatively easily surmounted in regions where the labor, assets, and output of the regional economy were concentrated within a particular economic sector and/or among a few particularly large enterprises.

DILEMMAS OF COLLECTIVE ACTION

Having identified the key players, and the increasing power of enterprise directors following the collapse of the command economy, I now move to explain why some were able to cooperate both with each other and with the regional government to produce higher-performing regional political institutions.

Dilemmas of collective action are so important to this aspect of my argument that they are worth reviewing in more detail. Quite simply, "Collective dilemmas arise when choices made by rational individuals lead to outcomes that no one prefers."[49] Indeed, it is often easier to comprehend why cooperation does not take place—why groups do not form—than why they do. An oft-cited passage from eighteenth-century political philosopher David Hume sums up the fundamental dilemma of collective action:

> Your corn is ripe to-day; mine will be so to-morrow. 'Tis profitable for us both, that I shou'd labour with you to-day, and that you shou'd aid me to-morrow. I have no kindness for you, and know you have as little for me. I will not, therefore, take any pains upon your account; and should I labour with you upon my own account, in expectation of a return, I know I shou'd be disappointed, and that I shou'd in vain depend upon your gratitude. Here then I leave you to labour alone; you treat me in the same manner. The seasons change; and both of us lose our harvests for want of mutual confidence and security.[50]

Others have presented this dilemma as "the tragedy of the commons"—the failure of an individual to limit his or her own use of a common pool

---

[49] Robert H. Bates, "Contra Contractarianism: Some Reflections on the New Institutionalism," *Politics and Society* 16, nos. 2–3 (1988): 387.

[50] David Hume (1740), book 3, part 2, section 5, as cited in Putnam, *Making Democracy Work*, p. 163. For more on Hume and collective action dilemmas, see also Russell Hardin, *Collective Action* (Baltimore, Md.: The Johns Hopkins University Press, 1982).

resource (for example, a meadow on which sheep graze) even when the individual knows that unlimited use by everyone will mean the destruction of the common resource which will cause universal hardship, including his or her own.[51] Similar logic is involved in the classic prisoner's dilemma.[52]

In all these examples, the pursuit of one's rational self-interest leads to socially irrational and undesirable outcomes—unharvested crops, the disappearance of grazing lands, and conflict-ridden governments.[53] Putnam notes that "even if no party wishes harm to the other, and even if both are conditionally predisposed to cooperate—I will, if you will—they can have no guarantee against reneging, in the absence of verifiable, enforceable commitments."[54]

Economists, sociologists, social psychologists, and political scientists have devoted considerable time and energy to studying how collective action dilemmas might be solved. Among the classic works is Mancur Olson's solution in the *Logic of Collective Action*.[55] Olson posits that a qualitative difference exists between the behavior of large groups and that of small groups in pursuing a collective benefit (or public good). He argues that "small groups are more likely to be able to provide themselves with collective goods without relying on the coercion or positive inducement apart from the collective good itself."[56] Simply, individual incentive to cooperate decreases as group size increases.

Olson attributes this to the fact that in small groups, each member, or at least one of the members, will find that his or her personal gain from having the collective good is greater than the total cost of providing some amount of the good. Thus "in a very small group, where each member gets a substantial portion of the total gain simply because there are few others in the group, a collective good can often be provided by the volun-

---

[51] See Elinor Ostrom, *Governing the Commons: The Evolution of Institutions for Collective Action* (New York: Cambridge University Press, 1990).

[52] Under this well-known scenario, two prisoners are held in separate rooms. Each prisoner is told that if she turns in her partner (thereby "defecting"), she will get off lightly. If, however, she remains silent (cooperates) and her partner confesses (defects), she will be punished more severely (the sucker's payoff). If both prisoners remained silent (cooperate), they would get off lightly. But because they cannot communicate to coordinate their actions, each is better off confessing (defecting) regardless of what the other prisoner does. Thus pursuing the rationally "best" strategy makes each prisoner worse off. See Robert Axelrod, *The Evolution of Cooperation* (New York: Basic Books, 1984), pp. 8–9.

[53] Putnam makes a similar point in his *Making Democracy Work*, p. 164.

[54] Ibid.

[55] Olson, *The Logic of Collective Action*.

[56] Ibid., p. 33. Olson notes (p. 33, n. 53) that David Hume also argued that small groups could achieve common benefits where large groups could not.

tary self-interested action of the members of the group."[57] Thus individually rational action in the context of a small group (what Olson calls "privileged" or "intermediate" groups) provides a socially desirable outcome—the provision of a collective benefit.[58]

The Concentration of a Regional Economy and Collective Action

The concentration of a regional economy in a single industry, or within several enterprises, assisted in the resolution of regional collective action dilemmas. First, as noted above, by limiting the number and variety of actors in the economy, it encouraged the formation of economic interest groups that collectively pursued access to state resources. Second, in encouraging formalized interest representation, it facilitated the systematic inclusion of these interests in government.

The dynamic is not unlike that of a "company town." In a company town, in the West or East, the primary employer is a dominant company or corporation. Most people living in the area are either directly or indirectly employed (in a supporting enterprise, for example, a supplier) by the corporation. Thus the fate of the town (including its tax base, political recruitment, employment, commercial sector, and other supporting enterprises) is inextricably linked to the company's success or failure. Further, political, economic, and societal actors anywhere "are embedded in concrete, ongoing systems of social relations."[59] Elite actors' norms and expectations, created by the social structures of a company town, affect the behavior of the political system and the government's capabilities.

Economic Interest Group Formation

Briefly, with respect to the rationally self-interested behavior of economic actors, following Olson, economic concentration limits the number of actors who would potentially share a public benefit. In this case, the collec-

[57] Ibid., p. 34.

[58] Olson does not dispute the fact that large groups form and can achieve collective benefits for their members, but he argues that any achievements they may make as lobby groups comes not from their formation as a lobby group, but because they serve some other purpose. For example, a doctor's association lobbies on behalf of its members, but it was formed not for this purpose but to put doctors in touch with one another in order to exchange information on medical issues. See ibid., pp. 132–133.

[59] Mark Granovetter, "Economic Action and Social Structure: The Problem of Embeddedness," *American Journal of Sociology* 91 (1985): 482.

tive good that such a lobby would pursue is access to state resources. Limits on group size increase the likelihood that an interest lobby will form.

Enterprise directors in a concentrated regional economy found themselves members of what Olson refers to as "privileged" or "intermediate" groups. These smaller groups were more likely to ensure the provision of a collective benefit. Privileged groups are those "in which each of its members, or at least some one of them, has an incentive to see that the collective good is provided, even if he has to bear the full burden of providing it himself." In an intermediate group, "no single member gets a share of the benefit sufficient to give him an incentive to provide the good himself, but which does not have so many members that no one member will notice whether any other member is or is not helping to provide the collective good."[60]

In contrast, regions with economies dispersed among a large number of small actors were more likely to witness "latent" group behavior on the part of enterprise directors. Large groups are "latent" lobbies because, unlike privileged or intermediate groups, they "are distinguished by the fact that, if one member does not help provide the collective good, no other one member will be significantly affected and therefore none has any reason to react."[61] Thus concentration of a regional economy among a few actors imposed a limit on group size, and this encouraged collective action.

But aside from this, the concentration of a regional economy provided a separate benefit that further supported collective action among enterprise directors in those regions. When we situate them within the context of "company towns," the repeated interactions of long-time directors of the largest and most important regional enterprises, and their previous personal and professional networks helped support collective action.

Organized Interests and Collective Action

Not only did the concentration of a regional economy encourage economic group formation, thus overcoming one collective action problem, it also assisted in overcoming a second collective action dilemma—cooperation between organized economic interests and the regional government. Surmounting this second collective action problem had a positive effect on regional government performance.

The company town syndrome, noted above, created increased congru-

[60] Olson, *The Logic of Collective Action*, pp. 49–50.
[61] Ibid., p. 50.

ence between the interests of economic and political actors. Both had a greater shared stake in maintaining some stability and consensus in the political and economic environment. In these regions, enterprises were so large, accounting for such a significant portion of regional economic assets, output, and employment of the regional labor force, that if they went bankrupt, the regional government would suffer tremendously. It would have been held responsible for resulting high unemployment, a poor economy, and other social ills that voters might have linked to the closure of mammoth regional enterprises.

When asked in a 1993 survey how they would react to a hypothetical decision by Moscow to close a large enterprise in their region at which they were *not* employed, more respondents in Nizhnii Novgorod (where employment, regional economic assets, and output were all highly concentrated among a few enterprises in the defense sector) than in the other three provinces indicated that they would actively oppose the central government in closing the enterprise. Further, more "Nizhegorodtsy" responded that they would urge the regional government also to oppose the plant's closure.[62]

While in these regions government was dependent on business, business was similarly dependent on government. For example, directors of large enterprises faced problems specific to their size—including a desperate lack of resources necessary to continue financing the cradle-to-grave services (like housing, exercise facilities, child care, schools, and food subsidies) that under the Soviet system they had traditionally provided. Other economic woes, including dwindling federal subsidies and soaring inter-enterprise debt, were not specific to very large enterprises but, because of often more complex coordination issues, were felt more severely by them than by smaller enterprises.[63]

[62] This question is drawn from the 1993 survey described in chapter 1. Respondents were presented with the following scenario: "Let's say that the government of the Russian Federation decided to close a large industrial enterprise in this oblast. This decision would lead to unemployment in the short run. You don't work at this enterprise, however. Which of the following responses best describes your thinking on this issue? (i) I would support the government's decision; (ii) I would fight against this decision; (iii) I would do nothing; or (iv) Hard to say." Where 1 is support the center and 3 is oppose the center, the mean of respondents in Nizhnii Novgorod was 2.18 as compared, for example, to 2.04 in Saratov. The difference between means is statistically significant at .05.

[63] For example, the largest enterprise in Saratov, SEPO, reportedly had 955 domestic suppliers for its refrigerator production line. The fact that many of these suppliers were in deep financial trouble after 1990 wreaked havoc on SEPO's production capabilities ("Russian Federation Defense Conversion: Two Enterprises in Transition," Case Studies Prepared by the International Finance Corporation and Company Assistance, Limited, August 1992).

Given the increased interdependence between economic and political actors fostered by the concentration of the regional economy, assuming rational behavior, we should expect to observe cooperation on the part of economic and political actors. *However, interdependence and congruent interests, as Hume's parable, the tragedy of the commons and the prisoners' dilemma noted earlier, are not always sufficient to guarantee collective action.* In a region with an economy concentrated within a particular sector or among a few particularly large and important enterprises, the issue of social and structural context, or what Mark Granovetter refers to as "embeddedness," played a key role in explaining behavior and political outcomes.[64]

The embeddedness of the actions of political and economic interests in such an environment meant first that there was a more limited and specialized pool from which to draw regional political actors. While a fuller discussion of this appears in chapter 6 (where evidence of the effect of cooperation between economic and political actors is linked specifically to performance measures), it is important to note here briefly that in both Nizhnii Novgorod and Tiumen', for example, the regional governors were previously employed in the key sectors of the regional economy. In Tiumen' the first governor, Iurii Shafranik, was the director of one of the region's main oil concerns—Langepas. In Nizhnii Novgorod, not only Governor Boris Nemtsov but the then chair of the regional legislature, Evgenii Krestianinov, were both previously employed in one of the leading regional technical support institutes in the defense (specifically radio physics) industry. Although they graduated ten years apart, observers reported a certain "meeting of the minds" that Krestianinov and others attributed to their common backgrounds and the relationship to regional industry (in terms of understanding) that this yielded.[65] In a concentrated regional economy, therefore, the likelihood of bureaucratic capture by economic interests is increased.

Second, the embeddedness of economic and political behavior in a concentrated economic community promoted horizontal networks between political and economic actors that in turn promoted credible commitments. Chapter 6 demonstrates systematically that the embeddedness of the interactions of political and economic actors in a "company town"

---

[64] Granovetter, "Economic Action and Social Structure." See also Karl Polanyi, *The Great Transformation: The Political and Economic Origins of Our Time* (Boston: Beacon, 1944).

[65] Author's interview with Kozlov, May 10, 1993.

environment had a positive effect on government performance. (This line of causality is depicted in Figure 1.1.)

Aspects of this theory are perhaps reminiscent of traditional elite analysis and theories of elite pacting familiar to Latin Americanists in particular. But several areas distinguish my theory from these approaches.

Traditional elite analysis generally holds that similar backgrounds of elite actors assist in the mutual understanding and cooperation of elites.[66] But elite analysis (for it does not really constitute a theory) fails to capture the give and take of politics that is embodied in the theory of coalitions and cooperation in higher-performance Russian regional governments. This is because the elite approach focuses almost exclusively on how the backgrounds and training of elites condition their behavior. However, the added value of focusing on the effects of relative economic concentration on elite behavior is precisely that it explains why it is rational for elites of similar backgrounds to cooperate in certain circumstances, rather than in all instances as elite analysis suggests. Thus focusing on elite backgrounds alone would lose the contractual aspect of the relationship between rationally motivated political and economic elites where the supporting condition is economic concentration.

The literature on elite convergence and pacting is similarly lacking relative to the theory presented here. A consistent theme of John Higley's work, for example, is that the unity of elites is one of the most important determinants of regime form (authoritarian or democratic).[67] This literature argues that a successful transition to democracy requires a consensually unified elite where there is "essential agreement and consensus about the desirability of a politically stable system, usually in something like its current form, and about the goals, if any, toward which the system

---

[66] Examples of traditional elite theory include C. Wright Mills, *The Power Elite* (New York: Oxford University Press, 1956); Gaetano Mosca, *The Ruling Class*, ed. Arthur Livingstone (New York: McGraw-Hill, 1939); Floyd Hunter, *Community Power Structure* (Chapel Hill: North Carolina University Press, 1953); and Robert Michels, *Political Parties: A Sociological Study of the Oligarchical Tendencies of Modern Democracy* (New York: Dover, 1959).

[67] See, for example, John Higley and Michael G. Burton, *Democratic Transitions and Democratic Breakdowns: The Elite Variable* (Austin: Texas Papers on Latin America, Working Papers of the Institute of Latin American Studies, University of Texas at Austin, 1988); G. Lowell Field and John Higley, *Elitism* (Boston: Routledge and Kegan Paul, 1980); and John Higley and Richard Gunther, eds., *Elites and Democratic Consolidation in Latin America and Southern Europe* (New York: Cambridge University Press, 1992).

is ostensibly moving."[68] Conflict can and does occur within such a system—but "within a tradition of political contest."[69]

Although Higley and his coauthors identify elite settlements and elite convergence as two possible ways in which a previously disunified elite may achieve consensual unity, their work contains little generalizable theory or clear causal logic. A recurring theme is the apparently necessary supporting condition of economic development. This, however, cannot explain situations in sufficiently developed cases where elite unity has not occurred. As a result, the description of elite unity provided by Higley et al. merely indicates when elite unity is unlikely (but still possible?) to occur (when countries are underdeveloped), rather than expressly spelling out with a clear causal argument when elite unity is likely to occur. Linked to this problem is that the conclusions for elite behavior drawn here appear to be applicable to a limited number of cases. Indeed, Higley and Burton themselves note that "our concepts steer a middle course between grand theory and a retreat to local history."[70]

In focusing on elite pacting in transitional situations, Guillermo O'Donnell, and Philippe Schmitter touch on similar themes but also share similar shortcomings with Higley.[71] Elite pacts are described as informal agreements. Pacts are often temporary and secretive agreements among a small group of actors seeking to redefine the rules governing the exercise of power to their own advantage. Like Higley's settlements, pacts are not always possible or necessary in bringing about a democratic transition, but, according to O'Donnell and Schmitter, they can play an important role in any process of regime change that is brought about gradually. A problem that the notion of elite pacting shares with Higley's work on elite settlements is that, although O'Donnell and Schmitter provide a general discussion of economic, military, and political "moments" when a pact may come about, a generalizable theory as to why pacting is possible in some cases and not in others is missing. Too much appears to hang on contingency and chance.

In contrast, the theory of convergence and coalition formation in Russian regional government is far more generalizable because of its reliance

---

[68] John Higley, G. Lowell Field, and Knut Groholt, *Elite Structure and Ideology: A Theory with Applications to Norway* (New York: Columbia University Press, 1976), p. 28.

[69] Ibid., p. 32.

[70] Ibid., p. 27.

[71] Guillermo O'Donnell and Philippe Schmitter, *Transitions from Authoritarian Rule: Tentative Conclusions about Uncertain Democracies* (Baltimore, Md.: The Johns Hopkins University Press, 1986).

on the structural variable of economic context. It is the behavioral norms and social structures that are derived from economic context that explain differences in the performance of political institutions.[72]

THEORETICAL CONTRIBUTIONS

This study of Russian regional government performance makes three main theoretical contributions to the study of simultaneous political and economic transitions. First, it emphasizes the importance of the structure of economic factor endowments in bringing about cooperative behavior between economic and political elites in times of great change. In making this argument, this study challenges those approaches to democratization that stress only political culture, modernization, or institutional design as key variables.[73] Although these factors can be, and often are, important in some circumstances, the relationships formed as a result of the structure of the economy are also important in explaining political outcomes during simultaneous political and economic transitions.

Second, with respect to some neo-institutional arguments in particular, this study demonstrates that successful reform efforts involve more than merely getting the institutions right. Neo-institutionalism has had a special appeal to students of Russia's transition since rarely does one find as good examples of institutional destruction and creation—one of the main projects of neo-institutionalist analysis—as in formerly communist countries. The literature has so far been used largely to explain the collapse of the old system rather than focusing on the creation and opera-

[72] Terry Karl has made similar observations in Latin America. Karl notes that without identifying the structural determinants of the transitional context, pacting would simply be the product of astute leaders. She argues that structural constraints (socioeconomic and political) are confining conditions that determine the range of choice open to elite actors. Although the theory of coalition formation in this study of Russian regional government performance shares the general emphasis on the influence of economic structural conditions on elite behavior, Karl's work focuses on how structural conditions bring about regime change rather than on institutional behavior once the decision to transit to democracy has been made. Further, Karl overlooks the importance of behavioral resources—like close, cooperative communities—that can further undergird collective action between political and economic actors. See Terry Lynn Karl, "Dilemmas of Democratization in Latin America," *Comparative Politics* 23 (1990): 1–21.

[73] For example, Putnam, *Making Democracy Work*; Robert C. Fried and Francine Rabinovitz, *Comparative Urban Politics: A Performance Approach* (Englewood Cliffs, N.J.: Prentice-Hall, 1980); Gabriel Almond and Sidney Verba, *The Civic Culture: Political Attitudes and Democracy in Five Nations* (Princeton, N.J.: Princeton University Press, 1989).

tion of the new system. Perhaps for this reason, the emphasis has been primarily on the rational choice variant of neo-institutionalism, focusing on the incentives that institutions provided strategically minded political actors.[74]

The logic of some institutional analysis in Russia is that institutional change—from authoritarian to democratic, for example—will change actors' incentives and thus change their behavior. This perception of the relationship between institutions and behavior was the logic behind the reform of political and economic institutions (and shock therapy in particular) in formerly communist countries. Indeed, institutional reform in post-Soviet Russia has been implemented with the understanding that democratic and market-oriented institutional change should produce concomitant societal and elite behavioral change necessary to bring about a consolidated democracy and a market economy.[75]

But this study of Russian regional government performance shows that "new institutions are adopted in a world already replete with institutions."[76] Contrary to rational choice neo-institutional analysis, the point of origin for transitional societies is not "one of freely contracting individuals, but one based on an institutional landscape that already embodies fundamental asymmetries of power."[77] The relative concentration of regional economies, legacies of the command economy, is a crucial case in point.

The important corrective that this study makes to a straightforward rational choice institutionalist analysis, then, is that new institutions, and

---

[74] See, for example, Roeder, *Red Sunset*; and Solnick, "The Breakdown of Hierarchies."

[75] See Peter C. Ordeshook, "Institutions and Incentives: The Prospects for Russian Democracy," California Institute of Technology, unpublished mimeo, 1994. Ordeshook argues that the incentives in the new Russian political institutions (post-December 1993) are simply "wrong" and thus democracy is unstable there. Ordeshook believes that if we can somehow alter the institutions so the incentives are "right" (as they are in the United States constitution, for example) we should see increased democratic stability in Russia. The problem with this argument is that without looking at how exactly the residue of the old institutional framework combines with the incentives provided by weak new institutions, it is difficult to understand just exactly where, or whether, institutional incentives can be "tweaked." It is also difficult to understand why political actors benefiting from the current amalgam of institutions would allow such changes to occur. Ordeshook's analysis thus appears rather static.

[76] Peter Hall and Rosemary Taylor, "Political Science and the Four New Institutionalisms," paper presented at the Annual Meeting of the American Political Science Association, New York, September 1994, p. 20.

[77] Ibid.

political and economic actors that operate within them, do not start with a tabula rasa. Behaviors emanating from institutional context and history influence the way actors respond to the incentives that new political institutions provide.[78] The argument here therefore indicates that we need to combine contextual and structural variables in order to better understand political outcomes in transitional situations.

Finally, in arguing that the more concentrated the economy, the higher is regional government performance, this study points to the critical impact that cooperation between economic and political actors can have on regime governability—particularly in times of crisis. In doing so, the argument draws both on the literature on corporatist solutions to governing in hard times in Western Europe and on the insights of the rich and more recent political economy literature that focuses on the importance of economic factor endowments in structuring politics.

The concluding chapter discusses in detail the implications of this theory. The most obvious normative possibility is that although cooperative coalitional behavior between economic and political elites may be beneficial in the short term, in the longer term it has troubling implications for the further development of democracy and a market economy. This is because of the risk that emergent societal interests will be excluded from the relationship and inefficient enterprises will be protected by governments dependent on the support of their enterprise directors where the greater good of economic efficiency might otherwise require them to shut down unprofitable enterprises.

Before exploring these potentially troubling implications, chapter 3 delves further into the process of exploring how variations in preexisting economic structure, and the resulting relationships between political and economic elites, influence institutional performance.

---

[78] Again, this general point is also made by North in *Institutions, Institutional Change, and Economic Performance.*

Decentralization and Democratization: The Development of Regional Government Institutions

BEFORE MEASURING differences in institutional performance in chapter 4 and testing theories that might explain variance in institutional behavior in chapters 5 and 6, it will be useful to examine the development of Russian regional government institutions.

The thawing of the Soviet system brought about dramatic changes in center-periphery relations and regional government structures. The late 1980s saw the initiation of dual processes of democratization and decentralization in the USSR as a whole (leading eventually to the demise of the Soviet Union in December 1991), and in Russia in particular.[1] Mikhail Gorbachev came to power as the last general secretary of the CPSU with a mandate for change because cracks had appeared in the monolithic system of economic and political control. The highly centralized, vertical system of administration, with the Party at its apex, which Lenin established and Stalin perfected, had become, under Brezhnev's long tenure, increasingly incapable of sustaining growth. As the economy grew more sophisticated, the Party lost the ability to manage it through planning mechanisms.[2] Moreover, with the completion of industrialization, Lenin's revolutionary Party, designed initially for high societal mobilization, became little more than a bureaucratic behemoth.

That Gorbachev's initial intention was to reform the system, rather than ruin it, seems clear. However, once he began to tinker with the Party, centrifugal forces spun the process of reform out of control. Democratizing the Soviet system, and the displacement of the Party as the vanguard of the society and the economy, led to decentralization and an increase in regional power. Multi-candidate, competitive elections in the Russian

---

[1] Indeed, throughout the 1980s, in the regions of Russia (and especially in Siberia), there was growing pressure to decentralize economically and politically.

[2] This is Peter Rutland's argument in *The Politics of Economic Stagnation in the Soviet Union: The Role of Local Party Organs in Economic Management* (New York: Cambridge University Press, 1993).

heartland created an impetus for increased regional power over policy. Not unreasonably, if local politicians were to be held accountable to their constituents, then they insisted on having more control over policy.

This chapter discusses the relationship between democratization and decentralization during the first few years of Russia's transition. Treating the reformed regional governments as a dependent variable, I examine the development of regional government structures and the nature of their power over policy by the early 1990s. I begin with a brief explanation of the organization of regional government historically and during the Soviet period before the reforms proposed initially at the Nineteenth Party Conference in 1988. A description of the first competitive elections to regional soviets in 1990 follows. These elections led to increased demands for more local control over local affairs. As a result, political conflicts between the Russian center and the periphery ensued. I then discuss the respective wins and losses of Moscow and the regions in these altercations over the future shape of the Russian Federation. Although the regions certainly did not gain everything they set out to, on balance the formal powers of regional governments increased through 1993. Indeed, so powerful had regions become that by the end of the first nine months of 1993, Moscow was losing 800 billion rubles in withheld tax revenue to regional governments.[3]

REGIONAL GOVERNMENT IN HISTORICAL PERSPECTIVE

Pre-Revolutionary Provincial Institutions

The Soviet Union, and the Russian Empire before it, had relatively limited traditions of local self-government. Although there had been a brief flirtation with local self-government in sixteenth-century Muscovy, it did not last, and after the Time of Troubles, the state relied on military governors, initially called "*namestniki*" and then "*voevody*." Their task was to extract revenue for the prince and to maintain law and order.[4] These representatives of the throne were appointed by the emperor but were often difficult to control from Moscow and later St. Petersburg. With primitive transportation systems, the farther one traveled across the Ural

[3] See *Foreign Broadcast Information Services* (hereafter, *FBIS*), November 4, 1993, p. 29.

[4] See Nicholas Riasanovsky, *A History of Russia*, 4th ed. (New York: Oxford University Press, 1984), p. 192; and Richard C. Robbins, *The Tsar's Viceroys: Russian Provincial Government in the Last Years of the Empire* (Ithaca, N.Y.: Cornell University Press, 1987), p. 5

Mountains into Siberia, the increasingly corrupt and self-interested these provincial governors became.[5]

Under Peter the Great, the demands on local administrations grew more complex. As a result, Peter undertook further administrative reform at the local level. Initially the country was divided into eleven large regional governments, called *gubernii*. Local officials were now to be responsible for regional welfare and economic growth. By 1719 Peter had divided the country into fifty provinces (*provintsii*), headed by voevody. These in turn were divided further into districts (*uezdy*), headed by commissars appointed from the gentry class.

Richard Robbins notes that in making these initial changes, Peter set the stage for what would prove to be some of the enduring challenges of Russian governance: (1) How should the functions of the state be divided between the center and the provinces? (2) How much discretion and power should local leaders be given over policy? and (3) To what degree and in what capacity could local people participate in the government of the regions?[6]

To better address these issues, Catherine the Great completed more redistricting in the late eighteenth century, but with an eye to further decentralization.[7] She drew new boundaries that abolished provintsii and left only gubernii and uezdy. An appointed governor became the head of the administration of each guberniia. Catherine drew on many of Peter's ideas and even attempted a partial separation of legislative, executive, and judicial powers, "without, of course, impairing her autocracy or ultimate control from St. Petersburg."[8] She restored the vice-regal status of governor and made him responsible to herself and the senate. She ultimately appointed a namestnik—or governor general—above the governor who was to be her official representative in the provinces.[9]

Her reorganization of the local apparatus at the uezd level was designed to co-opt the landed gentry into government in return for their

[5] See W. Bruce Lincoln, *The Conquest of a Continent: Siberia and the Russians* (New York: Random House, 1994), ch. 18, which describes the corruption of military governors in Siberia in the late eighteenth and early nineteenth centuries.

[6] Robbins, *The Tsar's Viceroys*, p. 6.

[7] Riasanovsky, *A History of Russia*, p. 261.

[8] Ibid., p. 262.

[9] Robbins, *The Tsar's Viceroys*, pp. 8–9. Significantly, the term *namestnik* was appropriated informally in 1991 to describe the new position of presidential representative in the provinces. Neither Catherine's *namestnik* nor Yeltsin's ever wielded the power in the regional apparatus that the creators of the office had intended. Yeltsin's representative in the provinces is described in greater detail in a later section of this chapter.

support for her rule in the wake of the Pugachev rebellion. This enabled the local gentry to participate at the guberniia and uezd levels in local administration. Catherine's contribution to the development of the imperial system of provincial rule was to create a comprehensive system of provincial government institutions. However, because the serf majority had no place in this arrangement, these institutions did little to represent the political will of the Russian masses.

The system that Catherine the Great introduced remained more or less intact until the Great Reforms of the 1860s. It was replaced by Alexander II's attempt to stimulate local initiative and activity through the *zemstvo* system of grass-roots legislatures and town dumas (legislatures). Under this reform, representative zemstvo assemblies were created at district, town, and provincial levels. Membership in these assemblies, however, was proportional to land ownership, and this limited the broadly representative nature of these bodies. Further, the office of appointed governor was retained.

Although gubernatorial power over provincial administration generally increased, the zemstvos for the first time confronted the governor with a reasonably powerful and independent counterbalance. Robbins reports that governors frequently had to employ *sluzhebnyi takt*, or "service tact": "This term had no precise definition but in a broad sense meant the ability to maintain authority without giving offense, a willingness to cultivate, and if necessary, to appease powerful local forces, or the knack for reconciling conflicting parties and resolving differences."[10] The political influence of the local gentry was of the utmost importance by 1917. Of particular significance for the theory of regional government performance advanced in chapter 2, "without cooperation from the nobility, a governor could not rule effectively."[11]

The Revolution of 1917 and the Establishment of the System of Soviets

Soviets rose to prominence following the October Revolution, but they initially appeared in 1905. The word *soviet* comes from the Russian word meaning "advice" or "counsel." Soviets were intended initially to be the primary instruments by which workers could participate in factory committees to negotiate with owners, and did not initially connote mass participation in government.

[10] Ibid., p. 126.
[11] Ibid., p. 149.

According to communist doctrine, soviets, as elected bodies of workers, were to have supreme legislative authority. The Declaration of Rights of the Toiling and Exploited People, issued in January 1918, announced that "Russia is declared a republic of soviets of workers', soldiers', and peasants' deputies. All power in the center and locally belongs to these soviets."[12] Despite Lenin's call for "All power to the soviets!" and the Communists' stated intention that soviets become one of the primary mechanisms by which workers would participate in government, following the October Revolution power lay primarily with the Communist Party.

As the vanguard of the proletariat, the Communist Party was to lead every aspect of life. The First Bolshevik Party Program of 1919 established the relationship that would enslave the soviets to the Party:

> The Communist Party strives particularly for the realization of its program and for the full mastery of contemporary political organizations such as the Soviets. . . . The Russian Communist Party must win for itself undivided political mastery in the Soviets and de facto control of all their work, through practical, daily, dedicated work in the Soviets [and] the advancement of its most stalwart and devoted members to all Soviet positions.[13]

The constitution of the Russian Socialist Federation of Soviet Republics (1918) and the 1923 Constitution of the Soviet Union instituted this relationship between Party and state structures at all levels. Throughout the summer of 1918, local government was transferred from the zemstvo assemblies at the uezd and guberniia levels to local soviets.[14] At the same time a parallel Party structure was erected at all levels.

The 1936 "Stalin Constitution" further enshrined this system of relatively powerless legislatures dominated by overbearing Party structures. The words *oblast* and *krai* (literally, "region" and "land," respectively) entered the Russian political lexicon shortly after the revolution, but with

---

[12] As cited in Richard Pipes, *The Formation of the Soviet Union: Communism and Nationalism 1917–1923*, rev. ed. (New York: Atheneum, 1964; originally published by Harvard University Press, 1954), p. 243.

[13] Program of the Russian Communist Party (1919), in TsK, RKP(b), Rossiiskaia Kommunisticheskaia Partiia (bol'shevikov) v rezoliutsiiakh ee s'ezdov i konferentsii (1899–1922) (Moscow-Petrograd, 1923), as quoted in Pipes, *The Formation of the Soviet Union*, pp. 255–256.

[14] That transfers of power were consolidated in Saratov as early as January 1918 is reported in Donald Raleigh, *Revolution on the Volga: 1917 in Saratov* (Ithaca, N.Y.: Cornell University Press, 1986), pp. 302–306.

the regional reform of 1929 through the mid-1930s Stalin redrew many of the old guberniia (provincial) borders, thereby forming the majority of the administrative units that persisted as oblasts and krais into the post-Soviet era.[15]

Various attempts were made to decentralize the system of subnational government during Nikita Khrushchev's tenure as first secretary, most notably the sovnarkhoz reform and the attempt to bifurcate the Party, but these experiments were shelved, along with Khrushchev, by 1964–65.[16] Official criticism of the soviets as nondemocratic organs was not tolerated, and, as a result, further efforts to improve their status as representative institutions came to naught.[17] Thus the outlines of the local government system that appeared in the 1920s, and were further developed in the 1936 Constitution, endured more or less until the sweeping reforms that were initiated in 1988 and enacted through multi-candidate elections of soviets at all levels in 1990.

No Power to the Soviets

To appreciate fully the impact of democratization, and the decentralization of the Russian state that accompanied it beginning in 1990, it is crucial to understand the extreme centralization that characterized the Soviet system.

With few exceptions, the contours of the Soviet state remained constant from Stalin's death in 1953 until the declarations of sovereignty in 1990 that began in the Baltic republics and spread to Ukraine, Russia, and beyond. Until then, the Soviet Union was composed of 15 union republics, 20 autonomous republics (ASSRs), 8 autonomous oblasts, 10 autonomous okrugs, 120 oblasts, and 6 krais (Figure 3.1).

As the largest of the fifteen union republics, the Russian Socialist Federated Soviet Republic (RSFSR) was home to eighty-eight subnational

[15] See Merle Fainsod, *Smolensk under Soviet Rule* (Boston: Unwin Hyman, 1958; reprinted 1989).

[16] For more on Khrushchev's bifurcation scheme, see Barbara Chotiner, *Khrushchev's Party Reform: Coalition Building and Institutional Innovation* (Westport, Conn.: Greenwood, 1984); and Barbara Chotiner, *Dismantling an Innovation: The 1964 Decision Reunifying Industrial and Agricultural Organs of the CPSU* (Pittsburgh: Center for Russian and East European Studies, 1985).

[17] Michael E. Urban, *More Power to the Soviets: The Democratic Evolution in the USSR* (United Kingdom: Edward Elgar, 1990), pp. 16–17.

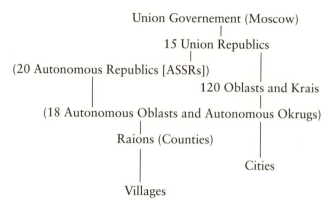

Figure 3.1. The Basic Arrangement of Subnational Units under the Soviet System. *Note*: Only some Union Republics had autonomous republics and oblasts and krais. (The Russian Republic had both.) Further, only some ASSRs and oblasts and krais had autonomous oblasts and autonomous okrugs located within their borders. In subnational units without autonomies, the next highest level was the raion. Furthermore, not all cities were subordinate to the raion, but were directly subordinate to the oblast and krai.

units divided into three categories, including (i) sixteen ASSRs; (ii) forty-nine oblasts and six krais, plus the two "special status" cities of Moscow and Leningrad[18]; and (iii) fifteen autonomous oblasts and autonomous okrugs (geographically located within the borders of ASSRs, oblasts, and krais).

The republic was organized according to the "national-territorial" principle such that ASSRs and the autonomous oblasts and okrugs were organized around one or several of the hundred or so ethnic groups located on the territory of the RSFSR. Oblasts and krais were essentially administrative units. Oblasts, populated primarily by ethnic Russians, were not attributed any particular ethnic character, whereas krais combined characteristics of both oblasts and ASSRs. Autonomous republics and oblasts had essentially the same powers on paper, with ASSRs sup-

---

[18] For most of the Soviet period it is more accurate to say that only Moscow had special status. For this, and more about Party prefectoralism, see especially Timothy J. Colton, *Moscow: Governing the Socialist Metropolis* (Cambridge, Mass.: Belknap Press of Harvard University Press, 1995).

posedly having slightly more independence from Moscow. The oblast and krai level remains the basic subnational unit in which more than 80 percent of the country's population lives. In order to hold the variables of institutional design and ethnicity constant in examining the issue of government performance, the oblast and krai level is the focus of this study and the discussion that follows.

The 1977 "Brezhnev Constitution" of the USSR declared the country to be "a unified, federal multinational state formed on the principle of socialist federalism" (Article 70). It is difficult, however, to reconcile the notion of the planned economy and the monoparty system of the Soviet Union with Western understandings of federalism.[19] Indeed the Soviet Union and the RSFSR, as one of its fifteen union republics, were federations in name only. Jerry Hough and Merle Fainsod point out, in reference to the soviet constitution, that the sovereignty of the union republics was limited "only in all the areas in which they might want to take action."[20] Similarly, in the RSFSR, the sovereignty of its subnational units was severely circumscribed.

The high degree of centralization in the Soviet Union and the Russian Republic was owing, in no small part, to the omnipresence of the CPSU and the centralization of Party structures. As Richard Pipes aptly noted:

> If the soviets were to be the supreme legislative organs of the new state; if they, in turn, were to be subjected to de facto control by the Communist Party; and if, finally, the Communist Party itself . . . was to be completely subordinated to the Central Committee, then clearly actual sovereignty in all Soviet areas belonged to the Central Committee of the Russian [later Soviet] Communist Party. Soviet federalism did not involve a distribution of power between the center and the province; only a corresponding decentralization of the Communist Party would have made the establishment of genuine federal relations possible.[21]

There was, then, a basic collision between the requirements of the division of jurisdictions required by a federal system and the high degree of

---

[19] An early discussion of Soviet understandings of federalism can be found in Vernon Aspaturian, "The Theory and Practice of Soviet Federalism," *Journal of Politics* 12, no. 1 (1950): 20–51. For very brief, but more recent discussions of Soviet federalism and the impact of nationalism , see Gregory Gleason, *Federalism and Nationalism: The Struggle for Republican Rights in the USSR* (Boulder, Colo.: Westview, 1990); and Stephen Kux, *Soviet Federalism: A Comparative Perspective* (Boulder, Colo.: Westview, 1990).

[20] Jerry F. Hough and Merle Fainsod, *How the Soviet Union Is Governed* (Cambridge, Mass.: Harvard University Press, 1979), p. 483.

[21] Pipes, *The Formation of the Soviet Union*, pp. 245–246.

centralization envisioned by a state dominated by a highly centralized political party.

At the local level, the dominance of the Party was translated into practice through the establishment of Party organizations at the union republic level and below. The RSFSR, however, had no union republic Communist Party (until 1990) and was included in the all-union Party structures. The Party organizations in the RSFSR, beginning with the oblast level, were, in descending order, oblast Party organizations, district or county (*raion*) Party organizations, city Party organizations, and village Party organizations, all the way down to primary Party organizations (PPOs) in all places of work. Each level was dominated by the next highest level such that the oblast Party organization was at the top of the territorial hierarchy and, in the RSFSR, was subordinate only to the Central Committee of the CPSU. The first secretary of the oblast Party committee (*obkom*) was therefore the undisputed political boss of the oblast.

Since Party organizations were designed to parallel state organs of power, the basic state units were (in descending order of administrative authority) oblast soviets, raion soviets, city soviets, and village soviets.[22] In 1989 the Soviet Union had 49,176 soviets, in which some 2.3 million part-time deputies served, elected for two-and-one-half-year terms.[23] Ronald Hill argues that despite modest attempts at reform in the 1960s and 1970s, "administration at the local level was effectively an extension of central authority."[24] This was because, as with Party organizations, the soviets were supposed to be subordinated to the next highest administrative level (and effectively also to corresponding Party structures all the way up to the Central Committee). Thus, officially at least, the city soviet (*gorsoviet*) was subordinate to the oblast soviet (*oblsoviet*). Each level was bound (at least in theory, if not always in practice) to follow the decisions made at the next highest level. This created a unitary system of soviets and was contrary to the idea of meaningful local self-government.

Soviets were further bound together by the principle of democratic centralism which was incorporated into Article 3 of the 1977 USSR Con-

[22] These generalizations apply to the RSFSR. The reader should recall the exceptions to these organizational arrangements noted in Figure 3.1.

[23] Seweryn Bialer, "The Changing Soviet Political System: The Nineteenth Party Conference and After," in Seweryn Bialer, ed., *Politics, Society, and Nationality inside Gorbachev's Russia* (Boulder, Colo.: Westview, 1989), p. 230.

[24] Ronald J. Hill, "The Development of Soviet Local Government since Stalin's Death," *Soviet Local Politics and Government*, ed. Everett M. Jacobs (Boston: Allen and Unwin, 1983), p. 18.

stitution. This concept rendered the system of soviets more "centralist" than "democratic." Theoretically, however, the "democratic" aspect referred to the "elected" status (discussed below) of deputies in the soviets and their accountability to their electorate. It also incorporated the rights of lower-level soviets to make proposals and recommendations to higher organs in policy areas that affected the lower level.

The "centralist" element, however, contradicted this in that it instituted the obligation of lower-level soviets to execute the decisions made by the soviet at the next highest level and also by the CPSU, regardless of the recommendations of lower levels. Further, if a superior soviet considered a decision by a lower-level soviet illegal, it could overturn it. Finally, although theoretically local soviets were supposed to decide local spending priorities on their own, the "centralism" of democratic centralism meant that the primary source of revenue for local soviets came from Moscow and had to be spent according to the economic priorities of the national plan.

Of course the soviets were also dominated by corresponding Party organizations. Brezhnev had modernized the Bolshevik principle of Party supremacy in the 1977 Constitution's Article 6, which established the CPSU as "the leading and guiding force of Soviet society and the nucleus of its political system, of all state organizations and public organizations." Theoretically, this was based on the idea that the parts of socialist society were inextricably bound to one another in an organic whole, and thus individual interests were the interests of all and no part was to gain at the expense of the others. Because there was but one common interest, only one political party could exist in communist society. In practical terms, this meant that the Party maintained control over local soviets, often "supplanting" their authority.

Although the soviets were officially regarded as the hallmark of socialist democracy, in reality soviets only faintly resembled Western understandings of representative government. The Party dominated the soviets through a range of other instruments, not the least of which was control over the nominations of deputies to sit in oblast soviets.[25] Candidates to the soviet represented territorial election districts but were nominated at their workplaces. No one received a nomination without the support of

[25] For a comprehensive treatment of exactly how local elections were conducted under the Soviet system, see Jeffrey W. Hahn, *Soviet Grassroots: Citizen Participation in Local Government* (Princeton, N.J.: Princeton University Press, 1988), pp. 97–107. An earlier, similarly comprehensive study is Theodore Friedgut's *Political Participation in the USSR* (Princeton, N.J.: Princeton University Press, 1979).

the PPO and, depending on the importance of the district, the obkom. This ensured that in noncompetitive, single-candidate elections, only candidates who were warmly regarded by the Party were allowed to participate.

Further, a certain number of candidacies were set aside for important Party figures. Hahn estimates that at the oblast level as many as 25 percent of elected deputies worked full-time as bureaucrats in the soviet organs and the Party.[26] The oblast Party first secretary was assured a seat in the soviet, along with the second secretary and other key Party functionaries. This was the first obstacle to democratic, competitive elections. The system of quota selection of candidates, by which the Party ensured the proportional representation in the soviet of various population groups (workers, intellectuals, farmers, women, and so on) also limited the competitive nature of the electoral system. Finally, the Party controlled the right of *nomenklatura*—lists of important appointments to various bureaucratic posts.

The two hundred to three hundred deputies (depending on the region's size) to the soviets were "elected"—in most cases "unanimously"—by 99 percent of the voting population in what could scarcely be described as free elections. Only one candidate's name was printed on the ballot, and voting, for all intents and purposes, was obligatory. Indeed, Theodore Friedgut and Jeffrey Hahn report that Soviet citizens participated in these elections largely to avoid drawing unfavorable attention to themselves for not voting.[27] In describing voting procedures under the Soviet regime, Friedgut explains: "The act of voting becomes almost an obeisance. Should he wish to demonstrate his support for the candidate, the voter may receive his ballot from the election officials and deposit it directly into the ballot box. Thus, support of the regime requires no undue action or effort."[28]

Once "elected" in this manner by their constituents, deputies in the soviets then elected an executive committee (*ispolkom*). In reality, the Party controlled election to the ispolkom, and generally the overlap between the chief functionaries of the local Party organization and the ispolkom was significant. Hough and Fainsod reported that in 1975, for example, the executive committees of oblast soviets had memberships of eight to eleven people. This almost invariably included the first secretary

---

[26] Hahn, *Soviet Grassroots*, p. 101.

[27] Ibid., pp. 106–107; Theodore Friedgut, *Political Participation in the USSR*, p. 108.

[28] Friedgut, *Political Participation*, pp. 108–109.

of the oblast Party committee and the heads of five or six of the twelve or so executive departments. [29] Soviet sessions were held four times a year, with the ispolkom meeting twice each month. There were also departments and administrations subordinate to the executive agencies of oblast governments (up to thirty or so of these in larger oblasts). These departments included, according to Hough, roughly five in the agricultural realm, four or more in light industry, several in construction, and at least one each in social security, communications, justice, health, and so on.[30] Further vertical centralization was ensured by subordinating these administrative agencies to the department or ministry at the next highest level:

> Thus, the city education department is subordinated to both the executive committee of the city soviet and the oblast education department. The oblast education department in turn is responsible both to the executive committee of the oblast soviet and the republican ministry of education. The executive committee itself is subordinated to both the local soviet and the executive committee (or Council of Ministers) at the next territorial level.[31]

This dual subordination (*dvoinoe podchinenie*), in combination with the soviet's subordination to the oblast Party organization, effectively limited the soviets' role in political life. Further, the dictates of the planned economy meant that local soviets had virtually no independent authority to establish their own spending priorities—this was essentially decided by the Moscow bureaucracy. In short, local soviets had broad responsibilities on paper, but in reality the system of "multi-subordination" ensured a high degree of centralization and rendered the soviets administrative, not policy-making, organs. Regional policy was set in Moscow, with little room for local initiative even on the part of local Party organs.[32] Indeed, so centralized was the Soviet system that a foreign traveler, to her horror, discovered a number of years ago that even local train schedules in Ukraine were run according to Moscow time![33]

---

[29] Hough and Fainsod, *How the Soviet Union Is Governed*, p. 485.

[30] Ibid., p. 490.

[31] Ibid.

[32] Indeed "localism" (*mestnichestvo*) was actively discouraged, and Party secretaries were at times scolded for pushing local over national interests at Central Committee meetings. Howard Biddulph notes the "modest impact" of Party secretaries on policy in "Local Interest Articulation at CPSU Congresses," *World Politics* 36, no. 1 (1983): 28–52.

[33] This had been the case since June 1930.

More Power to the Soviets: Institutional Reform
and the 1990 Elections

As part of his policy of restructuring (perestroika), as early as 1986 the last general secretary of the CPSU, Mikhail S. Gorbachev, spoke of the need for decentralization: "Excessive centralization exists in tackling issues that are far from always clearly visible from the center and can be handled much better on the spot. That is why we are resolutely directing one course toward enhancing the independence and the level of activity of local organs of power."[34]

Citing Lenin's original vision for the soviets, Gorbachev wanted to resolve the problem of excessive administrative capture of the soviets by the Party's administrative apparatus and resuscitate the soviets as actual governing institutions. Proposals for institutional change were further pursued at the January 1987 plenum of the CPSU, which produced a concrete resolution supporting Gorbachev's declaration that "we need democracy like we need air."[35] Experimental elections to soviets were held in several regions in 1987.

Systematic institutional reform, however, did not come until Gorbachev introduced concrete proposals to the Nineteenth Party Conference in June 1988. In his speech to the conference, Gorbachev further emphasized the need to resurrect the soviets' political role. He called for "the demarcation of the functions of the Party and state organs" and complained that although one-third of the adult population of the Soviet Union was technically elected to various state and public agencies, "the great majority of them were kept out of any real participation in the handling of state and public affairs."[36]

To remedy this, Gorbachev declared that the system of soviets would become real legislatures—more or less. He recommended: (1) multicandidate elections to soviets at all levels; (2) separation of the legislative and executive arms of state organs; (3) elimination of the effective fusion of the ispolkom and the Party such that joint resolutions would no longer be permitted; (4) increased economic and financial resources to local soviets such that they could enlarge their spheres of activity;

[34] Mikhail S. Gorbachev, speech to the Central Committee, February 25, 1986, as reported in *Daily Report of the Foreign Broadcast Information Service*, pp. 1–25.

[35] "Zakliuchitel'noe slovo general'nogo sekretaria Tsk KPSS, M.S. Gorbachv na plenume Tsk KPSS, 28 ianvaria 1987 g." *Izvestiia*, January 30, 1987.

[36] "Gorbachev Sizes Up Restructuring," *Current Digest of the Soviet Press* (hereafter, *CDSP*), 40, no. 26 (July 27, 1988): 12, 24.

and (5) the creation of an elected presidium and a permanent chair of the soviet.[37]

The presidium was to handle the soviet's organizational work, including organizing the work of the soviet's legislative committees, as well as ensuring that the soviet's decisions were properly implemented.[38] Its members were drawn largely from the chairs of the soviet's standing committees. The presidium was intended to strengthen the soviet relative to the bureaucracy and was effectively the resurrection of an institution that predated Stalin's 1936 Constitution. There had also been a presidium of the ispolkom that predated Gorbachev's reform.

Somewhat peculiarly, Gorbachev forced the approval of a proposal to declare it desirable that the local first Party secretary become the chair of the freely elected soviet. This was likely done to reassure the powerful first Party secretaries (whose support Gorbachev still needed in the Central Committee) that their futures would be guaranteed in any new order, but it would also make them popularly accountable for the first time. To put to rest further the concerns of more conservative Party functionaries, the law on elections to the USSR Congress of People's Deputies—the new super-parliament—allotted one-third of the 2,250 seats to public organizations (like Komsomol and the trade unions) and to the CPSU itself.

The undemocratic character of these last two proposals upset many reformers, and the 1989 electoral law for the Russian regional and national elections dropped these requirements. Instead, the 1990 elections were conducted according to the principles of universal adult suffrage, secret ballot and without pre-assigning seats to public organizations—including the CPSU. In contrast to the pre-1989 system, where candidates could only be nominated at their workplace, in the 1990 elections candidates could be nominated either at their workplaces, by officially registered public organizations, or at their places of residence. In particularly stark contrast to the old system, in 1990 no limit was set on the number of candidates that could run in each single-member district.

Significantly, there were no officially designated seats in the reformed soviets for high-ranking Party functionaries—in particular, obkom first secretaries (although many still won seats). From 1989–90 on, Party members were increasingly turning in their membership cards, and alternative political movements were slowly on the rise particularly in Moscow and Leningrad (as the city was so named at the time). The culmina-

[37] Ibid.

[38] For an interesting analysis of the reorganization at this point in Soviet history, see B. N. Gabrichidze "Sovet, presidium, ispolkom: sootnoshenie i razgranichenie funktsii," *Sovetskoe gosudarstvo i pravo*, no. 3 (1991): 77–86.

tion of this, just after the 1990 elections, was the removal from the constitution of Article 6, which had declared the Party to be the leading force in Soviet society. In short, these were the first elections held on Russian soil in which all "mentally competent" citizens over the age of eighteen were eligible to vote and had a choice from among several candidates representing a wide variety of viewpoints.

RUSSIA AT THE POLLS

Although the 1990 elections were not perfect by North American standards, it is hard to argue that they were not democratic. The electoral rules in force for the first round of local soviet elections on March 4, 1990, were sufficiently complicated. Candidates, if elected, would hold office for five years and had to receive at least 50 percent of the votes cast in their districts in order to be elected. Further, at least 50 percent of all eligible voters in each district had to turn out for the vote to be valid. The result was usually several rounds of run-off elections—sometimes running well into the summer of 1990. In a few cases, seats were left empty where turnout of 50 percent of eligible voters proved impossible.

In the weeks before the elections candidate biographies appeared in the oblast newspapers, and many candidates were listed "b/p" (*bezpartiinyi*), or without a party. Few political parties and movements that were popular in Moscow managed to penetrate the Russian periphery. In all four of the provinces examined in this study, Democratic Russia and the CPSU enjoyed the broadest representation, although Popular Front movements were also favored in some areas, including Yaroslavl'. Candidates held rallies and meetings with voters before the elections, and many printed and distributed their own campaign literature, often paid for out of their own pockets. Undoubtedly the CPSU had an advantage in terms of available resources—telephones, cars, and the mass media—but often a discrepancy also exists between the resources available to candidates in Western elections, and this should not necessarily be regarded as a distinct campaign advantage. Further, given the Communist Party's general unpopularity at this point in Russian history, it is difficult to argue that being a Party member was invariably a significant electoral advantage.

By most accounts, these were fairly run and free elections.[39] With few exceptions, voters were able to choose from among several candidates.

[39] Gavin Helf and Jeffrey Hahn, "Old Dogs and New Tricks: Party Elites in the Russian Regional Elections of 1990," *Slavic Review* 51, no. 3 (Fall 1992): 511–530; Timothy Col-

Although some electoral districts here and there had only one candidate on the ballot, in Yaroslavl', Nizhnii Novgorod, Saratov, and Tiumen' most seats were contested by at least two candidates. Further, even in single-candidate districts, a candidate still had to garner 50 percent of those eligible to vote with a 50 percent turnout so that running unopposed was by no means an automatic victory. Electoral districts in some cases appeared to favor communist incumbents, but gerrymandering did not appear to be widespread.[40] Although opportunities certainly existed for electoral fraud and the manipulation of votes and voters, throughout the country the elections were generally regarded as honest. In response to a survey conducted by Hahn in Yaroslavl' in 1990, for example, 70 percent of respondents felt that the elections had been fair and 16 percent felt that they had not been fair. By 1993, Hahn reports, the latter figure had dropped to 13 percent.[41]

Voter turnout in the first round of elections to oblast soviets was 70.0 percent in Yaroslavl', 75.9 percent in Nizhnii Novgorod, 80.8 percent in Saratov, and 68.9 percent in Tiumen'—remarkably high by Western standards but much lower than the 99 percent standard of old Soviet-style elections. In what is assumed to be a typical situation, one observer visited voting precincts in Yaroslavl' and reported:

> Voters went first to a table where ten to fifteen members of the election commission sat and had their names verified on a voter list. They were then given four differently colored ballots, one for each level of government where seats were to be filled: borough, city, oblast, and RSFSR. In contrast to previous practice, Russian voters were now required to take their paper ballots into a curtained booth to be marked. . . . A few older voters tried to go directly to the red ballot boxes on the other side of the booths to deposit their unmarked ballots as in the old days and had to be gently reminded that things were different now.[42]

Further, an observer in one electoral district in Moscow reported that "the spirit, if not the letter of the revised [electoral] law was respected."[43]

---

ton, "The Politics of Democratization: The Moscow Election of 1990," *Soviet Economy* 6, no. 4 (October–December 1990): 285–344.

[40] Helf and Hahn demonstrate this statistically in Yaroslavl'.

[41] Jeffrey Hahn, "The Development of Local Legislatures in Russia: The Case of Yaroslavl'," (paper delivered at Conference on Democratization in Russia: The Development of Legislative Institutions," Harvard University, October 29–31, 1993, p. 13.

[42] Hahn, "The Development of Local Legislatures," p. 12.

[43] Colton, "The Politics of Democratization," p. 295.

(For an overview of the composition of the oblast soviets elected in 1990 in Nizhnii Novgorod, Tiumen', Yaroslavl', and Saratov, see Table 1.2).

When a sufficient number of deputies had been elected for soviets to meet the required two-thirds quorum for a session (usually by June 1990 at the latest), oblast soviets held their first organizational sessions where they elected chairmen of the soviets, the presidiums, the chairs of the soviets' various standing committees, and the executive committees—still called ispolkomy—and approved the heads of various departments of the ispolkomy. The executive was to be bound by the decisions of the legislative branch (the oblast soviet). The oblast soviet retained the right to pass the oblast budget and was to receive reports from the ispolkom on the fulfillment of policy initiatives. The soviets' standing committees were to meet regularly and provide reports to full sessions of the soviet and the chair of the soviet, which was a permanent position.

Despite these reforms, however, institutionally the balance of power was still tipped in favor of the executive arm of government. One deputy in Yaroslavl' in 1990 explained this relationship: "We may pass the budget, but it is the ispolkom that spends it." Another noted, "The ispolkom is involved more with current, everyday issues; the soviet with general policy, so the ispolkom has more power."[44]

True to Gorbachev's proposals at the Nineteenth Party Conference in 1988, however, the most significant change the elections wrought was the Communist Party's diminished influence as the controlling institution at the local level. Although in many cases (but not all) the obkom first secretary was elected in 1990 to the oblast soviet, and even to the chairmanship of the soviet or the ispolkom, a measure of accountability to the soviet now existed above even the Party. The elections fundamentally changed the point of reference of these officials. Where previously Moscow and the Central Committee were their source of power, after the elections even the obkom was far more dependent for power on its domestic constituency than on an increasingly weakening Moscow.

The mounting discord within the Party at the national level, and the factionalization that bubbled to the surface at the Twenty-eighth Party Congress in July 1990, contributed further to the change in allegiances that the elections wrought. It was at this last Party congress that Boris Yeltsin, the newly elected chairman of the Russian legislature, formally broke with the CPSU. Throughout the remainder of 1990 Yeltsin became increasingly hostile to the CPSU, and by June 1991, as president of the

---

[44] As quoted in Hahn, "The Development of Local Legislatures," p. 16.

RSFSR, he issued a decree prohibiting Party organizations in all work-places on Russian soil. Arguably, this was one of the precursors to the August 1991 coup attempt against Mikhail S. Gorbachev.

The elections initiated simultaneous processes of democratization and decentralization within Russia and signaled the decline of the CPSU's grip on local governments. Given that regional legislators were now ac-countable to their constituents, it is not surprising that they began to demand increased authority over local affairs. Thus the 1990 elections also initiated a struggle over the shape of the new Russian federal system and an ongoing power struggle between the Russian center and the periphery.

CENTER VERSUS PERIPHERY: THE INCREASING POWER OF THE PROVINCES

Just before the attempted coup at the end of the summer of 1991, Boris Yeltsin, as Russia's newly elected president, announced his intention to make a few changes in the structure of regional government. Yeltsin had only just issued his decree on Party organizations in the workplace, and, in the absence of its unifying influence, many of these changes were in-tended to strengthen the center's hold on the increasingly independence-minded regions. At the oblast level, these institutional reforms included the creation of two new offices—that of presidential representative (*predstavitel' prezidenta*, informally referred to as "namestnik" after Catherine's governors general and the powerful representatives of Mus-covy before that) and that of oblast head of administration (*glava admin-istratsii*), which also became known as governor (*gubernator*). The pre-sidium was renamed the *malyi soviet*, or small soviet, and its functions were altered slightly in an effort to quell unrest in soviets in the wake of the coup attempt. In contrast to the presidium (largely comprised of chairs of standing committees), the malyi soviets were elected from the soviet's general membership and were a method of governing the legisla-ture between sessions of the full soviet, rather than being exclusively an organizational body. (Figures 3.2 and 3.3 show the structure of regional governments at the time of the 1990 elections and the changes made in 1991, respectively. Figures A.1 and A.2 in Appendix A show the setup of the different branches of government).

The office of presidential representative was the most overt attempt to reassert central executive control over the oblasts. Hahn reports that this

LEGISLATIVE SIDE	EXECUTIVE SIDE
Chair of the Oblast Soviet	*Oblastnoi Ispolkom*
— elected at first session of oblast soviet in 1990	*(Oblast Executive Committee)*
— is a full-time position	— chair elected by oblast soviet
— has at least one deputy chair	— effective cabinet with a membership of executive department heads
Presidium	— accountable to oblast soviet
— comprised of heads of soviet committees	— elected by soviet in first session, March 1990
— handles organizational work of soviet	*Departments of the Ispolkom*
Oblast Soviet	— heads of these elected at first session of soviet
— elected in competitive elections in 1990	
— approximately 250 deputies on average	
— meets by law no less than two times per year	
— has deputy committees paralleling Ispolkom departments	

Figure 3.2. The Structure of Newly Elected Governments, March 1990. *Source*: Information is based on organizational charts provided by Nizhnii Novgorod, Saratov, and Tiumen' oblast soviets and oblast administrations and the March 1992 Russian Federation Law, "On Oblast and Krai Soviets and Oblast and Krai Administrations."

idea was initially floated at the union level in 1990 at the Twenty-eighth Party Congress as a method of strengthening central control over the implementation of reform at the oblast level.[45] Yeltsin and his supporters rejected it then, but by 1991, with his election as president of Russia, Yeltsin supported the idea. By July 1991, only a month after taking office, President Yeltsin publicly announced his plan "to appoint a personal envoy to every region to bring home presidential and government decisions to the local administrators and dispatch objective information about the actual state of things there."[46] Another report described the role of these

[45] Ibid., p. 17.
[46] As reported and translated in *FBIS*, August 12, 1991, p. 48.

LEGISLATIVE SIDE   EXECUTIVE SIDE

Presidential Representative

— explains federal law; reports on its implementation

Chair of the Oblast Soviet
(no changes to this position from
1990)

Small Soviet (malyi sovet)

— body comprised of no more than
  one-fifth of full oblast soviet
— meets two times per month
— elected from general membership
  of soviet
— handles daily business of soviet
  between sessions
— chair of oblast soviet is also chair
  of malyi sovet

Oblast Soviet
(no change from 1990)

Oblastnaia Administratsiia
  (Oblast Administration)
Head of Administration/Governor
  (Glava Administratsii/Gubernator)

— formally appointed by the
  president on the
  recommendation of oblast soviet
— has a vice governor
— appoints heads of executive
  departments, with oblast soviet
  approving these appointments
— accountable to oblast soviet and
  can be removed by oblast soviet
  and by the president

*Departments/Committees of
Administration*

— each has a department head;
  some have deputy governor
  status bestowed by the governor
— departments/committees vary
  between oblasts, but generally
  include health, finance,
  education, transportation, social
  welfare, agriculture, trade,
  sports, culture, law, and so on

Figure 3.3. The Structure of Regional Governments after September 1991 until Spring 1994

new representatives of the center in the periphery as "the emperor's eye in the localities."[47]

Yeltsin insisted, however, that the presidential representatives were not to interfere in the activity of local authorities. In a decree signed on August 22, 1991, Yeltsin officially created the office and made it directly accountable to the control directorate (*kontrol'noe upravlenie*) of the

[47] Ibid., p. 49.

presidential administration. Unfortunately, the decree never clearly outlined exactly what presidential representatives were empowered to do. It simply stated: "Leaders and officials of ministries, departments, and other organizations of the RSFSR, and organs of executive power, are instructed to assist the RSFSR presidential representatives in the fulfillment of the functions vested in them." These "functions" were merely identified as fulfilling the president's instructions, which could have appeared to denote a very broad mandate indeed. Valerii Makharadze, the head of the control commission of the presidential apparatus in charge of the presidential representatives, further underscored that the presidential representative "has no right to interfere directly in the affairs of the administration [of the oblast], but is to monitor whether or not its activity accords with the laws and normative acts and the president's decrees."[48]

Yeltsin immediately began appointing presidential representatives to virtually all oblasts and krais in the Russian Federation. His appointees were generally from the locality to which they were assigned, and many were deputies from those localities in the Russian Supreme Soviet. Although these appointees were supposedly hand-picked by Yeltsin, and were ostensibly reform-oriented, some analysts argued that conservative elements had slipped in: "The president hastily appointed representatives who often included individuals removed from their current positions in connection with the events of last August."[49]

By August 26, 1991, presidential representatives had been appointed in Yaroslavl', Saratov, and Tiumen'. In Nizhnii Novgorod, an appointment was made in September. In all but Saratov, where the appointee was the former chairman of the city of Saratov Party committee (*gorkom*), the presidential representatives in the provinces examined in this study were deputies in the Russian Supreme Soviet representing the oblasts to which they had been appointed.

In early reports from the provinces, it was clear that the presidential representative's role was ill defined and that the officials themselves did not share a consensus regarding their actual mandates. For example, in Yaroslavl', during his first working day, presidential representative Vladimir Varukhin explained that his role was to include monitoring and supervising the localities in implementing the president's decrees. However, in direct contradiction to Yeltsin's and Makharadze's public statements, Varukhin noted: "Naturally, if officials do not obey, they must be

[48] Ibid., September 12, 1991, p. 75.
[49] Cited in *Current Digest of the Post-Soviet Press* (hereafter, *CDPSP*) 44, no. 9 (1992): 26.

relieved of their posts."[50] In contrast, the new presidential representative in Novosibirsk, Anatolii Manokhin, saw his duties more narrowly and stated that he would be " 'neither a prosecutor, a governor general, nor a Pontius Pilate,' and that his tasks did not include removing anyone from their jobs."[51]

In reality, the office of presidential representative did not carry with it much influence in regional political affairs. In an interview with the author eighteen months after taking office, Vladimir Varukhin of Yaroslavl' described the most difficult aspect of his job as establishing and asserting his authority in the absence of "a single unified approach to the institution of presidential representative."[52] In the year and a half he had been in office, he had reported two instances to Moscow where local authorities had not implemented presidential decrees, but far from resulting in the removal of officials in the administration or soviet, no action was taken on these reports. Further, considering the breadth of his duties on paper, the Yaroslavl' presidential representative had a remarkably small staff of two—a secretary and an assistant. In terms of technical support, he was in office more than a year before receiving a photocopier and a fax machine.

It is indicative of the role the presidential representative played that, in Tiumen', officials in the oblast soviet, when asked, could not remember who held the position (it was Stanislav Selezev). In an unusual twist of events in Nizhnii Novgorod, Boris Nemtsov had only just been appointed presidential representative when the oblast soviet nominated him to be governor. He held both posts simultaneously (to my knowledge, this was the only case where one person held both positions) until he requested to be removed as presidential representative in April 1994.[53] By all accounts, including his own, Nemtsov never acted as anything but governor, and he agreed with the chair of the oblast soviet that the position of presidential representative was a powerless and unnecessary infringement on the legitimate authority of elected governments in the provinces.[54]

[50] *FBIS*, August 30, 1991, p. 102.

[51] Ibid.

[52] Author's interview with Vladimir Varukhin, Presidential Representative, Yaroslavl', January 5, 1993.

[53] See "Nemtsov Resigns as Yeltsin's Representative in Nizhnii Novgorod," *Radio Free Europe/Radio Liberty Reports* (hereafter, *RFE/RL*), no. 75, April 20, 1994. He was replaced, at his own request, by E. Krestianinov, then former chair of the oblast soviet.

[54] Author's interview with Evgenii Krestianinov, Chair of the Nizhnii Novgorod Oblast Soviet of People's Deputies, Nizhnii Novgorod, December 19, 1992.

Of the four oblasts in this study, only in Saratov was the presidential representative an independent political force. This had little to do with the power of the office itself, however; the presidential representative there had previously been the first secretary of the city of Saratov Party committee (gorkom) and simply transferred that powerful apparatus into the offices of the presidential representative. Deputies in the oblast soviet insisted that he used the position to further his own interests and not the business of the president. Moreover, there was a consensus in interviews in both Moscow and the provinces that the office of presidential representative proved to be a failed attempt by Yeltsin to gain an institutional foothold in regional politics.[55]

The office of head of administration, or governor, however, turned out to be far more powerful and represented a significant change in regional government structure. The administration that the governor was to lead replaced the ispolkom and created a clear separation of the legislature and the executive. Where the ispolkom and its chairman had been elected at the first session of the oblast soviet, governors were to be popularly elected and would appoint department heads with the approval of oblast soviets. The governor, however, was also supposed to be accountable to the presidential administration in a move that echoed the old unitary system of state organs. Governors were initially appointed by the president on the recommendation of the oblast soviets until elections could be held. Initially, these elections were scheduled for December 1991, but in October, fearing that conservative forces would sweep the regions, Yeltsin postponed the elections indefinitely. As a result, the process of the soviets nominating gubernatorial candidates with the presidential apparatus approving the nominations continued until 1993 when some regions insisted on holding elections for governor. Elections were held in eight regions, but because President Yeltsin's preferred candidates did poorly (losing seven of eight races), he did not permit further gubernatorial elections until 1995 and even then in only thirteen regions (including Nizhnii Novgorod) where he was more certain his preferred candidates could win. In these later elections, his preferred candidates won ten of thirteen races. Finally making good on his promise to institute popularly elected heads of regional executives, Yeltsin mandated guber-

---

[55] This conclusion is based on the author's interviews with deputies in all four of the oblasts included in this study as well as with Sergei Timofeevich Vaskov, Head of Sector, Interregional Affairs Committee, Russian Federation Supreme Soviet, Moscow, March 1992, and with Professor Georgii Barabashev, Faculty of Law, Moscow State University, Moscow, March 19, 1992.

natorial elections across Russia in the autumn of 1996 when incumbents and candidates backed by Moscow met with mixed results in the face of strong oppositional candidates.[56]

With the creation of the office of governor, in many cases the locus of executive power shifted further to the executive side of government. Still, because the executive was accountable to the legislature to a degree, an uncooperative oblast soviet could certainly stand in the governor's way, as proved to be the case in Saratov.

The formal relationship between the oblast soviets and the administrations was set out in the March 1992 Russian Federation "Law on Oblast and Krai Soviets and Oblast and Krai Administrations."[57] Although Yeltsin clearly had intended the office of glava administratsii, like that of presidential representative, to guarantee another central stronghold in governing the provinces, Article 46 of this law enabled oblast soviets to remove heads of administration from office. Five oblast soviets, like, for example, Sakhalin oblast, took advantage of this. To the chagrin of Moscow, they unilaterally removed the governor and held new gubernatorial elections in the spring of 1993.

Further, although Yeltsin, by exercising some control over the final appointments, attempted to ensure that the first heads of administration would be somewhat loyal to the center, in practice this did not always prove to be possible. As with his presidential representative appointees, in some cases Yeltsin and his team did not always have a firm grasp on who was coming to power in the provinces (as, for example, in Ulianovsk where a seemingly conservative Communist was appointed). Indeed, many of these new governors later spearheaded their oblasts' efforts to gain increased independence from Moscow. Finally, in the four cases examined here, the heads of administration were far from capable of unilaterally imposing their wills on their oblast legislatures, and, for the most part, their loyalties clearly lay with their respective provinces rather than with Moscow. Despite Yeltsin's best efforts, some measure of executive accountability to the legislature (rather than to Moscow) was upheld.

Also, in the fall of 1991, on the legislative side of government, the

---

[56] Full results from the gubernatorial elections of 1966 were not available at the time of writing.

[57] Although Hahn, in "The Development of Local Legislatures," reports that the Supreme Soviet passed this law and Yeltsin withheld his signature from it, in all four oblasts that the author visited officials cited this law as the authority for their governments' operations. Thus even if the law was not in force de jure, it was operational de facto.

malyi soviet was created to provide some balance to the executive. Malyi soviets were elected by oblast soviets from September 1991 through March 1992. The malyi soviet was required to meet at least two times each month, and its meetings were run by the chairman of the oblast soviet. It was to act in place of the oblast soviet in its dealings with the administration between sessions of the oblast soviet. Further, where the presidium was not supposed to have any real legislative power,[58] the malyi soviet could protest decisions made by the oblast administration (the executive) and even rescind them. The oblast soviet, in turn, retained the right to reverse the decisions of the malyi soviet. That malyi soviets could overturn executive decisions ensured another line of legislative-executive accountability that had been absent previously. In malyi soviet sessions attended by the author, heads of departments of the oblast administration were regularly invited to give reports, and members of the malyi soviet asked questions and prepared legislation (*resheniia*) based on those reports.

In sum, although the changes in regional government structure that Yeltsin instituted in 1991 were designed to strengthen central control over the maverick provinces of Russia, in practice these changes were not as effective as he might have hoped. Ironically, his struggle with Russia's regions paralleled a battle that Yeltsin himself had waged against the union government since Russia's own declaration of sovereignty from the USSR at the first session of the new Congress of People's Deputies on June 12, 1990. Parallel and simultaneous processes were taking place at the union level the hallmark of which was the "parade of sovereignties" of the fifteen union republics and the subsequent "war of laws" (where republics and the union wrote laws that contradicted those of the other) between the union government under Gorbachev and the increasingly autonomous republican governments.

Many scholars and analysts within the halls of the Russian parliament itself thought that Yeltsin had set a bad precedent for regional leaders to declare themselves independent of Russian central authorities.[59] Further, Yeltsin's invitation to autonomous republics to "take as much indepen-

---

[58] In practice, some presidia apparently did attempt to legislate. See, for example, Gabrichidze, "Sovet, presidium, ispolkom," p. 79, where he reports that both the presidia of the Moscow city soviet and the Ivanovo oblast soviet passed normative decisions beyond their official purviews.

[59] Author's interview with Vaskov, March 1992; author's interview with Nikolai Deev, chief researcher, Institute of State and Law, Russian Federation Academy of Sciences, Moscow, February 20, 1992.

dence as you can handle" was clearly heard in the provinces.[60] Russia's declaration of sovereignty was quickly followed by similar declarations of sovereignty from Russia itself of almost all sixteen of the ASSRs within its borders by the fall of 1991 (eleven of sixteen by October 1990).[61]

The ASSRs changed their names to "republics" to denote what they considered to be their newly independent status. Four (including Adigai, Gorno-Altai, Karachai, and Khakassia) of five autonomous oblasts within the RSFSR similarly declared themselves sovereign and also unilaterally raised their status to that of republic. This, too, was the beginning of a dangerous precedent. By declaring themselves republics, these autonomous oblasts grabbed increased jurisdiction over their own territories. They did this so that their governments, not Moscow, had first access to their economic resources.

At the same time, a few of the newly elected oblast governments attempted to free themselves further from the yoke of central authority by threatening to withhold taxes from collection by the federal treasury.[62] Some—for example, Krasnoiarsk krai—even went so far as to eventually declare themselves republics in "a kind of protest against the parade of sovereignties, a demonstration to the parliament where Russia [was] headed."[63]

These events precipitated a reconsideration of the shape of Russia's federal system by both the center and the periphery. A brief recounting of this process brings to light the wins and losses of Russia's regions—particularly the new oblast-level governments—and demonstrates that newly elected subnational governments were able to go quite far in asserting local interests. Indeed, so uppity did many of the soviets become in their dealings with the center that Yeltsin, in the course of his final bloody battle with the Russian Supreme Soviet in October 1993, opted to suspend the local soviets entirely. In so doing, Yeltsin unconstitutionally brought a close to the First Russian Republic and Russia's initial experi-

[60] *Komsomol'skaia pravda*, March 14, 1991.

[61] For a convenient compilation of these declarations of sovereignty, see *K soiuzu suverennykh narodov: sbornik dokumentov KPSS, zakonodatel'nykh aktov, deklaratsii, obrashchenii i prezidentskikh ukazov, posviashchenykh probleme natsional'no-gosudarstvennogo suvereniteta* (Moskva: Institut teorii i istorii sotsializma TsK KPSS, 1991). Prof. Edward A. Bagramov, chairman of the editorial committee of this volume, kindly provided this document to the author.

[62] Cf. ch. 1, n. 4, regarding Irkutsk's refusal to pay taxes into the federal budget.

[63] See Aleksei Tarasov, "Krasnoiarsk Territory Wants to Become the Yenisei Republic," *Izvestiia*, February 25, 1992, p. 2, as summarized in *CDPSP* 44, no. 8 (March 25, 1992): 5.

ment with democracy in the provinces. Elections to smaller regional legis-latures (renamed dumas, or regional assemblies) averaging thirty-two deputies began in December 1993 and continued in the provinces throughout 1994.[64] Approximately twenty-four oblast dumas stood for reelection in the fall of 1996.

CENTER VERSUS PERIPHERY: TWO INTERPRETATIONS OF FEDERALISM

As in the late nineteenth century when federal issues were hotly contested in Russia,[65] from the outset of the debate on the new shape of the Rus-sian Federation, two competing visions were evident. Although there was division at the center, Moscow's view of how best to deal with the coun-try's diversity was generally far more unitary than the system that provin-cial leaders envisioned. Indeed, one might conceptualize the center's view as "national" federalism, whereas the provinces preferred a federation of a more "contractual" nature. According to Samuel Beer, whereas a con-tractual federal system is the result of a "treaty among several sovereign independent states, each of which has delegated certain limited powers, such as defense, to a general government," a national federal system "is based not on a contract, but on an order by the single sovereign power . . . who creates two levels of government, a general government and

[64] See report by Nikolai V. Petrov translated in *FBIS*, June 9, 1995, p. 5, for more details on the 1994 provincial elections. Elections took place initially in Moscow, Tula, and Ark-hangelsk. New regional legislative organs were constructed on the basis of Yeltsin's presi-dential decree no. 1723, "On the Establishment of New Organizations of State Power in the Subjects of the Russian Federation." Elections to a forty-five-seat assembly were held in Nizhnii Novgorod in March 1994. The oblast soviet met right up to the election of the new legislative assembly. In Tiumen' a smaller duma of twenty-five seats was also elected in March 1994. Similar to the situation in Nizhnii Novgorod, the oblast malyi soviet contin-ued working right up to the first meeting of the new duma. In Yaroslavl', elections took place somewhat earlier (in February 1994), but the oblast soviet stopped work before the elections and seating of the new twenty-three-seat duma. Finally, in Saratov, the work of the soviet was suspended in the fall of 1993, and elections took place in May 1994 to a twenty-five-seat duma. Deputies in all these new regional institutions had a two-year mandate. As of December 12, 1994 (exactly one year after the initiation of the reform of legislative organs throughout Russia), elections to new regional legislative organs had taken place in fifty-four of fifty-five regions.

[65] See Frederick Starr, *Decentralization and Self-Government in Russia: 1830–1870* (Princeton, N.J.: Princeton University Press, 1972).

several state governments, delegating to each certain limited powers."[66]
Thus, while the subnational governments of Russia envisioned a "ground
up" approach to national reconstruction, the central government was
unwilling to forfeit much of its authority.

The first session of the Russian Supreme Soviet in June 1990 elected a
constitutional commission charged with producing a draft constitution
that was to incorporate a revised statement of the distribution of powers
between center and periphery. Although central authorities, including the
secretary of the constitutional commission, Oleg Rumiantsev, paid lip
service to federalist ideas—that is, some division of powers between the
central government and territorial governments—the proposals they offered were slanted in favor of maintaining central control over the provinces rather than sharing power with them.

Further, the constitutional proposals envisioned the maintenance
of a multi-tier federal system that encompassed a special "national-
territorial" status for the twenty RSFSR republics as opposed to the lesser
"territorial-administrative" status of the fifty-five oblasts and krais. This
meant that only the republics were to be considered "subjects" of the
federation and signatories to any federative treaty, whereas oblasts were
to remain nothing more than branch representatives of central power,
bound to the center in a unitary system of government and not through a
federative treaty. Republics were to have a president and a supreme soviet
and were to retain more control over their own affairs than were oblasts.
If they surrendered some power to the republic level, central authorities
were unwilling to give up their claim to control over oblast-level
government.

Nowhere, in all the proposals that Rumiantsev's constitutional commission put forward, was this more evident than in the fall 1991 proposal to redraw the boundaries of the oblasts and create "*zemli*"
(lands)—or the equivalent of German "länder." Ostensibly the purpose
of redrawing boundaries, such that in some cases several oblasts would
be consolidated into a single "zemlia" (land), was to simplify territorial
administration and to render the status of oblasts "subjects" of the
federation—effectively giving them the same authority as republics (except that they would not have formal constitutions).[67]

---

[66] Samuel H. Beer, in "Federalism and the National Idea: The Uses of Diversity" (Cam-
bridge, Mass.: Harvard Graduate Society Newsletter, Fall 1991), p. 8. See also Beer's *To
Make a Nation: The Rediscovery of American Federalism* (Cambridge, Mass.: Belknap
Press of Harvard University Press, 1993).

[67] "O glavnykh zamechaniiakh k proektu. Interv'iu s professorom, rukovoditelem grup-

At first glance one would think that this would have greatly benefited the oblasts in that they would no longer be merely "territorial-administrative" units but actual "subjects" of the federation. In reality, however, this rather ill-considered notion satisfied neither oblast- nor republic-level governments. Oblast leaders perceived it as an attempt by Moscow to erode provincial authority further by redrawing geographical boundaries in a thinly veiled effort to do away with the most vocal (and conservative) regional leaders. Moreover, many believed that the zemli would not, in the end, have that much increased authority over their own affairs. One analyst noted that "they would not have been as strong as American states," whereas this seemed to be the oblast leaders' goal.[68]

For their part, republic authorities thought that the creation of zemli from the combination of several oblasts would mean effectively the creation of at least forty-five new republics with forty-five new presidents and forty-five new parliaments that would overwhelm the special interests of the ethnic republics in further negotiations with Moscow.[69] The subsequent rows that took place between the federal government and Russia's constituent units, and between the levels of constituent units (republic versus oblast), resulted in the relatively rapid (and quiet) abandonment of the whole zemli idea.

This represented the Russian provinces' first victory over Moscow in the contest to redefine center-periphery relationships. In focusing on appeasing the ethnic nationalism of many of the republics (the combined populations of which constituted less than 20 percent of Russia's population as a whole) rather than the oblasts, the center had underestimated the growing influence of regionalism at the oblast level. The regionalist flame had been fanned by democratic elections and the resulting accountability of regional leaders to constituents.

Among the most important signs of increased regional power was the establishment of regional political and economic associations. Although some of these were little more than formal declarations of cooperation

---

poi ekspertov konstitutsionnoi komissii RSFSR V. Zor'kinym," *Konstitutsionnyi vestnik* no. 8 (Moskva: Konstitutsionnaia komissia RSFSR, oktiabr' 1991): 12–13. Also, author's interview with Vsevolod Vasiliev, (former) Director of the Institute of Legislation and Comparative Law of the Supreme Soviet of the Russian Federation, February 10, 1992.

[68] Author's interview with Deev, Moscow, February 20, 1992.

[69] Author's interview with Barabashev, Moscow, March 19, 1992. Professor Barabashev was a key architect of both the Federative Agreements and the 1992 Law on Oblast and Krais Soviets and Oblast and Krais Administrations; author's interview with Vikor Sheinis, member of the Constitutional Commission, Russian Federation Supreme Soviet, March 10, 1992. (The author is grateful to Sergei Markov of Moscow State University and now of the Carnegie Corporation's Moscow office for arranging this interview.)

between oblasts, others, like the Siberian Agreement, one of the largest and most active of these associations, established rather remarkable organizations designed to promote economic, social, and political collaboration independent of Moscow.[70] Whereas before 1990 inter-oblast trade and cooperation was virtually nonexistent, after the 1990 election members of the Siberian Agreement, for example, cooperated on pressing the center on such issues as tax reform, budgetary authority, and increased rights over the extraction of local natural resources. Many oblasts also freely and independently pursued foreign trade agreements and economic agreements with members of the Commonwealth of Independent States.

The move for increased regional control over local affairs led to the adoption of three "Federative Agreements" in March 1992 that formally introduced the notion of jurisdictional rights into Russian constitutional practice. The texts of the Federative Agreements themselves, however, represent a more mixed result for the oblasts. Initially, as noted above, the central government had no intention of including oblasts and the autonomous oblasts and okrugs as signatories of any formal treaties between Moscow and the "subjects" of the federation—the republics.[71] But following the defeat of the zemlia proposal, oblast leaders became more proactive in pressing their concerns with the center. By February 1992 many articles appeared in the Russian press describing the similarities between the processes that had led to the disintegration of the Soviet Union—when its constituent units declared themselves independent and refused to sign the Union Treaty.[72] The difference was that, in Russia, in many cases it was ethnic Russians at the oblast level declaring sovereignty within their own country. As one journalist explained, "The separatism of the krais and oblasts is a form of their self-defense against the uncontrolled disposal of natural resources by the center."[73] Indeed, in the spring of 1992, "razviazat'sia Rossii" (the undoing of Russia) was the catch phrase of Russian political pundits.[74]

[70] Chapter 4 discusses the genesis of regional associations and the participation of Nizhnii Novgorod, Tiumen', Yaroslavl', and Saratov in regional associations.

[71] Author's interview with Barabashev, Moscow, March 19, 1992.

[72] See, for example, "How Close Is Russia to Breaking Up? *CDPSP* 44, no. 8 (March 25, 1992): 1; "The Russian Federation of Independent States," *Rossiiskaia gazeta*, January 31, 1992, p. 1.

[73] Aleksei Aliushin, "Constitutional Reform, Goals, Tasks, Problems," *Rossiiskaia gazeta*, March 2, 1992, p. 1.

[74] Even ostensibly ethnic claims to independence made, for example, by the Tatar republic contained a "Russians against Russia" element. This is clear if one looks to the results of

That the oblasts were included in January and February drafts of a formal federal treaty signaled their increased influence and accomplished the important goal of raising the oblasts' status to that of "subjects" of the federation. Georgii Barabashev of Moscow State University, an adviser to Moscow on the federative deals, explained that Moscow insisted on signing separate agreements with each level of government in part to appease the republics and reassure their leaders that their status was above that of oblasts. In fact, the oblasts "were economically and socially equal vis-à-vis the republics, but not politically equal" in that republics were granted the right to write a constitution, to establish rules on citizenship, to have presidents, and to grant republic service awards (for example, awards for achievements in politics and the arts).[75]

In many ways these were little more than cosmetic advantages over oblasts. Where republics had constitutions, in Article 4 of the 1992 Law on Oblast and Krai Soviets and Oblast and Krai Administrations, oblasts were commissioned to write *ustavy*—regulations of government conduct—that essentially amounted to constitutions. Their citizens would be citizens of the Russian Federation (as it was called by the spring of 1992) alone, and they had none of the less significant power to grant service awards. Finally oblasts would have no presidents, but governors instead. For oblasts, however, the important victory was an economic one. The oblasts' authority to retain, for the first time in their histories, some control over their economic resources was guaranteed in Article 3 of the federative agreement between the Russian Federation and oblast- and krai-level governments:[76]

---

the March 1992 Tatar referendum regarding its status as an independent territory within the Russian Federation. Considering that the breakdown of the population in Tatarstan is such that Tatars make up 48.5 percent of the population while ethnic Russians make up 43 percent (with the remainder of the population divided between Ukrainians, Chuvash, and other smaller ethnic groups), and 61.4 percent of the voting population voted in favor of increased independence for the republic, then a good proportion of the ethnic Russian population backed independence.

[75] Author's interview with Barabashev, Moscow, March 19, 1992. Despite these efforts, unanimous approval was elusive and only eighteen of twenty republics signed the Federative Agreement, with Tatarstan and Chechenia declining. Tatarstan eventually formally joined the federation in the spring of 1994 .

[76] The agreement was signed March 31, 1992, and was officially called the "Agreement between the Federal Organs of Power and Organs of Power of Krais, Oblasts, and the Cities of Moscow and St. Petersburg of the Russian Federation." Moscow and St. Petersburg, because of their economic, historical, and political significance as large population centers, had traditionally always been granted oblast-level status. The other two federative treaties

Questions of the ownership, use, and distribution of land, mineral wealth, water, timber, and other natural resources are regulated by the basic legislation of the Russian Federation and the legal acts of krais, oblasts, and the cities of Moscow and St. Petersburg. The status of federal natural resources will be defined by mutual agreement of the federal organs of state power of the Russian Federation and the organs of power of krais, oblasts, and the cities of Moscow and St. Petersburg.

Although regional leaders expressed optimism when they signed the oblast- and krai-level federative treaty, many of its provisions proved vague in practice and others went unfulfilled. Most important, although the federative agreement with the oblast- and krai-level governments established joint federal-provincial jurisdiction over the establishment of general principles of tax assessment, the agreement did not in any way resolve the very sticky issues of budget and tax reform. Both these systems remained highly centralized and were continuing sore points in center-periphery relations. Further, Article 3 established oblast- and krai-level governments as "independent participants in constructing internation [*mezhdunarodnye*, i.e., within Russia and the Commonwealth of Independent States] and foreign economic [*vneshekonomicheskie*] ties as long as these did not contravene the Constitution and laws of the Russian Federation." Significantly, though, the agreement left "coordination" (*koordinatsiia*) of these ties with "federal organs of power of the Russian Federation jointly with organs of power of krais and oblasts," which was clearly intended to limit the "independence" of the oblasts and krais as participants.

By early 1993 many regional government officials were lamenting that the central authorities had not honored the intent of the federative agreement. The federative agreements continued in force following the adoption of the 1993 Constitution, but Krestianinov, the chair of the Nizhnii Novgorod oblast soviet, noted that although all three federative agreements had the positive effect of hastening the pace at which the Russian parliament passed decentralizing legislation, they still did not provide sufficient powers to the oblasts and there were no mechanisms for enforcing federal compliance.[77] Significantly, the 1993 Constitution contains two Articles (71 and 72) outlining federal and joint federal-regional jurisdiction but contains no article enumerating areas of exclusively provin-

---

between Moscow and the republics and Moscow and the autonomies were signed March 13, 1992 and March 31, 1992, respectively.

[77] Author's interview with Krestianinov, Nizhnii Novgorod, December 18, 1992.

cial jurisdiction. Beginning in 1994 some republics and gradually some oblasts sought to overcome this by signing bilateral power-sharing agreements with Moscow. As of the end of 1996, approximately twenty-six of these agreements existed and several more awaited signature. Although it is unclear exactly what these agreements will mean in practice, on paper at least they appear to guarantee regional leaders relatively broad authority over areas of specific interest to a particular region. Often these include taxation and increased control over economic resources, as well as specific policy areas like education. This rather arbitrary policy of assigning extra powers to some regions but not others, however, has created the potential for further uneven economic (and political) development across the Federation.

Conclusion

Despite the disappointing performance of the oblast and krai federative agreement, the early 1990s witnessed a marked increase in independent regional activity. In the space of only three and a half years the oblasts had traveled a remarkable distance toward achieving more control over local affairs. Finally liberated from the domineering presence of local Communist Party organs and overbearing central bureaucrats, many oblast governments moved to increase their spheres of action.

At last oblast authorities, free of the dictates of the plan and the yoke of central ministries, were able to establish their own public policy and managed to determine their own spending priorities, although their independent taxation authority was still limited.[78] Before Yeltsin capitalized on the opportunity to disband regional soviets (which by the fall of 1993 he viewed as bastions of opposition in his battle with the Russian Federation legislature), in conversations and interviews many regional policy makers, regardless of geographical location, insisted that Moscow and its problems were a long way away.

Democratization led somewhat uncontrollably to political decentralization and to a dramatic increase in regional governments' sphere of activity in Russia. Although institutional reform is perhaps better measured over decades or centuries, regional governments in Russia, in fewer than four years, were clearly transformed from bodies that did little more

[78] For more on the development of fiscal federal relations, see Daniel Treisman, "The Politics of Intergovernmental Transfers in Post-Soviet Russia," *British Journal of Political Science* 26 (1996): 299–335.

than execute the Party's will to those that functioned as representative governments with increasingly broad responsibilities. The 1990 elections altered legislators' point of reference in the provinces and initiated the notion of public accountability into Russian political life.

In reviewing the government performance of Nizhnii Novgorod, Tiumen', Yaroslavl', and Saratov, chapter 4 provides additional evidence of what regional governments actually accomplished in their first few years of operation. Chapter 4 demonstrates, however, that some of these new representative governments achieved more than others despite the fact that they all had undergone the same institutional transformations and, on paper, had equal opportunities to succeed.

Who Governs Russia *Well*? Measuring
Institutional Performance

SOCIAL SCIENTISTS as private people do not hesitate to pass normative judgments on governments, but professionally we prefer to leave performance evaluations to political philosophers, satirists, and journalists.[1] Undoubtedly, positivists are squeamish because of the combined difficulty of both arriving at nonarbitrary and meaningful evaluative criteria and then operationalizing these measures using reliable data on government behavior. The appropriate matching of theory and empirical evidence seems particularly difficult to attain in this exercise. Yet the question "What is good government?" has endured as one of the most central and basic problems of the study of politics. As foreign consultants and former Soviet bloc policy makers riding the "third wave"[2] of democratic transitions attempt to reconfigure political institutions, the question of why some democratic governments perform "better" than others is now especially pressing. Thus, although the task is a particularly difficult one, it seems that we are more obligated than ever to address it.

Although Plato, Machiavelli, and Mill pondered the "good government" question, there are but a few modern studies that can serve as guides to measuring *decisional efficacy* and *responsiveness*, the two most important dimensions of *democratic* government and the ones with which this study is concerned.[3] In the early 1970s, Harry Eckstein pro-

---

[1] Similar observations have been made by Robert Dahl, "The Evaluation of Political Systems," in Ithiel de Sola Pool, ed., *Contemporary Political Science: Toward Empirical Theory* (New York: McGraw-Hill, 1967), p. 167; and Robert D. Putnam, *Making Democracy Work: Civic Traditions in Modern Italy* (Princeton, N.J.: Princeton University Press, 1993), p. 63.

[2] For an analysis of democratic transitions in the last twenty years, see Samuel P. Huntington, *The Third Wave: Democratization in the Late Twentieth Century* (Norman: University of Oklahoma Press, 1991).

[3] Studies that deal conceptually with different aspects of performance do exist, of course, but these do not provide measurement frameworks. Instead they tend to focus on what governments do, not on how well they do it empirically. See, for example, Robert Dahl, *A Preface to Democratic Theory* (Chicago: University of Chicago Press, 1956); and Robert Dahl, *Polyarchy: Participation and Opposition* (New Haven, Conn.: Yale Univer-

duced a paper outlining the theoretical requirements of any study of the performance of political institutions.[4] Ted R. Gurr and Muriel McClelland then wrote a short paper attempting to operationalize many of Eckstein's theoretical postulates, with some success.[5] Perhaps the most comprehensive and impressive study of institutional performance to date is Robert Putnam's twenty-year study of Italian regional governments.[6] The current chapter attempts to refine these excellent examples.

Putnam's measures of government performance are the most rigorous. He argues that any meaningful assessment of government performance must pass four tests:[7]

1. Measures must be selected such that they are *comprehensive*. They must extend to as many areas of government activity as possible, including service provision, policy innovations, and operational management. The more measures the better.

2. Measures must be *internally consistent*. Often, some governments do certain things better than others. Any index of institutional performance will only be meaningful if the performance of each polity under consideration forms some pattern; that is, we ideally would like to see one case that scores quite well on all measures (in the aggregate) and another that scores poorly on all measures. Thus "*if and only if* our varied indicators turn out empirically to rank the regions in roughly the same way will we be justified in speaking summarily of institutional success and failure."[8]

3. Measures of performance must be *reliable* and consistent across time. If performance rankings change radically from year to year, then correlations may prove spurious. Since this study covers only the first three years of the existence of democratic regional governments, the quest for reliability is perhaps rather forward looking. Nonetheless, in an

---

sity Press, 1971); and Gabriel A. Almond and G. B. Powell, *Comparative Politics: A Developmental Approach* (Boston: Little, Brown, 1966). One attempt at measurement was Seymour Martin Lipset's rather arbitrary operationalization of a stable democracy as one that has lasted since World War 1. See Lipset's *Political Man: The Social Bases of Politics* (New York: Doubleday, 1963). Many of these works are summarized and critiqued in Harry Eckstein, *The Evaluation of Political Performance: Problems and Dimensions* (Beverly Hills, Calif.: Sage, 1971).

[4] Eckstein, *The Evaluation of Political Performance.*

[5] Ted Robert Gurr and Muriel McClelland, *Political Performance: A Twelve Nation Study,* (Beverly Hills, Calif.: Sage, 1971).

[6] Putnam, *Making Democracy Work.*

[7] Ibid., p. 64.

[8] Ibid.

attempt to increase the reliability of my measures, I selected indicators so that they extended across the still admittedly short life span of democratically elected regional governments. Further, in all oblasts, following the August 1991 attempted coup, many incumbent heads of oblast soviets changed, and in all of them new heads of administrations were appointed in the fall of 1991 and the spring of 1992. Thus, in most cases, there was a certain degree of incumbent turnover even before 1993 when, beginning in December in Moscow and stretching into the spring of 1994, elections for new regional legislatures were held across Russia. (A third round of elections to regional legislatures was held in a number of regions in the autumn of 1996.)

4. Finally, any "objective" measures of democratic governments must *correlate to the evaluations of constituents*. Democratic governments, after all, are supposed to be responsive to the wishes and needs of voters. "Customer satisfaction" is measured here in a survey with a total sample size of 3,774 residents of the four oblasts.[9]

It seems inevitable that a performance evaluation of any sort requires a numerical ranking scale. Yet the assignment of a score to a particular measure is often a rather arbitrary judgment. If any fault can be found in Putnam's performance evaluation index, it is that he fails to provide the reader with a detailed explanation of exactly how policies were scored relative to one another. We are forced to take on faith his assignment of scores to policies and the results that follow in his factor loading. Where, to his credit, Putnam dealt with twenty regional governments, one of the benefits of working with fewer cases is that one can supplement "scoring and scaling" with "thick description."[10] In supplementing my scales and scores with descriptions, I aspire to lead the readers through the scoring process and, ideally, to demonstrate that my judgments are not arbitrary but follow logically consistent evaluative criteria.

A frequent and justified criticism of assigning quantitative measures to

---

[9] As noted in chapter 1, we surveyed fewer residents of voting age in Tiumen' oblast primarily because the population density is low in the northern regions; further, some of these northern areas were accessible only by helicopter, the rental of which was beyond our means. We used random cluster samples of each oblast's population and randomly recontacted respondents to ensure that interviews actually took place. Respondents answered sixty-two questions in twenty-five- to forty-minute (depending on the respondent) person-to-person interviews. To enhance the comparability of our results and indexes, we used as many questions as possible from surveys conducted by Putnam et al. in Italy.

[10] Clifford Geertz, "Thick Description: Toward an Interpretive Theory of Culture," in Clifford Geertz, *The Interpretation of Cultures* (New York: Basic Books, 1973).

theoretical concepts is that the choice of indicators is often random. This "measurement-by-fiat" occurs when the researcher says that the concept is hard to measure and so announces that any available variables will do.[11] Hubert Blalock suggests that among the ways of obviating this problem is to ensure that the researcher not only employs many different indicators for each concept but also states explicitly the assumptions required to link theoretical constructs with their indicators. Where possible, one should also use measures that have been used elsewhere.[12]

All these recommendations, of course, further the generalizability of corresponding theories, which should be the object of any comparative inquiry. In view of this, I have attempted to employ many performance indicators used in other studies. It is important to remind the reader that we are focusing on decisional efficacy and responsiveness (as opposed to legitimacy and stability), and so indicators are keyed to these parameters. Although Gurr and McClelland provide convincing measures of the budgetary process and operations management (incumbent turnovers, elections), their focus is essentially limited to questions of process. In contrast, Putnam provides a much wider assessment of government performance, including: (1) *the policy process*—"Whatever else this institution is doing, is it conducting its crucial internal operations smoothly and with dispatch?" (2) *policy content*—"Are the governments prompt to identify social needs and propose innovative solutions? Does legislation enacted by the governments reflect a capacity to react comprehensively, coherently, and creatively to the issues at hand?" (3) *policy implementation*—"Are the regional governments successful in using the available resources to address the needs of a rapidly changing society? Have they succeeded in implementing their avowed policy objectives?"[13]; and (4) Do they *respond* to the demands of their constituents?

The current study roughly follows Putnam's format but incorporates some of Gurr's and McClelland's indicators. I use twelve indicators and rank each of the four oblasts on bipolar quantitative scales that range from 1 to 4, where 1 is the lowest score and 4 the highest.[14] In a few instances, two oblasts received the same score where their performances were virtually identical. Summed scores for each oblast across the perfor-

[11] Hubert M. Blalock, Jr., *Conceptualization in the Social Sciences* (Beverly Hills, Calif.: Sage, 1982), p. 19.

[12] Ibid., pp. 1–30.

[13] All references in this section are from Putnam, *Making Democracy Work*, p. 65.

[14] For more on bipolar scales, see Paul E. Spector, *Summated Rating Scale Construction: An Introduction* (Newbury Park, Calif.: Sage, 1992).

mance indicators appear later in this chapter in Table 4.15. The higher the summed score, the higher the performance of the oblast government.

POLICY PROCESS

The operating assumption of this section is that *if the process of making key decisions was frequently delayed in each case, this may indicate that a great amount of dissension existed within the polity.* As Eckstein notes, "The greater the observed dissension the less likely it is that polities can process efficaciously even routine pressures,"[15] not to mention the great challenges facing the Russian provinces in the post-Soviet period. A "normal" deliberative process indicates efficacious procedure, whereas an extended or extraordinary deliberative process may indicate inefficacy. This section incorporates indicators designed to measure: (1) the extent of dissension within the process of "internal allocation of authority"—the selection of political leaders; (2) the degree of professionalization of legislatures and the time spent on organizational as opposed to policy questions; and (3) the variation in oblast information services.

Internal Allocation of Authority

The major instance of elite personnel change, where great variation existed among the cases, concerned the nominations of gubernatorial candidates.[16] In almost all of Russia's forty-nine oblasts and six krais, the appointment of candidates for the newly created post of head of the regional administration (glava administratsii), or governor (gubernator), took place between September 1991 and the spring of 1992.[17] The position was officially created by presidential decree following the August 1991 attempted putsch, and effectively separated the legislative and the executive branches by establishing for the very first time the concept of what would eventually be an elected executive arm of regional government.

[15] Eckstein, *The Evaluation of Political Performance*, p. 77.

[16] In some oblasts, where heads of administrations whom President Yeltsin initially appointed were dismissed by the soviets, there have been two opportunities for personnel change. For example, Cheliabinsk, Sakhalin, and Smolensk were among five oblasts that replaced their appointed governors in 1993.

[17] These data were culled from *Vedemosti verkhovnogo soveta RSFSR* (September 1991–March 1992).

Evidence clearly suggests that Yeltsin had the idea of restructuring the old oblispolkom (oblast executive committee), which had been elected by oblast soviets, before the putsch in order to prevent communist-backed oblast soviets from dominating the executive arm of the government.[18] The attempted coup therefore merely hastened the realization of this plan. Following the coup attempt, gubernatorial candidates were nominated by oblast soviets and were then subjected to presidential approval and appointment until free elections for governor could be held.[19]

The process of selecting a candidate for governor is a good indicator of the extent of dissension within the legislative organs of power. In some cases, like that of Tiumen', the process of selecting a candidate on whom the soviet could agree, and who was likely to win presidential approval, was prompt and conflict-free. In Tiumen' the oblast presidium nominated the chairman of the oblast soviet—Iurii Shafranik—and the chairman of the ispolkom—Leonid Roketskii—and sent the names of these candidates to Yeltsin. Yeltsin chose Shafranik in early October 1991, and the oblast deputies confirmed him immediately thereafter. As if to underscore the amicability of the entire process, Shafranik then appointed Roketskii as his first deputy governor.[20]

In other instances, however, like in Saratov, the last region in Russia where a governor was appointed, the soviet was never able to decide on a gubernatorial candidate that could win presidential approval. As a result, President Yeltsin eventually appointed a candidate, Iurii Belikh, whom the soviet refused to approve until four months after his initial presidential appointment in February 1992. This was despite the fact that Saratov legislators sitting in the national parliament proposed Belikh's name to Yeltsin essentially behind the soviet's back.

---

[18] "Government Reorganization Plan Cited," July 10, 1991, and "Regional 'Representatives' Discussed," August 10, 1991, in *Foreign Broadcast Information Services* (FBIS-SOV-91–155), August 12, 1991, pp. 48–49.

[19] As noted in chapter 3, elections were originally scheduled for December 1991 but were canceled for fear that conservative, anti-Yeltsin candidates would win. In 1993 and 1995 several regions held gubernatorial elections. In 1995 Governor Nemtsov, of Nizhnii Novgorod, won reelection easily, perhaps indicating a high level of constituent satisfaction with his administration. Gubernatorial elections were held in the fall of 1996 and early 1997 for the remaining oblasts and krais where elections had not yet taken place.

[20] *Tiumenskaia pravda*, October 1–9, 1991. Author's interviews with deputies in July 1993 confirmed this version of events. Further, when Shafranik was appointed the federal minister of oil and gas in January 1993, the malyi soviet nominated Roketskii to replace him as head of administration. Yeltsin quickly confirmed the nomination.

In contrast, in both Nizhnii Novgorod and Yaroslavl' oblasts, the first choices of the majority of the oblast soviets were not sent for presidential approval because it was clear to all that they would not get it. As a result, in both oblasts, legislators came to a slightly forced consensus on compromise candidates. In Nizhnii, consensus gradually emerged around a political outsider—Boris Nemtsov. Agreement on Nemtsov was relatively prompt, especially compared to Saratov. In early November 1991 the Democratic Russia candidate was unable to get enough votes from the more conservative members of the oblast soviet and withdrew his candidacy. Nemtsov's name was put forward by the chairman of the oblast soviet (himself elected only two months earlier), and he was able to get enough votes for the nomination only as part of a combined ticket with the communist-backed candidate as running mate for deputy governor.[21] Therefore, by appeasing the dominant factions within the oblast soviet, and also by having the backing of Nizhnii's representatives in the national parliament (of which Nemtsov was one), Nemtsov became the youngest governor in Russia and, by many accounts, one of the most radical.

In Yaroslavl' the situation was somewhat similar. As in Nizhnii Novgorod, the selection of a governor took place in November 1991, with presidential approval following in early December. While the former chief of the ispolkom and communist-backed candidate, Vladimir Kovalev, received the most votes in the oblast soviet (ninety-seven), the third place candidate, Anatolii Lisitsyn, was ultimately appointed governor with only fifteen votes. (The second-place candidate, who was the first choice of the "democratic" faction in the oblast soviet, received forty-five votes.) The oblast soviet ultimately settled on Lisitsyn because it was well known that Kovalev was unlikely to get Yeltsin's approval (as a deputy in the Russian Supreme Soviet, Kovalev had several times opposed Yeltsin), and other candidates were thought unlikely to garner enough votes in the oblast soviet. Lisitsyn therefore, like Nemtsov in Nizhnii, represented a compromise between the major factions within both oblast soviets.

Whereas the selection processes of the head of the oblast administration in Tiumen', Nizhnii Novgorod, and Yaroslavl' oblasts were relatively calm and consensual, in Saratov the process could scarcely have been more drawn out and divisive. In a few other oblasts in Russia, oblast soviets refused to accept Yeltsin's appointment and eventually turned

[21] Author's interview with Evgenii Krestianinov, chairman of Nizhnii Novgorod Oblast Soviet of People's Deputies, December 18, 1992.

TABLE 4.1
Selection of Gubernatorial Candidates

Score	Process	Oblast Ranking
4	No conflict over selection of candidate. No delay. Local and national representatives agree quickly.	Tiumen'
3	Some conflict over selection of candidate. Candidate ultimately selected as a compromise between competing factions within legislature. Some delay. Local and national representatives eventually agree.	Nizhnii Novgorod; Yaroslavl'
2	Intense conflict and debate over candidate within legislature. Soviet and national representatives decide on candidate together only after an extended delay.	
1	Intense conflict and debate over candidate within legislature. Soviet and national representatives cannot decide on candidate together. Appointment not approved by soviet until after candidate officially takes office. Severe delay.	Saratov

that appointee out of office. By this measure, therefore, elites in Tiumen', Nizhnii, and Yaroslavl' appear to have handled this matter with relative dispatch and managed to avoid major upset over the appointments. These comparisons are shown in Table 4.1.

Gurr and McClelland, Eckstein, and Putnam also compare the nature of budgetary processes as a measure of dissension during routine decision making. If the passage of budgets was frequently delayed, this may indicate regular legislative inefficiency. Although this is an effective and useful measure in other contexts, unfortunately it cannot as yet be used in the Russian case. This is primarily due to the still awkward nature of the budget process in the Russian Federation as a whole.

Certainly conflicts over budget allocations occurred, but the conflicts were largely between the federal government and oblast governments rather than merely within the oblast itself. From 1990 to 1993 oblasts still had little power to levy taxes. Instead they received shares of federally determined taxes, and the proportion of revenues that an oblast received was negotiated on a case-by-case basis with the federal Ministry of

Finance. Oblast budgets were therefore often delayed as a result of ongoing negotiations with the federal government over budgetary allocations. Oblast officials traveled to Moscow to negotiate their annual budgetary needs and to lobby the central government for funding. To a certain extent, the revenue an oblast was ultimately awarded depended on the negotiator's skill and the regional economic structure. There was therefore little transparency in the distribution process. Thus budgetary delays were at least as much a result of center-periphery conflict as internal oblast conflict. Further, until January 1993 oblasts were not permitted much discretion in determining their own spending priorities. In Russia, moreover, until the budgetary process has changed such that oblast governments are given more power over revenue collection and allocation, it was not a reliable tool to analyze internal political processes in Russia.[22]

Degree of Professionalization of Political Life

Gurr and McClelland, Eckstein, and Putnam used the degree of cabinet stability as a metric of policy process and internal operations. In the four Russian provinces analyzed here, however, no variation along these lines existed. In part this may have been because of the absence of well organized political parties in the Russian provinces since the collapse of the CPSU. It therefore became necessary to seek out another process indicator similar in nature to government stability.

A thorough comparison of various aspects of the policy process in each case revealed rather wide variation in the relative degree of professionalism of political life. Some oblasts had a relatively high degree of professionalism in their soviets such that a comparatively large number of deputies were working as full-time legislators and were able, at least in

---

[22] This information was largely provided by Beth Mitchnek, Assistant Professor, Department of Geography and Regional Development, University of Arizona. Professor Mitchnek is currently researching taxation issues in Russian cities and oblasts. Her research is supported by a grant from the National Council for Soviet and East European Studies. For a brief, although somewhat confused analysis of Russian fiscal federalism, see Christine I. Wallich, *Fiscal Decentralization: Intergovernmental Relations in Russia*, Studies of Economies in Transformation, Paper No. 6, The World Bank, 1992. See also Christine Wallich, ed., *Russia and the Challenge of Fiscal Federalism* (Washington, D.C.: The World Bank, 1995); and Daniel Treisman, "Intergovernmental Transfers in Post-Soviet Russia," *British Journal of Political Science* 26 (1996): 299–335. The foremost work on Soviet fiscal federalism is Donna Bahry's *Outside Moscow* (New York: Columbia University Press, 1987). Professor Bahry's focus, however, is primarily the union republic and not the oblast level.

principle, to devote their full attention to policy matters. Further, some oblasts repeatedly had difficulties maintaining a quorum in meetings of the oblast soviet, thereby frequently delaying policy decisions. Finally, the four cases exhibited relatively wide variation in the amount of time allocated to making policy decisions versus organizational and personnel choices in oblast institutions.

Nizhnii Novgorod and Saratov oblasts lie at two extremes. The Nizhnii Novgorod oblast soviet never had a single meeting of the soviet without a quorum (two-thirds of the deputy corps) since its election in 1990.[23] Further, in Nizhnii, 21 of 255 deputies (or 8 percent) were permanently employed by the oblast soviet. In contrast, in 1993 the chairman of the Saratov oblast soviet, Nikolai Makarevich, complained that oblast soviet sessions "are still far from fully using their potential. It is sad, but on session agendas, the problem of obtaining a quorum has appeared. Practically one-third of the deputy corps passively fulfills their obligations."[24] He proceeded to specifically name deputies who had not fulfilled their duties and noted policy areas that were ignored in the oblast as a direct result.[25] Further, only 6 of 298 deputies (or 2 percent) were permanently employed in the soviet and were able to devote themselves full-time to the policy process.[26]

Yaroslavl' oblast also repeatedly had difficulties maintaining a quorum in soviet meetings. As in Saratov, Yaroslavl' also had very few deputies (about 2 percent) permanently employed in the soviet.

Tiumen' oblast reported one instance during the summer of 1993 when the soviet did not have a quorum. Moreover, in Tiumen' only 6 of 297 deputies (or 2 percent) were permanently employed in the soviet. In 1990 the soviet reportedly considered the question of increasing the professionalization of their deputy corps by employing more deputies full-time, but the proposal was rejected[27] (See Table 4.2).

Finally, an analysis of the legislative priorities of all four oblasts reveals striking variation in the amount of time oblast malyi soviets spent on

[23] Author's interview with Irina D. Obriadina, Head of the Protocol Section, Nizhnii Novgorod Oblast Soviet of People's Deputies, May 7, 1993.

[24] Saratovskii oblastnoi sovet narodnykh deputatov, informatsionnyi biulleten' no. 6, "O trinadsatoi sessii Saratavskogo oblastnogo soveta narodnykh deputatov dvadtsat' pervogo sozyva," Saratov, 1993, p. 10.

[25] Ibid., pp. 14–15.

[26] Ibid., p. 11.

[27] Author's interview with Vladimir Oseichuk, chairman of the Tiumen' Oblast Soviet Committee on the Work of the Soviet, Tiumen', July 19, 1993.

TABLE 4.2
Ability to Raise a Quorum for Meetings of the Oblast Soviet

Score	Relative Frequency of No Quorum	Oblast Ranking
4	Always had quorum.	Nizhnii Novgorod
3	At least one report of no quorum.	Tiumen'
2	Two reports of no quorum.	
1	Repeated lack of quorum.	Saratov; Yaroslavl'

organizational versus policy questions.[28] The underlying assumption of this indicator is that the more time decision makers spent on organizational matters, the less time they spent responding to policy challenges. Over a ten-month period in 1992 (February to December), the Nizhnii Novgorod malyi soviet adopted 303 decisions, only 54 of which, or 17.8 percent, were concerned with internal soviet organizational and personnel matters.[29] In approximately the same period, the Yaroslavl' oblast malyi soviet adopted 125 decisions, 31 of which, or 20.0 percent, were organizational.[30] In contrast, the Saratov malyi soviet adopted 148 decisions, 46 of which, or 31.1 percent, concerned organizational and personnel matters, and the Tiumen' malyi soviet adopted 227 decisions, 104 of which, or 45.8 percent, were organizational in nature.[31] These comparisons are expressed in Table 4.3.

[28] I employ data from malyi soviets because oblast soviets met only four times a year, on average, whereas malyi soviets met bimonthly and generated most of the legislation that eventually was presented to oblast soviets. Further, the data available on oblast soviets in Saratov and Tiumen' were insufficient to make reliable comparisons. To construct this measure, I read through all the available malyi soviet legislation from all four oblasts that was passed in late 1991 through 1992. I classified this legislation according to subject (agriculture, industry, social services, social welfare, privatization, price policy, and organizational and personnel matters). I then counted the number of decisions made in each category and calculated these as percentages of the total number of decisions made by each malyi soviet.

[29] Information for Nizhnii Novgorod oblast comes from *Biulleten' Nizhegorodskogo oblastnogo soveta narodnykh deputatov* (February–December 1992) (Nizhnii Novgorod: Nizhegorodskaia oblastnaia tipografiia, 1992).

[30] Information for Yaroslavl' oblast comes from (spravochniki [handbooks]) *Resheniia malogo soveta Yaroslavskogo oblastnogo soveta narodnykh deputatov* (March–November 1992) (Yaroslavl' Oblast Department of Soviet Affairs).

[31] Information from Saratov comes from *Informatsionnyi biulleten' Saratovskii oblastnoi sovet narodnykh deputatov* (December 1991–December 1992) (Saratov Oblast Soviet of People's Deputies). Information for Tiumen' comes from *Vestnik oblastnogo soveta narodnykh deputatov* (December 1991–November 1992) (Tiumen': Tiumenskaia oblastnaia tipografiia).

TABLE 4.3

Comparison of the Percentage of Time Malyi Soviets Spent on Organizational versus Policy Matters, 1992

Score	Percentage of Time Spent on Organizational and Personnel Matters	Oblast Ranking
4	0–20	Nizhnii Novgorod; Yaroslavl'
3	21–30	
2	31–40	Saratov
1	41 or more	Tiumen'

Statistical Information Services

This measure is directly borrowed from Putnam's performance index. As he explains, "Other things being equal, a government with better information about its constituents and their problems can respond more effectively."[32] Just as Putnam found in the twenty regions of Italy, the Russian provinces exhibited considerable variation in the scope and breadth of available information services.

This indicator could almost as easily be placed under the rubric of innovations as under responsiveness, for the presence of such services is new in the former Soviet Union. Under the communist system, information on just about anything was, of course, tightly controlled. While hard numbers are probably nonexistent, one can relatively safely assert that photocopiers and fax machines, not to mention computers and electronic mail, were (and still are) scarce in the offices of bureaucrats in provincial capitals. The collection of information was highly secretive, and access to it was carefully monitored and protected by both central and provincial officials.

All four regions are rated in Table 4.4 according to the breadth of their information-gathering facilities. Again, at the two extremes are Saratov and Nizhnii Novgorod, with Yaroslavl' and Tiumen' ranking closer to the latter than the former. A simple test of the breadth of information services available in each oblast arose by "naively" asking for what I knew to be previously unavailable information—such as gross oblast product, gross oblast production output, survey and polling results of oblast residents, oblast unemployment statistics, and the like.

[32] Putnam, *Making Democracy Work*, p. 67

TABLE 4.4
Information Services

Score	Services Available	Oblast Ranking
4	Produced own publications; extensive original data collection and processing services.	Nizhnii Novgorod; Tiumen'
3	Original data collection and processing services.	Yaroslavl'
2	Data collection services.	Saratov
1	No improvements over what already existed before 1990.	

Nizhnii Novgorod was able to provide by far the most comprehensive information in the least amount of time. This is owing in no small part to the establishment of the "Nizhnii Novgorod Research Fund." The Fund employed several dozen people and collected social and economic statistics never before compiled in one place. It also produced publications regarding Nizhnii Novgorod oblast's economic and human resource potential. It operated as a subdivision of the oblast administration's Economic Prognosis Department.

Similarly, Tiumen's oblast soviet established an information-analysis center in 1992. The center employed about twenty people, including political analysts, economists, and sociologists and collected original economic and sociological data.[33] The oblast soviet in December 1992 instructed this center, jointly with the regional Goskomstat (state committee on statistics) branch to modernize and systematize the oblast's system of information collection so that it would conform to international standards. To assist in this process, the oblast government funded a U.S.$4 million computer network designed to link more than two hundred organizations within the oblast, including:

"the oblast soviet, city, and raion soviets; the oblast administration's committee on economics; the economic organs of the administrations of autonomous okrugs, cities, and raions; the privatization funds and com-

[33] Author's interview with Vladimir A. Filipov, chairman of Info-Tsentr, Department of the Activities of the Soviet, Tiumen' Oblast Soviet of People's Deputies, July 26, 1993.

mittees of the oblast, the okrugs, cities, and raions; the oblast library; and the oblast school of people's deputies."[34]

This computer network received funding from the oblast hard-currency fund and was installed in July and August 1993. Although other oblasts considered this sort of system (including Yaroslavl' and Nizhnii), Tiumen' was the first oblast to establish such a network.[35]

Yaroslavl' established a research organization, employing twenty-six people including programmers, analysts, and administrators and offering statistical services based on the Nizhnii Novgorod model. In Yaroslavl', however, these workers were not able to produce the same breadth of information as was available in Nizhnii Novgorod or Tiumen' oblasts even given more time to compile it. The *city* of Yaroslavl' had an extremely active sociologist on staff, and the oblast had recently acquired a staff sociologist charged with conducting surveys of oblast residents on various issues (privatization, housing, and so on).

In contrast, Saratov was really at the infant stage in this process and was able to provide only a fraction of what was present in either Nizhnii Novgorod, Tiumen', or Yaroslavl' oblasts. The Saratov oblast administration did, however, establish a modest information sector, and the chairman of the oblast soviet appointed a small information department with a staff of three.

POLICY OUTPUT AND IMPLEMENTATION

This section reorients the study from *how* governments do things to *what* governments do. Here I examine the policy pronouncements each oblast government made in self-declared priority areas, and then compare the degree to which these policies were implemented. Specifically, we are looking to see if mechanisms were created for policy implementation. It is important to note that the deliberate focus is on policy *output* rather than policy *outcomes*. The reason for this, as Putnam and Eckstein have noted, is that policy outcomes are results of more than just government legislation. For example, a recorded drop in the amount of pollutants in the air between time A and time B can be as much a result of the direction

[34] "Ob organizatsii pervoi ocheredi regional'noi informatsionno-komp'iuternoi seti Tiumenskoi oblasti," no. 208 ot 25.11.92), *Vestnik oblastnogo soveta narodnykh deputatov* 24, no. 15 (December 1992): 25 (Tiumen').

[35] For more information on the establishment of this network, see *Kommersant-Daily*, no. 133 (July 16, 1993): 13.

of the wind on the day of measurement as much as to the successful implementation of local pollution control legislation.

Eckstein notes that "it is ludicrous to expect polities to attain goals that they do not want to attain, but surely reasonable to expect them efficaciously to pursue those that are in fact strong preferences."[36] Therefore, rather than randomly selecting policy areas on which I thought governments should focus, I arrived at the policy areas below by asking a dozen or so legislators in each oblast "What are the most pressing problems in this region?" Not surprisingly, because all Russian regional governments faced similar challenges with the collapse of the Soviet system, the legislators' self-declared priorities had a high degree of overlap. These deputy appraisals were double-checked against the decisions (*resheniia*) taken by the oblast and malyi soviets in 1992. I assess policies in each of the areas below according to their coherence, scope, and level of creativity.

The policy areas break down into (1) Regional Economic Development, which includes (a) regional trade policy, and (b) programs to improve the general performance of the regional economy; and (2) Education.

Regional Economic Development Policy

In all four oblasts, economic development was a prime goal. Comparing economic development policies provides an excellent opportunity to examine how governments responded to the major challenge of restoring supply lines to their oblasts in the wake of the collapse of the Soviet super-ministries. Concrete measures here are (1) the extent and scope of attempts to promote interregional and foreign trade; and (2) general efforts to improve the performance of the local economy. Comparison along these lines reveals that Nizhnii Novgorod and Tiumen' oblasts were far more proactive in developing their regional economies. The leaderships of both these governments actively sought out interregional and foreign trade opportunities, as well as writing and initiating comprehensive regional development programs. In contrast, Yaroslavl' oblast devoted its policy efforts to stabilizing the regional economy rather than actively developing its economic opportunities. Where Yaroslavl' had not produced far-reaching development programs, Saratov was somewhat successful in this regard but fell short at the implementation stage.

---

[36] Eckstein, *The Evaluation of Political Performance*, p. 68.

REGIONAL TRADE POLICY

The immediate response of most regions to the collapse of the central command administration system was to enact independently their own inter-oblast barter agreements. Gradually, however, several oblasts developed trade associations and arranged their own trade agreements with other regions within the Russian Federation and other members of the Commonwealth of Independent States.

The economics section of the Novosibirsk branch of the Academy of Sciences under Anatolii G. Granberg helped promote the idea of freer inter-oblast trade throughout the 1980s.[37] This effort culminated in the establishment, in July 1991, of the first inter-oblast trade association—the Siberian Agreement (*Sibirskii Soglashenie*)—between the oblasts and krais of Siberia.[38] It was the first of twelve such agreements signed by almost all of Russia's subnational units, designed "to promote economic decentralization and development."[39] Some of these associations proved more active than others, and this was owing in no small part to the zeal with which oblast signatories approached the task of promoting inter-oblast trade. Further, some oblasts began to pursue more elaborate independent trade initiatives beyond these agreements. These were clear attempts to promote local industry and to prevent high unemployment of constituents.

All four oblasts in this study were members of interregional trade associations. The nature of their participation in these organizations, however, clearly differed qualitatively. Further, whereas Nizhnii Novgorod and Tiumen' oblasts were among the first regions to pursue indepen-

[37] See, for example, Anatolii G. Granberg, *Sintez regional'nykh i narodnokhoziastvennykh modelei i zadach territorial'nogo sotsialno-ekonomicheskogo razvitiia*, Doklad, vtoroi sovetsko-zapadnogermanskii seminar "Modelirovanie razvitiia territorial'nikh sotsialno-ekonomicheskikh sistem," Novosibirsk, 1983; and Anatolii G. Granberg, *Intensifikatsia ekonomicheskoi i mezhregional'noi integratsii*, Chetvertoe sovetsko-bolgarskoe rabochee soveshcanie "Sovershenstvovanie form territorialnoi organizatsi proizvodstva," Novosibirsk, 1984.

[38] See "Regional'naia ekonomika—zelenyi tsvet," *Sovetskaia sibir*, July 3, 1991. Technically, the other trade associations were formed by the spring of 1991, but the Siberian Agreement was the first to become operational. For more on the Siberian Agreement, see James Hughes, "Regionalism in Russia: The Rise and Fall of the Siberian Agreement," *Europe-Asia Studies* 46, no. 7 (1994): 1133–61.

[39] Ukaz prezidenta RSFSR no. 194, November 1991. For a list of these associations, see "Spisok mezhregional'nykh assotsiatsii po RSFSR," March 13, 1991, produced by the Supreme Soviet's Committee of Inter-Republic Relations and Regional Policy and provided to the author by the committee's staff in April 1992.

dently arranged trade agreements with other regions, Yaroslavl' and Saratov stuck primarily to more traditional barter agreements.

Nizhnii Novgorod oblast's interregional trade activity was part of a larger, coherent regional economic development plan written, at the request of the oblast leadership, by the well-known young Russian economist (and politician) Grigorii Yavlinsky.[40] In his plan Yavlinsky noted that "today, the powers of the Russian provinces take upon themselves the function of cultivators and conductors of their internal economic and social policy."[41] In keeping with this, Yavlinsky urged the increased integration of regional governments and the establishment of horizontal ties between the provinces to replace the traditional vertical lines of dependence on Moscow. Yavlinsky was in favor of increased free trade between the provinces and jointly creating "favorable conditions for attracting domestic and foreign investment." To this end he encouraged the leaders of Nizhnii Novgorod oblast to make their membership in the regional association Bol'shaia Volga (meaning "Greater Volga" in reference to the river that passes through each oblast in the association) a meaningful vehicle for trade and economic development. In addition, Nizhnii pursued many horizontal trading agreements outside the parameters of Bol'shaia Volga. These agreements far surpassed traditional barter agreements and included arrangements for establishing, on the territory of the partner province, trading houses and banks as well as the sale of locally produced products for money.[42] The agreement that Nizhnii Novgorod oblast signed with two oblasts (Taldykorgan and Karagandinsk) in Kazakhstan enabled the former to sell its products to China.

Beyond the establishment of trade relationships within the confines of the former Soviet Union, Nizhnii Novgorod oblast also tried to promote its international trade ties.[43] The oblast government also made use of the

---

[40] See *Ekonomika i politika v Rossii: Nizhegorodskii prolog* (Epitsentr: Nizhnii Novgorod, June–September 1992). Since working in Nizhnii Novgorod, Yavlinsky has founded a national political party, Yabloko, and ran a distant fourth in the 1996 presidential elections behind Boris Yeltsin, Gennadi Zyuganov of the Communist Party of Russia, and Alexander Lebed.

[41] *Ekonomika i politika v Rossii: Nizhegorodskii prolog*, p. 5.

[42] See, for example, "Agreement on the Economic, Technical, and Cultural Collaboration between the Administrations of Tiumen' and Nizhnii Novgorod Oblasts," (1993); "Agreement on the Economic, Technical, and Cultural Collaboration between Two Oblasts of Kazakhstan and Nizhnii Novgorod Oblast" (November 1992).

[43] The oblast has been inhibited in this regard by restrictions placed on it by Moscow, which continues to envision a more unitary approach to trade. Author's interview with Lev Beldor, Foreign Economic Ties and Trade Department, Nizhnii Novgorod Oblast Administration, January 5, 1993.

historic Nizhnii Novgorod Iarmarka—a pre-Revolutionary trade fair—to display goods produced by the region's factories for sale abroad.

Similarly, Tiumen' oblast made a concerted effort to increase its interregional trade opportunities. It participated in two interregional trade associations (Sibirskii Soglashenie and Bol'shoi Ural), as well as signing a number of trade agreements with other oblasts. As part of an arrangement with the federal government, the oblast was allowed to trade freely 10 percent of the oil and gas extracted in the region. Tiumen's trade agreements therefore usually involved the sale of Tiumen' oil and gas in exchange for the purchase of food stuffs and consumer goods. Although Tiumen's trade deals were plentiful, those of Nizhnii Novgorod surpassed them in quality. For example, Tiumen' did not include in its deals the establishment of trading houses or banks. Still, the Tiumen' government established trading deals with Ukraine and even had a permanent Ukrainian representative in residence in the oblast soviet building. Moreover, Tiumen's pursuit of trade opportunities, like Nizhnii Novgorod's, was part of a general effort to improve capital flow into the region with the hope of improving the state of the area's economic base.

Although Yaroslavl' was more active than Saratov in promoting trade opportunities, the oblast was not nearly as aggressive in this regard as Nizhnii Novgorod or Tiumen'. Yaroslavl' was a member of the association of oblasts and cities of the central region of Russia. This association was little more than a symbolic institution used for political rather than economic purposes.[44] The chairman of the Yaroslavl' oblast soviet certainly met regularly with the leaders of neighboring oblasts, but in comparison with Nizhnii Novgorod and Tiumen' oblasts, there was little evidence of resulting concrete accomplishments with regard to interregional trade.[45] Instead, in Yaroslavl', trade deals were limited primarily to barter agreements with other oblasts (for example, there was a barter arrangement with Murmansk oblast for fish in exchange for Yaroslavl's consumer goods). Other elements of the oblast's trade policy were limited to exchanges that existed under the Soviet system between enterprises in Yaroslavl' and those in other oblasts. Finally, although foreign trade opportunities arose in Yaroslavl', in 1993 the most the oblast could boast of in this regard was the purchase of medical supplies and agricultural machinery from the West.[46]

[44] Author's interview with Viktor Zharikov, chairman of the Department of Foreign Economic Activity, Yaroslavl' Oblast Administration, January 5, 1993.

[45] Author's interview with Aleksandr Veselov, chairman of Yaroslavl' Oblast Soviet of People's Deputies, January 6, 1993.

[46] Author's interview with Zharikov, Yaroslavl', January 5, 1993.

TABLE 4.5
Trade Policy

Score	Policy Description	Oblast Ranking
4	Active creation of interregional trade opportunities through trade association and comprehensive independent trade agreements. Extensive foreign development opportunities.	Nizhnii Novgorod
3	Promotion of interregional trade opportunities through trade associations and establishment of independent trade agreements. Extensive foreign development opportunities.	Tiumen'
2	Some activity in interregional trade association, few inter-oblast trade agreements, and some foreign development opportunities.	Yaroslavl'
1	Some activity in interregional association, no inter-oblast trade agreements, and some foreign development opportunities	Saratov

Although Saratov was a member of Bol'shaia Volga, it had no other interregional trade agreements.[47] The chairman of the oblast soviet recognized a need for interregional trade and produced a protocol announcing Saratov's desire for increased interregional collaboration but, at the time of writing, little had come of it.[48] Foreign trade agreements were also few and far between in Saratov, although the oblast signed several contracts with foreign companies for the development of some of its industries.[49]

The differences between the four oblasts' trade policies is shown in Table 4.5.

[47] Author's interview with Valerii Sukunin, head of the Foreign Trade Department, Saratov Oblast Administration, and author's interview with Dimitri Kibirskii, Department of Social and Economic Problems and International Relations, Saratov Oblast Soviet of People's Deputies, April 27, 1993.

[48] See "Protokol namerenii o sotrudnichestve" (Protocol on intention of collaboration), Saratovskii oblastnoi sovet narodnykh deputatov, Spring 1993.

[49] For example, ELF oil and gas of France.

PROGRAMS TO IMPROVE REGIONAL ECONOMIC DEVELOPMENT

Aside from increasing their trading sphere, oblast governments had the ability to manipulate other policy instruments to promote regional development. The extent to which regions availed themselves of these opportunities, however, varied considerably. The following brief discussion of the general economic development activities of these four cases again reveals that Nizhnii Novgorod oblast more actively pursued this self-avowed policy priority.

First, of the four cases, in 1992 Nizhnii Novgorod oblast's malyi soviet devoted the largest proportion (17.5 percent) of its legislative output to agricultural and industrial development issues.[50] Second, Nizhnii Novgorod oblast sought to fulfill Yavlinsky's development plan by attempting to enable regional enterprises to keep more money to devote to capital investment. The oblast leadership employed several approaches here. Under the Soviet system, large enterprises paid for their employees' social services. As the nation shifted slowly to market mechanisms and allowed prices to float, these enterprises in some instances were pinched between old and new such that they were using as much as 80 to 100 percent of their profits to continue paying for social services (housing, transportation, medicine, and schooling).[51] Nizhnii Novgorod oblast's economic development strategy therefore included plans to free enterprises from the stifling burden of paying for workers' and their families' social services, and provided tax incentives for investment and privatization.

One of the prime objectives of the Nizhnii Novgorod economic plan was to create an economic middle class through ownership of private property.[52] To this end, the oblast leadership pursued a rapid and thorough privatization effort of large and small enterprises and hastened the pace of land sales. Indeed, Nizhnii Novgorod oblast was the model for effective privatization in Russia.[53] Further, in an effort to encourage the transformation into a market economy, Nizhnii Novgorod oblast sim-

[50] See notes 29, 30, and 31, above, regarding sources for the ranking of oblast legislative priorities.

[51] *Ekonomika i politika v Rossii: Nizhegorodskii prolog*, p. 41.

[52] Ibid., p. 28.

[53] The International Finance Corporation (IFC) participated in some of the small-scale privatization in Nizhnii Novgorod oblast and produced several brochures on the "Nizhnii Novgorod model" to assist other oblasts in privatizing. It is notable that the IFC attempted to assist other oblasts in privatizing and yet did not enjoy the success it did in Nizhnii Novgorod oblast. Allen Bigman of the IFC, in an interview with the author on November 24, 1992, attributed the IFC's success in Nizhnii to the cooperation and support of the oblast leadership—specifically Governor Nemtsov and Evgenii Krestianinov, the chairman of the oblast soviet.

plified the process of registration of small businesses, effectively legalizing previously labeled black market operations. Finally, because an estimated 60 to 85 percent of the oblast's industrial sector was oriented to defense production in a time when Russia's defense needs were diminishing, Nizhnii Novgorod oblast encouraged the process of production conversion.[54] Although there was a federal-level conversion fund, many oblasts with economies devoted to military industrial production complained that federal funding was insufficient. Nizhnii Novgorod oblast, however, supplemented the available funds for conversion by creating the Nizhegorodskii Bankerskii Dom (Nizhnii Novgorod Banking House), which was able to generate enough capital to lend money to some enterprises for conversion. The bank was written into the oblast's trade deals, discussed above, such that each of the oblast's trading partners was obligated to assist in the establishment of a branch of the bank. The bank's director also managed to establish branches in France and England with foreign financing.[55]

Moreover, the leadership of Nizhnii Novgorod oblast produced a comprehensive regional economic development plan and created mechanisms for its implementation.

Tiumen' oblast also produced a comprehensive regional development program but was slightly hampered by its inability to implement all facets of the program. In September 1991 President Yeltsin signed an *ukaz* (executive order) regarding "the Development of Tiumen' Oblast." Before its inception, the oblast had no independent authority to sell any share of the oil and gas extracted on its territory. This was strictly the purview of the central government. The ukaz gave the oblast the authority to "freely use" (sell or trade) 10 percent of the oil and gas extracted by centrally owned enterprises located on the oblast's territory and 10 percent of other products produced by enterprises in the region.[56]

The decree was the product of extended planning on the part of the Tiumen' oblast soviet. At the soviet's first session following the 1990 elections, the then soviet chairman, Iurii Shafranik, declared the legislature's intention to initiate a regional development plan in order to improve the province's disastrous socioeconomic situation.[57] The soviet

---

[54] Estimates of the size of the defense sector come from author's interview with Boris Brevnov, chairman of the Nizhegorodskii bankerskii dom, November 22, 1992.

[55] Author's interview with Brevnov, November 22, 1992.

[56] Ukaz prezidenta RSFSR, "O razvitii Tiumenskoi oblasti," no. 122 (September 19, 1991): 2.

[57] "Zaiavlenie o sessii Tiumenskogo oblastnogo soveta narodnykh deputatov," *Tiumenskaia Pravda* (May 16, 1990): 1.

leadership eventually presented several versions of the decree to the central authorities, and it was ultimately signed following the August coup attempt. The enabling documents were not initiated, however, until March 1992. This was probably owing in part to the center's unwillingness to surrender control of any hard-currency earning resources to the regional government. Thus, although the oblast authorities were able to produce this general plan, its implementation suffered from enduring jurisdictional disputes between center and periphery. The expected benefits from the program were only partially realized.

Whereas Tiumen' and Nizhnii Novgorod oblasts were concerned with the politics of development, during the same time period Yaroslavl' concerned itself with the politics of subsidies.[58] Although the chemical and machine-building industries were the largest sectors of the oblast economy, in 1992 as much as 50 percent of oblast spending was ploughed into agricultural subsidies. In 1993 a projected 52 percent of spending was to go into subsidizing agriculture.[59] Normatively, this may appear an irrational policy (Why, for example, wasn't the focus on industry instead of agriculture, given the small size of the agricultural sector in Yaroslavl'?), but the oblast leadership must nonetheless be credited as effective in implementing its subsidies initiative.

Aside from its heavy subsidies in agriculture, Yaroslavl' had little or no overarching economic development plan beyond that of stabilizing the regional economy.

In contrast, Saratov produced regional economic policies but was weak in finding ways to implement them. Saratov, like Nizhnii Novgorod oblast, had a large military industrial complex. An estimated 60 percent of the output of all industrial enterprises in the oblast have military applications.[60] The oblast administration's committee on the industrial complex produced a plan in the autumn of 1992 for the conversion of its defense plants. The plan hoped to divert production to consumer goods, buses, chemical production, communications, agricultural machinery, and environmental cleanup. Difficulties arose, however, in implementing this plan when the oblast administration was unable to get expected funding from the central government's conversion fund. Oblast authorities reported in the spring of 1993 that they were still looking for funding sources and were hoping this would come from increased trade ties.[61]

[58] Dr. Blair Ruble, Director, Kennan Institute, made this observation.

[59] Author's interview with Anatolii Lisitsyn, Governor, Yaroslavl' oblast, April 1993.

[60] This estimate comes from the Departments for Social and Economic Problems and International Relations, Saratov Oblast Soviet of People's Deputies, April 1993.

[61] Author's interview with Kibirskii, Saratov, April 27, 1993.

TABLE 4.6
Regional Economic Development Programs

Score	Policy Description	Oblast Ranking
4	Produced comprehensive development plan and created mechanisms for implementation.	Nizhnii Novgorod
3	Produced comprehensive development plan, but implementation proceeded slowly.	Tiumen'
2	Produced limited plan but was able to implement it.	Yaroslavl'
2	Produced plans but had little ability to implement them.	Saratov

To its credit, Saratov's leadership also produced a comprehensive agricultural development program as well as a program for the development of small businesses. Although the programs were comprehensive, the small business development plan was largely dependent on supporting legislation from the central government and the agricultural program was stalled for a lack of funds. Moreover, although Saratov was able to produce programs, it did not have much success in implementation.

While this is merely a sampling of some of the more striking differences between the four oblasts' regional development policies, it demonstrates that these governments clearly differed in what they were able to accomplish. These differences are shown in Table 4.6.

Before ending this section, it is important to reiterate that regardless of the normative orientations of policy in each case, these policy areas were self-declared priorities. All four governments expressed concern over these areas and noted themselves that these were areas they were trying to improve. Thus, regardless of how they approached these challenges (through the establishment of market mechanisms in Nizhnii Novgorod and Tiumen', for example, or through subsidies in Yaroslavl'), Nizhnii Novgorod oblast produced comparatively more comprehensive, coherent, and creative policy outputs and demonstrated a greater ability to implement them. Yaroslavl' produced and implemented less creative and comprehensive policy outputs but was able to implement them. Tiumen' and Saratov rated higher on policy output than did Yaroslavl', but compared to Nizhnii Novgorod and Yaroslavl' implementation was a problem.

Education Policy

Revamping the old Soviet educational system was also a self-declared priority for all four oblast governments. Policy makers agreed that major societal change required reform of the educational system. Yet, although all acknowledged that educational reform was important, there were of course significant variations in policy output and the degree of policy implementation.

The 1992 Russian Federation Law on Education allowed for a significant degree of regional discretion in devising educational programs, including "the development and realization of regional programs for the development of education . . . taking into account ethnic and regional socioeconomic, ecological, cultural, demographic, and other particularities."[62] Further, at the time of this writing, a select few oblasts availed themselves of the opportunity to sign agreements with the Russian Federation Ministry of Education regarding the independence of the oblast Departments of Education. These agreements, in principle, enabled signatory oblasts to go further in developing their educational programs by taking increased responsibility in such areas as teacher accreditation, retraining, and the licensing of schools.

Three of the four cases, Nizhnii Novgorod, Yaroslavl', and Tiumen' signed such agreements with the federal Ministry of Education. Nizhnii Novgorod and Tiumen' oblasts, however, went even further in devising educational programs. Nizhnii developed a rather expansive educational program focusing on promoting student interest and ability in the humanities—an area long ignored by the Soviet educational system. Some of the more remarkable aspects of the program included the development of the oblast's own textbook for the humanities called *Chelovek i obshchestvo* (Man and society), which promoted learning about the development of competitive markets. The Nizhnii Novgorod Department of Education also established a computer laboratory and job (re)training center for both teachers and students. Finally, the department devised its own teacher accreditation and promotion system. This was to address the problem of good teachers leaving the profession for new, higher-paying private sector jobs. As a result, when Moscow ordered a teacher salary increase of 1.4 percent, Nizhnii officials raised salaries by a few percentage points more to reward good work.

---

[62] See 1992 Zakon Rossiiskoi federatsii ob obrazovanii, razdel 3, stat'ia 29 (v).

TABLE 4.7
Education Reform Policy

Score	Policy Description	Oblast Ranking
4	Regionally produced textbooks; teacher retraining; implementation of new regional programs; exchanges.	Nizhnii Novgorod; Tiumen'
3	Teacher retraining.	
2	No significant changes in preexisting educational services.	Saratov, Yaroslavl'
1	Deterioration of existing services.	

Tiumen' matched Nizhnii Novgorod's initiatives in all these areas. The Tiumen' oblast Department of Education also produced its own textbooks, reestablished programs for the humanities, established a teacher retraining center, and implemented its own teacher accreditation and promotion system.[63]

In contrast, although Yaroslavl' also signed an agreement with the federal Ministry of Education enabling it to develop regional education more freely, it did not take full advantage of the agreement. Instead, the focus remained on more traditional Soviet-style approaches to education, as well as promoting exchanges between students in Yaroslavl' and the United States (these exchanges lasted three months on average and only accommodated a handful of children). Saratov did not sign an independence agreement with Moscow, but its programs appeared on a par with Yaroslavl's. In an interview, the director of the Saratov oblast Department of Education preferred to discuss regional accomplishments that took place three to five years earlier rather than boast about what the department had done since the election of the new regional soviet.[64] In Saratov and Yaroslavl' few new programs were written, no new regionally produced textbooks were in circulation, and few educational reforms were implemented.

Differences in educational reform policy are shown in Table 4.7.

[63] Author's interview with Zoia Zvonkova, Chief Specialist, Committee on Education, Tiumen' Oblast Administration, July 27, 1993.

[64] Author's interview with Valentina Antonchenko, head of the Department of Education, Saratov Oblast Administration, April 20, 1993.

RESPONSIVENESS

I am not measuring all types of polities but rather new representative polities. Representative institutions have a particular obligation to adhere to societal demands. Having already measured the degree to which these four cases were effective, I have yet to measure the specifically democratic component of their performance—responsiveness. Drawing from extensive survey results, I examine whether constituents ranked these governments in the same way I did using "objective" measures of effectiveness.[65]

Constituent Evaluations of Performance

Using survey data from a sample of 3,774 constituents of these four oblasts, a clear ranking of the oblasts appeared across five questions regarding various aspects of performance.[66] Of course citizen satisfaction with government services, used in isolation, is not a thoroughly reliable measure of overall performance. The satisfaction levels that constituents express may not, for example, reflect true service performance because citizens do not always recognize what policy output governments are

[65] An informal measure of responsiveness concerns legislators' accessibility. In each of the four oblast soviets and administrations, I tested "open door" policies. This simple test concerned the ease with which I was able to walk into government buildings without an employee escort or a special pass (in Russian, a *propusk*). The logic of this test is rather simple. If constituents (or even foreign observers) cannot gain easy access to elected representatives, how can representatives know and respond to constituent concerns?

There is a rather striking correlation between this measure of responsiveness and the other measures of performance discussed in this chapter. Although all four oblasts posted guards at their entrances, in Tiumen' and Nizhnii the guards did little more than blink at me the dozens of times I walked through the same doors. Passage in or out of the buildings was uninhibited. In Yaroslavl' I was generally stopped and asked why I was in the building. After a brief explanation, I was allowed to continue on my way. In Saratov, however, I was never once able to slip past the guards' watchful eyes. Without exception, they directed me to the house phone to call the person I was interviewing so that he or she could escort me into the building. Although this test may seem trivial, its significance should not be underestimated. Many of these buildings were completely closed to nonemployees during the Soviet period. In the post-Soviet period, the guards at the doors operated on direct instructions from oblast heads of administration and chairmen of oblast soviets.

[66] Breakdowns of constituent appraisals by urban versus rural dwellers and levels of education are in Appendix B.

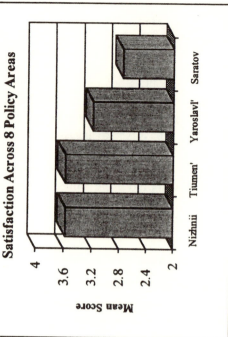

Composite Mean Scores of Constituent Satisfaction Across 8 Policy Areas

Nizhnii Tiumen' Yaroslavl' Saratov

(Respondents ranked their degree of satisfaction on a scale of 1 to 9 across eight policy areas.)

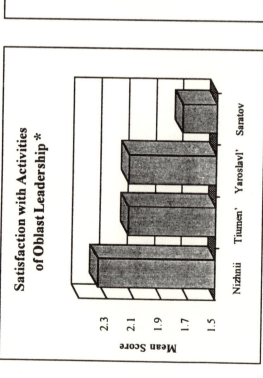

Satisfaction with Activities of Oblast Leadership *

Nizhnii Tiumen' Yaroslavl' Saratov

Q. "How satisfied are you with the activities of the leadership of this oblast?"

Figure 4.1. Summary of Constituent Evaluations of Government Performance. *Note:* Asterisks following bar graph titles indicate that scoring has been reversed from that described in the text so that a high mean score corresponds to high performance.

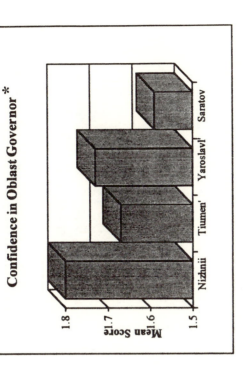

Confidence in Oblast Governor *

Mean Score

1.8
1.7
1.6
1.5

Nizhnii   Tiumen'   Yaroslavl'   Saratov

Q. "Do you believe that the following political actors and organizations are capable of solving the concrete problems of your region?"

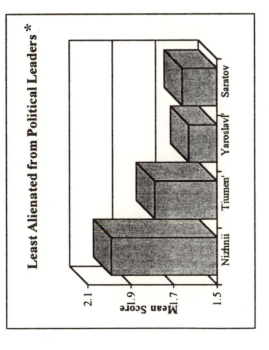
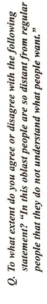

Least Alienated from Political Leaders *

Mean Score

2.1
1.9
1.7
1.5

Nizhnii   Tiumen'   Yaroslavl'   Saratov

Q. To what extent do you agree or disagree with the following statement? "In this oblast people are so distant from regular people that they do not understand what people want."

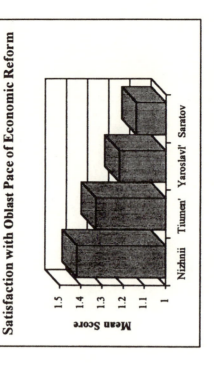

Confidence in Oblast Soviet *

Mean Score

1.7
1.6
1.5
1.4

Nizhnii   Tiumen'   Yaroslavl'   Saratov

Q. "Do you believe that the following actors and organizations
are capable of solving the concrete problems of your region?"

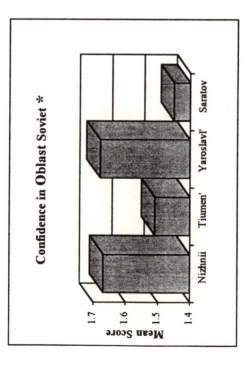

Satisfaction with Oblast Pace of Economic Reform

Mean Score

1.5
1.4
1.3
1.2
1.1
1

Nizhnii   Tiumen'   Yaroslavl'   Saratov

Q. "Do you think that economic reform in this oblast is going
too quickly, too slowly, or at the right pace?"

responsible for nor what is beyond government control.[67] Nonetheless citizen appraisals, *in combination* with other measures of effectiveness, provide compelling evidence of variation in regional government performance. In all but a few cases, citizen appraisals were highly correlated with the foregoing "objective" measures of performance. In almost every measure of satisfaction with government performance, Nizhnii Novgorod oblast ranked highest and Saratov ranked lowest. Tiumen' and Yaroslavl' generally ranked second and third, respectively. These comparisons are clearly illustrated in Figure 4.1.

Readers should note that in a few cases differences between oblast mean scores were not statistically significant at the .05 level (Tables 4.8 and 4.9). It is important to note, however, that the general pattern of Nizhnii Novgorod oblast at the top and Tiumen' and Yaroslavl' oblasts in the middle, with Saratov at the bottom, occurred too often across all indicators to assume that even those differences in means that were not significant at a .05 confidence level or better occurred merely by chance. Indeed, *all differences between the means of Nizhnii Novgorod and Saratov oblasts (except one) were significant at the .01 level or better!* With this in mind, I awarded oblast point scores throughout this section as though all paired differences in mean scores were significant at the .05 level or better.[68]

The first question deals with constituents' levels of satisfaction with regional leadership in each oblast. Numerical results appear in Table 4.10. Although in every oblast more respondents were dissatisfied than satisfied, the difference in the levels of satisfaction (columns 1 plus 2) between Nizhnii Novgorod oblast (47.6 percent) and Saratov oblast (14.3 percent) is striking. Saratov trailed behind Yaroslavl' (34.9 percent)

[67] For problems associated with this approach, see Brian Stipak, "Citizen Satisfaction with Urban Services: Potential Misuses as a Performance Indicator," *Public Administration Review* 39 (January–February 1979): 46–52.

[68] To do otherwise would wreak havoc on the point score system. For example, oblast A had a mean of 2.0, oblast B had a mean of 2.5, and oblast C had a mean of 3.0. If a lower mean indicates higher performance, and the difference between means of oblasts A and B was statistically significant at the .05 level, then oblast A should receive a higher point score (4) than oblast B (3). Problems arise, however, if the difference in means between oblasts A and C was not statistically significant at .05. We would then be forced to assign oblasts C and A the same point score even though the actual means of oblast A and oblast B are lower than that of oblast C. This situation arose in two instances, prompting the decision to treat all differences between means as though they were statistically significant at .05. I use a student t significance test to compare differences between two means of independent samples in Tables 4.8 and 4.9.

TABLE 4.8

Significance Levels for Differences between Oblast Mean Scores of Constituent Evaluations (two-tailed student *t*-test)

	Leadership	Alienation	Governor	Oblast Soviet	Economic Reform
Nizhnii-Saratov	< 0.01	< 0.01	< 0.01	< 0.01	< 0.01
Nizhnii-Tiumen'	< 0.01	< 0.01	< 0.01	< 0.01	< 0.01
Nizhnii-Yaroslavl'	< 0.01	< 0.01	< 0.01	*	< 0.01
Saratov-Yaroslavl'	< 0.01	*	< 0.01	< 0.01	< 0.01
Tiumen'-Saratov	< 0.01	< 0.01	< 0.11	< 0.05	< 0.01
Tiumen'-Yaroslavl'	< 0.05	< 0.01	< 0.01	< 0.01	< 0.01

*Significance > 0.30.

and Tiumen' (31.5 percent). Nizhnii Novgorod oblast had the best mean score (i.e., the lowest score), whereas Saratov had the worst.

A second question deals with the degree to which constituents felt alienated from regional political leaders (Table 4.11). The question examines people's perceptions of the extent to which leaders understand concrete political problems. A majority of respondents in all four oblasts expressed feelings of alienation from regional government (columns 1 plus 2) although, as we would expect, this feeling was highest in Saratov (81.7 percent), Yaroslavl' (82.8 percent), and Tiumen' (76.8 percent), but significantly lower in Nizhnii Novgorod (66.1 percent). Adding columns 3 and 4 produces "less alienated" scores. The pattern is virtually the same: in Nizhnii Novgorod oblast, 33.8 percent of respondents disagreed with the statement; in Tiumen', 23.1 percent disagreed; in Saratov, 18.4 percent disagreed; and in Yaroslavl', only 17.3 percent disagreed.

A brief look at the comparisons of statistical significance between the oblasts' mean scores in Table 4.8 reveals the same pattern. Again, in all comparisons but one (Saratov and Yaroslavl'), significance levels of differences between means were at the .01 level. Following the explanation of point assignments above, although there was no statistically significant difference between the mean scores of Saratov and Yaroslavl', the difference between means did form the pattern we have already observed so often. Thus, although we cannot prove in this one case that the differences were not at statistically significant levels, oblast point scores were assigned as if all differences were statistically significant.

Next, the survey asked respondents to assess how well regional gov-

TABLE 4.9

Significance Levels for Differences between Oblast Mean Scores of Constituent Evaluations across Eight Policy Areas

	Composite	Housing	Transport	Employment	Wages	Prices	Industrial Slump	Food	Environment
Nizhnii-Saratov	< 0.01	< 0.01	< 0.01	< 0.01	< 0.01	< 0.01	< 0.01	< 0.01	< 0.23
Nizhnii-Tiumen'	< 0.01	*	*	< 0.01	< 0.01	< 0.01	< 0.01	< 0.01	*
Nizhnii-Yaroslavl'	< 0.01	< 0.10	< 0.01	< 0.01	< 0.01	< 0.01	< 0.01	< 0.01	*
Saratov-Yaroslavl'	*	< 0.01	< 0.01	< 0.01	< 0.01	< 0.01	< 0.01	< 0.01	*
Tiumen'-Saratov	< 0.01	< 0.01	< 0.01	< 0.10	< 0.05	< 0.01	< 0.01	< 0.01	*
Tiumen'-Yaroslavl'	< 0.01	*	< 0.01	< 0.01	< 0.01	< 0.01	< 0.01	< 0.05	*

*Significance > 0.30.

121

TABLE 4.10

Satisfaction with Regional Leadership: "How satisfied are you with the activities of the leadership of this oblast?"

	1 (%)	2 (%)	3 (%)	4 (%)	Mean Score	N[a]	Oblast Point Score
Nizhnii Novgorod	8.2	39.4	32.9	19.4	2.6	743	4
Tiumen'	4.3	27.2	37.5	31.1	3.0	580	2
Yaroslavl'	3.7	31.2	41.4	23.7	2.9	781	3
Saratov	2.5	11.8	45.0	40.8	3.2	763	1

Note: Respondents ranked their degree of satisfaction with the leadership of the regional government on a scale of 1 to 4, where 1 was "fully satisfied"; 2 was "more satisfied than dissatisfied"; 3 was "more dissatisfied than satisfied"; and 4 was "fully dissatisfied." *A lower mean score therefore represents a higher level of satisfaction.*

[a]Because the original question offered a fifth response—"difficult to answer"—in order to prevent a score of 5 from skewing our results, we eliminated these responses from the total N for each oblast as well as for the calculation of the mean score. Significance levels appear in Table 4.8. All paired comparisons were statistically significant at the .05 level or better.

TABLE 4.11

Alienation from Oblast Political Leaders: "In this oblast, political leaders are so distant from regular people that they do not understand what people want."

	1 (%)	2 (%)	3 (%)	4 (%)	Mean Scores	N[a]	Oblast Point Score
Nizhnii Novgorod	44.4	21.7	22.7	11.1	2.0	765	4
Tiumen'	49.0	27.8	18.0	5.1	1.8	648	3
Yaroslavl'	58.2	24.6	13.1	4.2	1.6	817	1
Saratov	57.6	24.1	12.6	5.8	1.7	825	2

Note: We asked respondents to express the extent to which they agreed with this statement on a scale of 1 to 4, where 1 was "fully agree"; 2 was "agree more than disagree"; 3 was "disagree more than agree"; and 4 was "fully disagree." *A higher mean score therefore indicates a lower level of alienation.* Statistical significance levels for comparisons between mean scores appear in Table 4.8.

[a]Because the original question offered a fifth response—"difficult to answer"—in order to prevent a score of 5 from skewing our results, we eliminated these responses from the total N for each oblast as well as for the calculation of the mean score.

ernments addressed specific problems in certain policy areas, namely, housing, public transport, unemployment, wages, prices, provision of food supplies, industrial stagnation, and the environment (Table 4.12). Although the results reveal that Russians were generally rather unhappy with their governments in all these policy areas, they were more consistently dissatisfied in some oblasts than in others. Because some respondents may possibly have used "5" as the equivalent of "hard to answer," we look to the sums of the 1–4 scores versus those of the 6–9 scores. In *every area* respondents from Saratov oblast were the most dissatisfied with their regional government's handling of these issues. In contrast, in half of the eight areas included in the survey, Nizhnii Novgorod oblast's respondents were satisfied most consistently with their government's handling of the issues. In the areas where Nizhnii Novgorod's constituents did not rate highest in levels of satisfaction, they ranked second to Tiumen'. Where Tiumen's constituents did not rank highest in levels of satisfaction, they were second to constituents from Nizhnii in all but one policy area (the environment). Finally, respondents from Yaroslavl' oblast consistently ranked second or third in their levels of satisfaction across all eight policy areas.

When we examine the mean scores, the results are the same. Nizhnii Novgorod oblast received the highest approval rating, followed, in descending order, by Tiumen', Yaroslavl', and Saratov. The comparisons between the mean scores of each case and each of the three other cases was significant at a .05 level or greater, except in a few instances (see Table 4.9 for levels of statistical significance). The comparisons between the extremes—Nizhnii Novgorod and Saratov oblasts—across all policy areas (except the environment, where no differences in means were statistically significant) were significant at a .01 level.

The fourth question asks constituents to evaluate the abilities of political actors and institutions at the regional level. Respondents were asked to respond yes or no to whether they believed the governor and the oblast soviet were capable of solving regional problems (Table 4.13).

Again, in expressing confidence in their regional institutions, respondents from Nizhnii Novgorod and Saratov oblasts were at opposite extremes. Respondents in Yaroslavl' expressed more confidence in their governor than did respondents in Tiumen', although in both oblasts constituent ratings of the governor's capabilities were both significantly higher than in Saratov. With respect to confidence in the oblast soviet, the pattern was the same. Examining the mean scores of Yaroslavl' and Nizhnii Novgorod oblasts, respondents in both oblasts expressed higher

TABLE 4.12

Degree of Constituent Satisfaction with Regional Government in Eight Specific Policy Areas: "How satisfied are you with the way the leadership of this oblast is resolving the following problems?"

	Nizhnii Novgorod	Tiumen'	Yaroslavl'	Saratov
Housing				
Dissatisfied (%)				
(1–4)	60.7	63.1	65.2	85.3
Satisfied (%)				
(6–9)	19.1	16.9	15.4	4.9
Neither Dissatisfied nor Satisfied (%)				
(5)	20.1	19.9	19.5	9.8
Mean Score	3.48	3.41	3.28	2.24
Oblast Point Score	4	3	2	1
Transport				
Dissatisfied (%)				
(1–4)	51.0	52.1	57.2	66.8
Satisfied (%)				
(6–9)	21.3	26.0	16.0	10.8
Neither Dissatisfied nor Satisfied (%)				
(5)	27.7	8.1	9.9	22.3
Mean Score	3.94	4.05	3.59	3.21
Oblast Point Score	3	4	2	1
Unemployment				
Dissatisfied (%)				
(1–4)	41.3	37.8	52.5	60.5
Satisfied (%)				
(6–9)	25.6	30.3	13.8	13.8
Neither Dissatisfied nor Satisfied (%)				
(5)	33.2	31.9	33.7	25.7
Mean Score	4.48	4.79	3.74	3.57
Oblast Point Score	3	4	2	1

(continued)

TABLE 4.12 (*Continued*)

	Nizhnii Novgorod	Tiumen'	Yaroslavl'	Saratov
Wages				
Dissatisfied (%)				
(1–4)	70.9	62.4	78.2	82.3
Satisfied (%)				
(6–9)	13.4	13.6	7.5	5.1
Neither Dissatisfied nor				
Satisfied (%)				
(5)	15.7	24.0	14.4	12.5
Mean Score	2.92	3.40	2.64	2.31
Oblast Point Score	3	4	2	1
Prices				
Dissatisfied (%)				
(1–4)	77.4	72.4	83.5	89.5
Satisfied (%)				
(6–9)	11.4	11.4	7.0	3.1
Neither Dissatisfied nor				
Satisfied (%)				
(5)	11.1	16.2	9.5	7.4
Mean Score	2.52	2.84	2.23	1.88
Oblast Point Score	3	4	2	1
Provision of Food Products				
Dissatisfied (%)				
(1–4)	45.5	59.5	50.4	72.6
Satisfied (%)				
(6–9)	26.4	15.8	19.4	11.9
Neither Dissatisfied nor				
Satisfied (%)				
(5)	28.1	24.7	30.2	15.5
Mean Score	4.28	3.86	3.86	3.02
Oblast Point Score	4	3	3	1
Industrial Stagnation				
Dissatisfied (%)				
(1–4)	50.8	62.4	65.5	74.6
Satisfied (%)				
(6–9)	17.0	12.2	9.0	7.9

(*continued*)

TABLE 4.12 (*Continued*)

	Nizhnii Novgorod	*Tiumen'*	*Yaroslavl'*	*Saratov*
Neither Dissatisfied nor Satisfied (%)				
(5)	32.3	25.3	25.4	17.3
Mean Score	3.87	3.46	3.11	2.80
Oblast Point Score	4	3	2	1
Environment[a]				
Dissatisfied (%)				
(1–4)	68.5	71.0	67.0	72.0
Satisfied (%)				
(6–9)	15.1	12.1	12.8	14.2
Neither Dissatisfied nor Satisfied (%)				
(5)	16.5	16.8	20.1	13.8
Mean Score	3.12	3.03	3.07	2.99
Oblast Point Score	4	2	3	1
TOTAL OBLAST POINT SCORE	28	27	18	8

Note: Respondents were asked to indicate their level of satisfaction on a 9-point scale, where 1 is extremely dissatisfied and 9 is extremely satisfied. Those classified in the table as "more satisfied" responded anywhere from 6 to 9 on the scale; those classified as "more dissatisfied" responded anywhere from 1 to 4; those classified as "undecided" responded by indicating 5 on the scale. Higher levels of satisfaction therefore have higher mean scores. Significance levels for all comparisons appear in Table 4.9. Where results of percentages and mean scores conflict, oblast point scores are based on the differences in mean scores. Again, in four instances, the differences between means were not significant at greater than a .05 level. Nonetheless, the signs were all positive and, in most cases, the differences formed familiar patterns. *As a result, oblast point scores are assigned as though all relationships were statistically significant.*

[a]With respect to the environment, none of the differences between mean scores was statistically significant at greater than the .05 level.

degrees of confidence in the abilities of their regional legislatures to solve regional problems than respondents from either Tiumen' or Saratov.

These findings correspond fairly well to the pattern established with regard to "satisfaction with oblast leadership" shown in Table 4.10. Although in Yaroslavl' respondents expressed more confidence in the ability

TABLE 4.13

Abilities of the Governor and the Oblast Soviet to Solve Regional Problems:
"Do you believe that the following political actors and organizations are
capable of solving the concrete problems of your region?"

	Yes (%) (1)	No (%) (2)	Mean Scores[a]	N[b]	Oblast Point Score
The Governor					
Nizhnii Novgorod	79.6	20.4	1.20	746	4
Tiumen'	63.4	36.6	1.37	620	2
Yaroslavl'	73.3	26.7	1.27	757	3
Saratov	59.0	41.0	1.41	712	1
The Oblast Soviet					
Nizhnii Novgorod	66.9	33.1	1.33	636	3
Tiumen'	51.4	48.6	1.49	590	2
Yaroslavl'	68.3	31.7	1.32	675	4
Saratov	45.4	54.6	1.55	674	1

[a]Regarding the oblast soviet, all paired differences between means, except for Nizhnii and Yaroslavl', were significant at the .05 level or better (see Table 4.8). Regarding confidence in the governor, all paired relationships were statistically significant at the .01 level except for Tiumen' and Saratov. Point scores were assigned as though all relationships were statistically significant.

[b]Respondents were given three choices: "yes" (1); "no" (2); or "hard to answer" (3). We have treated the latter as opting out of the question and so subtracted these respondents from the N as well as in the calculations of the mean score and significance levels. *A lower mean score therefore indicates a higher degree of confidence in institutions and organizations.* Significance levels appear in Table 4.8 above.

of their governor and their oblast soviet to solve concrete problems than did respondents from Tiumen' (Table 4.13), the latter expressed slightly higher satisfaction with the activities of their regional leadership (Table 4.10). This slight reversal of middle positions, however, is still consistent with the general findings thus far.

Finally, a fifth question asked constituents to evaluate the pace of economic reform in the oblast (Table 4.14). In a sense, this provided a more general appraisal of regional economic policy. The oblast rankings formed an increasingly familiar pattern. Although many respondents had difficulty answering this question, in Nizhnii Novgorod and Tiumen' oblasts far more respondents approved of the pace of economic reform than in

TABLE 4.14

Evaluation of the Pace of Economic Reform: "Do you think that economic reform in this oblast is going too quickly, too slowly, or at the correct tempo?"

	Satisfied (%) (3)	Dissatisfied (%) (1 and 2)	Mean Score	N[a]	Oblast Point Score
Nizhnii Novgorod	42.5	57.4	1.42	568	4
Tiumen'	32.9	67.1	1.33	526	3
Yaroslavl'	22.4	77.5	1.22	582	2
Saratov	14.6	82.5	1.14	615	1

[a]Respondents were given four options: "tempo is too fast" (1); "tempo is too slow" (2); "tempo is about right" (3); and "hard to answer" (4). We combined responses 1 and 2 into a "dissatisfied" score; 3 is the proportion of respondents characterized as "satisfied." We discarded 4 so as not to bias our mean score and have recalculated our N appropriately. Significance levels appear in Table 4.8. All paired comparisons of mean scores were significant at the .01 level.

either Saratov or Yaroslavl'. The differences between the mean score comparisons of all four oblasts are significant at the .01 level (Table 4.8). Again, the performance pattern is pervasive. Nizhnii Novgorod and Tiumen' oblasts received higher satisfaction ratings than either Saratov or Yaroslavl'.

Moreover, across all the foregoing measures of responsiveness, Nizhnii Novgorod oblast, with few exceptions, ranked consistently higher than Tiumen' and Yaroslavl' and particularly Saratov. This is the same pattern we observed in our examination of effectiveness. Summed performance scores for all the foregoing twelve measures are shown in Table 4.15. Subtotals appear after each subset of performance—policy process, policy output and implementation, and responsiveness—to show that governments that have smooth policy processes were the same as those that were effective in their policy output and implementation and were most responsive.

Nizhnii Novgorod oblast scored thirteen points higher than Tiumen', which in turn scored thirteen points higher than Yaroslavl'. Saratov oblast scored significantly lower than the three other cases, with only about one-third the point score of Nizhnii Novgorod. Results indicate, therefore, a clear and consistent performance ranking among the four cases. Nizhnii Novgorod oblast rated high in all three categories of performance, whereas Saratov rated lowest in all three categories. Tiumen' and Yaroslavl' fairly consistently ranked second and third, respectively.

TABLE 4.15
Summed Performance Scores across Twelve Indicators

Table	Indicator	Nizhnii Novgorod	Tiumen'	Yaroslavl'	Saratov
4.1	Governor Selection	3	4	3	1
4.2	Quorum	4	3	1	1
4.3	Percentage of Time Spent on Organizational Matters	4	1	4	2
4.4	Information Services	4	4	3	2
	POLICY PROCESS SUBTOTAL	15	12	11	6
4.5	Trade Policy	4	3	2	1
4.6	Regional Economic Development Programs	4	3	2	2
4.7	Educational Reform Policy	4	4	2	2
	POLICY OUTPUT AND IMPLEMENTATION SUBTOTAL	12	10	6	5
4.10	Approval of Leadership	4	2	3	1
4.11	Alienation	4	3	1	2
4.12	Satisfaction with Performance in Specific Policy Areas (Not Counting Composite Scores)	28	27	18	8
4.13	Faith in Problem-Solving Abilities of Governor and Oblast Soviet	7	4	7	2
4.14	Pace of Economic Reform	4	3	2	1
	RESPONSIVENESS SUBTOTAL	47	39	31	14
	TOTAL INSTITUTIONAL PERFORMANCE SCORE	74	61	48	25

CONCLUSIONS

This chapter accomplished two tasks. First, it demonstrated that one can use positivist political methodology in measuring institutional performance. By devising a method of scoring and scaling, and combining it with description, I employed a method of measurement that should be applicable in other regions of Russia, as well as in a variety of other contexts. Second, the chapter showed that during Russia's first democratic experiment in the provinces, some regional governments were consistently higher achievers than others. Although Nizhnii Novgorod was by no means a post-socialist utopia, and compared to the performance of some Western subnational governments would likely have scored low, in the Russian context it was a region where policy processes were relatively smooth, policy outputs were more creative, and policy implementation abilities were better. Further, and central to the representative component of democratic performance, the regional government in Nizhnii Novgorod was more responsive to its constituents than were the other three governments examined here. Clearly some regions were better governed than others, although on paper their institutions were identical. Significant and consistent variation was evident in what the new representative Russian regional governments were able to accomplish. Why did these "local heroes"—higher-performance regional governments—exist in some places in the First Russian Republic but not in others? Chapter 5 looks for answers to this question by testing various theories of performance that appear in the comparative politics literature.

Testing Theories of Performance Variation: Economic, Social-Structural, and Cultural Hypotheses

THE COMPARATIVE POLITICS literature on both democratization and institutional performance provides a wide array of hypotheses that might explain the rather striking differences in the performance of the new government institutions. The four oblasts examined here represent diverse contexts in which to test the explanatory power of the most dominant comparative politics theories.

As noted in the introduction to this study, the four provinces roughly represent the four points of the compass and range in their physical size and distance from Moscow. They are, in short, geographically varied. Historically, the four oblasts range in age and importance to the Russian Empire, to its successor the Soviet Union, and to the present-day Russian Federation. At the time research for this study was completed, the economies of the four oblasts were also dominated by different economic sectors—the fertile wheat-growing regions of Saratov provided a valuable juxtaposition to the vast oil and gas fields of Tiumen', and Nizhnii Novgorod's heavy industrial and defense factories were in sharp contrast to the chemical refineries and lighter industry of Yaroslavl'.

The four oblast soviets elected in 1990 were also of varying political complexions—with Nizhnii Novgorod and Saratov having the highest incumbency rates as well as the highest rates of deputy membership in the CPSU.[1] Finally, although ethnically the four regions were predominantly Russian, some variations existed in the ethnicity of the four populations and in the average educational level of oblast residents. Finally, the data collected in the 1993 surveys tested for differences in popular attitudes among the four oblast populations.

In chapter 2 I asserted that *the more concentrated the economy, the higher was regional government performance* more accurately explained the performance variations observed in chapter 4 than the more dominant comparative politics theories of democratization and institutional

[1] See Table 1.2, ch. 1.

performance. To bolster my argument, this chapter tests the dominant hypotheses in the comparative politics literature, including the effects of variation in wealth and modernity among these four provinces; the possible effects on performance of differences in levels of social conflict; and, finally, cultural and social-structural variables. Despite comprehensive empirical testing, none of these theories persuasively accounted for the observed performance pattern: Nizhnii Novgorod and Tiumen' in the lead, followed by Yaroslavl', with Saratov consistently lagging.

WEALTH AND PERFORMANCE

Area specialists and comparativists alike might suggest initially that differences in wealth among these four provinces accounted for differences in regional government performance. Seymour Martin Lipset, for example, has asserted that higher levels of economic development are associated with the prevalence of democratic political systems.[2] More recently, in their study of comparative urban governments, Robert C. Fried and Francine Rabinovitz argued that of all the competing explanations for the performance differences that they observed, modernization was the most compelling.[3]

Logically, scarcity breeds conflict. Lower relative wealth can also potentially limit what governments can accomplish and may affect policy implementation. Wealth can also have a bearing on educational levels and citizen expectations of and attitudes toward government. Given, then, that wealth could affect all three aspects of government performance examined in chapter 4—the political process, ability to implement policy, and constituent evaluations of government—it seems reasonable to compare measures of relative oblast wealth.

[2] Seymour Martin Lipset, *Political Man: The Social Bases of Politics* (New York: Doubleday, 1950), especially ch. 2. Other examples of this argument are Robert A. Dahl, *Democracy and Its Critics* (New Haven, Conn.: Yale University Press, 1989); and Robert A. Dahl, *Polyarchy: Participation and Opposition* (New Haven, Conn.: Yale University Press, 1971). Samuel Huntington provides a useful review of the modernity and developmental literature in "The Goals of Development," in Samuel P. Huntington and Myron Weiner, eds., *Understanding Political Development* (Boston: Little, Brown, 1987).

[3] Robert C. Fried and Francine F. Rabinovitz, *Comparative Urban Politics: A Performance Approach* (Englewood Cliffs, N.J.: Prentice-Hall, 1980), p. 66, as cited in Robert D. Putnam, *Making Democracy Work: Civic Traditions in Modern Italy* (Princeton, N.J.: Princeton University Press, 1993), p. 84.

Further, area specialists and those more familiar with the characteristics of each of Nizhnii Novgorod, Tiumen', Yaroslavl', and Saratov will undoubtedly point to the expected political and economic gains Tiumen' might have enjoyed because it is a region rich in oil and gas. Indeed, in 1993, average salaries in Tiumen' were roughly four times higher than in the other provinces. Others might argue that because of its defense orientation, Nizhnii Novgorod might have benefited somehow from central investment during the Soviet era which would have had an enduring impact on the region after the collapse of the Soviet Union.

In the post-Soviet context, relative wealth is difficult to measure largely because of the peculiarities of the command economy. First, under the planned economy, communist authorities did not publish gross regional product statistics, and production statistics in general were purposely vague, often unreliable, and frequently manipulated for ideological purposes. Following the Soviet Union's collapse, the reform of methods for compiling statistics varied from oblast to oblast (see chapter 4). A second difficulty is that many of the measures of a region's wealth might be obscured by the fact that the communist economic system was directed by central planners situated in Moscow. Thus investment in human capital, in particular, did not necessarily follow from Moscow's investment in physical capital. In short, measures of wealth employed in the West do not yet reveal much when applied to former Soviet bloc economies.

To compensate for these difficulties, it is important to use as wide a variety of measures of wealth as possible. First, I use the measure of central capital investment in each oblast through the late-Soviet period to demonstrate which oblasts were a central economic priority and which may have continued to be economically important to the center through the early 1990s.[4] Second, I report average salary levels from the years 1991 and 1993 but also include other traditional measures of development for each of the four regions: infant mortality rates, telephones per hundred households, and average educational levels. These comparisons are shown in Table 5.1.

Table 5.1 demonstrates that there is little evidence to suggest that relative wealth and modernity explain the performance variation shown in chapter 4. Indeed, except for Tiumen', the oblasts vary little in terms of these traditional measures of wealth.

In the last decade of the Soviet period, Tiumen' had by far the highest

---

[4] This sheds some light on another important issue—relations with the central government—although, as regionalist demands for increased authority have demonstrated, economic power does not always translate into political power in post-Soviet Russia.

TABLE 5.1
Measures of Wealth and "Modernity"

	Nizhnii Novgorod	Tiumen'	Yaroslavl'	Saratov
Average Central Capital Investment per Capita (1981–89) in Rubles[a]	2,522 (4)[b]	21,230 (1)	2,806 (3)	3,062 (2)
Average Salary per Month at End of 1991 in Rubles[c]	5,055 (3)	9,403 (1)	5,170 (2)	4,964 (4)
Average Salary per Month at End of 1993 in Rubles	31,200 (3)	102,500 (1)	33,300 (2)	25,700 (4)
Infant Mortality per 1,000 Births (1991)[d]	16.2 (2)	18.7 (3)	19.6 (4)	14.2 (1)
Telephones per 100 Families (1991)[e]	20.8 (2)	19.1 (4)	21.8 (1)	19.7 (3)
Educational Levels[f] Higher/Unfinished Higher (University, Technical School) (%)	11.0	11.7	11.0	13.1
Middle School/Unfinished Middle School (High School) (%)	65.3	75.8	67.5	66.7
Elementary or No Formal Education (%)	23.7 (4)	12.5 (1)	21.5 (3)	20.2 (2)

(*continued*)

levels of central investment; Saratov followed, then Yaroslavl' and Nizhnii Novgorod. This was likely because of the capital-intensive nature of oil and gas extraction in Tiumen'. Salaries were also highest in Tiumen', jumping to more than 100,000 rubles per month in 1993. Salaries there were also higher on average than in the other three oblasts at the end of 1991, before prices were freed and both wages and inflation rose. Thus, on these two measures, Tiumen' appears to have been the wealthiest, but its regional government performance ranked a relatively distant second to that of Nizhnii Novgorod.

TABLE 5.1 (*Continued*)

	Nizhnii Novgorod	*Tiumen'*	*Yaroslavl'*	*Saratov*
Aggregate Modernity Score (Lower Scores Indicate *More* Modern)	18	11	15	16
Average Modernity Rank Score (Aggregate Score Over Six Measures Where 1 Is Most Modern and 4 Is Least Modern)	3.0	1.8	2.5	2.7

[a]Investment figures are averages of yearly data provided by Prof. Ronald Leibowitz, Middlebury College.

[b]Oblasts' ranking according to a 1 to 4 aggregate index of wealth and development measures, where 4 is high and 1 is low.

[c]Salary information from Russia Federation Goskomstat and kindly provided by Vladimir Gimpelson of the Institute of World Economy and International Relations (IMEMO), Russian Academy of Sciences. See also Appendix 8 in Vladimir Gimpelson, Darrell Slider, and Sergei Chrugov, "Political Tendencies in Russia's Regions: Evidence from the 1993 Parliamentary Elections," *Slavic Review* (Fall 1994): 711–732.

[d]*Pokazateli sotsial'nogo razvitiia respublik, kraev i oblastei Rossiiskoi federatsii* (Moskva: Respublikanskii informatsionno-izdatel'skii tsentr, 1992), p. 19.

[e]*Pokazateli sotsial'nogo razvitiia*, pp. 257–258.

[f]From the 1989 USSR Census.

This is significant because across both salary and central investment figures Nizhnii ranks third and fourth, respectively. Central investment in Nizhnii Novgorod in the last decade of communist rule was lower than in Saratov and Yaroslavl', both of which ranked significantly lower in terms of regional government performance. In terms of wages, Nizhnii Novgorod trailed Yaroslavl' and Tiumen'.[5] Average monthly salaries in Nizhnii Novgorod were less than 100 rubles higher than in Saratov in 1991 and slightly higher than in Saratov in 1993.

Central capital investment and higher wages, however, did not necessarily translate into material wealth or wealth in human services. This is evident in the more traditional measures of wealth and modernity where

[5] Monthly wages in Tiumen' were highest among oil and gas workers. Higher salaries there were an explicit attempt to attract and retain labor in the face of the extremely difficult working conditions in northern Siberia.

the pattern among the four regions shifts slightly. Here, Saratov scores well in that it had the lowest rate of infant mortality of the four oblasts, followed by Nizhnii and then Tiumen, with Yaroslavl' ranking lowest. The number of telephones per family, although low in all regions by Western standards, also reveals a small amount of variation across cases. Along this measure of development, Yaroslavl' rates highest, followed by Nizhnii, Saratov, and Tiumen'.[6]

Finally, if educational levels play a role in citizens' perceptions of government and their abilities to adapt to democratic forms of government, we might expect regions with higher educational levels to be regions where approval ratings of the new representative regional governments would be highest. Indeed, education is also often used as a measure of overall development. Yet, comparing relative levels of education among these four regions does not yield the expected performance pattern. In all four oblasts more than 10 percent of the population had higher postsecondary degrees or higher unfinished postsecondary degrees. Saratov, however, had the greatest proportion (13 percent) of people in this, the highest educational category. Tiumen' also ranks reasonably well on education, while Nizhnii Novgorod ranks the lowest. Thus little positive correlation appears to exist between educational levels and government performance.

To make comparisons more easily across all these wealth and development measures, I devised a simple aggregation index. Each oblast is ranked from 1 to 4 such that the most developed region rates closest to 1.0 and the least developed closest to 4.0. Rankings for individual measures appear in italics in Table 5.1. Aggregate figures appear at the bottom of Table 5.1 and are then divided by the number of development measures (six) to obtain a rank score from 1.0 to 4.0.[7]

The index demonstrates that relative wealth does not account for the pattern of performance variation observed in chapter 4. Whereas Nizhnii Novgorod rated highest on performance measures, it rated lowest (3.0) on these measures of development. Tiumen', the second highest performing regional government, rated highest in the aggregate in terms of development but did rather poorly on certain individual measures (number of telephones and infant mortality rates). Yaroslavl', where regional govern-

[6] This pattern seems to be related to distance from Moscow, reflecting perhaps that regions closer to the nation's capital enjoy greater access to modern services.

[7] With respect to educational levels, I used only those with elementary and without formal education in the index to avoid weighting education more heavily than the other measures of development.

ment performance trailed both Nizhnii and Tiumen', rated second highest across the development index. Finally Saratov, where government performance lagged consistently, rated higher than Nizhnii Novgorod in the aggregate ranking of development and modernity. Moreover, virtually no positive correlation exists between performance and relative modernity and wealth across a variety of measures. Specifically, what variations there were in relative modernity clearly do not account for Nizhnii Novgorod's high performance score, especially compared to Tiumen' and Yaroslavl'.

It is important to emphasize, however, the relative lack of variation (with the exception of Tiumen') among these four oblasts along these measures of wealth. As a result, the evidence here does not prove, of course, that relative wealth and modernity might not have made a difference in regional government performance if they did vary more. Given the extreme centralization of the planned economy under communism, however, and the absence of strong market forces that might have produced significant regional variations in wealth regardless of the oblasts one chose to examine, variations between regions along these measures would have been low through the early 1990s. In addition, because development decisions under the Soviet system were, for the most part, made by central planners in Moscow, in the early 1990s there was still little intercorrelation among these measures. Thus levels of socioeconomic modernity cannot account for performance differences.

Traditional Regional Importance to the Central Government in Moscow

As an alternative, the influence of a region's past and present political and economic relationships with the central government might also explain variations in regional government performance. If, for example, Nizhnii Novgorod or Tiumen' proved to be an especially vital economic region to Moscow, they might have been politically and economically favored and this might have had a positive influence on regional government performance.

As an initial proxy for political and economic importance to the central government in Moscow, Table 5.1 also compares central investment levels during the last decade of the Soviet era. Central investment, however, does not appear to play a role in accounting for regional government performance variations. Because of its oil and gas complex, Tiumen' was clearly a central investment priority compared to the other oblasts. Yet Moscow's preferential treatment of Tiumen' was more apparent than real—the region did not benefit in terms of human services. Indeed, by 1990, there was a severe housing shortage and a general dearth of social services. Furthermore, this preference did not translate into proportionately higher levels of new regional government performance, as Tiumen' trailed Nizhnii Novgorod rather significantly in this regard.

In support of this, Nizhnii Novgorod, the poorest of the four provinces in terms of central investment, did not appear to suffer when it came to regional government performance where it ranked highest. Thus a region's traditional importance to the national economy seems not to have had a bearing on regional government performance from 1990 to 1993. The evidence here therefore provides little support for the argument that regions traditionally favored by the center always were and always will be able to accomplish more than those regions not so favored.

On a related point, a Russian scholar suggested to me that defense regions, like Nizhnii Novgorod, were always materially favored and continued to be favored by the center (even with the end of the Cold War) because of their technological and trade potential. He argued that the fact that citizens were better treated under the Soviet era (given more and better housing and better access to schools and health clinics) probably had a positive effect on public perception in Nizhnii Novgorod of regional government performance. However, the data in Table 5.1 provide little to no evidence for such an assertion. Moreover, Clifford Gaddy demonstrates statistically that citizens of defense regions like Nizhnii Novgorod generally did *not* have higher salaries, better living standards including greater access to medical care, or more housing space than other urban areas.[8]

Finally, a third hypothesis regarding the influence of past relationships with Moscow concerns the possibility of a high degree of continuity in governing capabilities during and after the Soviet era; that is, regions that were well governed by successive Party organizations under communism may be the same ones that scored high in regional government performance even when regional governments were effectively democratized in 1990. Given the slightly higher proportion of deputies that previously sat in the old soviet that managed to regain their seats in the new soviet elected in 1990 in Nizhnii Novgorod (16.1 percent, compared to 6.1

[8] Clifford Gaddy, "Economic Performance and Policies in the Defense Industrial Regions of Russia," in Michael McFaul and Tova Perlmutter, eds., *Privatization, Conversion, and Enterprise Reform in Russia* (Stanford: Stanford University Center for International Security and Arms Control, 1994), pp. 103–36.

percent in Tiumen', 11.9 percent in Yaroslavl', and 19.8 percent in Saratov),[9] it was reasonable to consider this as a plausible hypothesis of high regional government performance. Those deputies with governing experience under the old system may indeed have had a positive effect on regional government performance. In short, high regional government capabilities before 1990 might have led to a similarly superior performance after 1990, especially where the turnover of deputies between old and new soviets was low.

This theory can be tested rather crudely if we consider high-performance regions under the old regime to be oblasts where Party organizations consistently were able to implement central plans and were politically important to the center. In the late 1980s John Willerton and William Reisinger ranked regions and their Party organizations in order to identify the prominent regional settings from which powerful Soviet politicians would come.[10] Willerton and Reisinger employed career mobility data for all regional Party first secretaries from 1950 to 1982 in forty-four regions of Russia. They then compared this to regional Party organization performance in achieving economic growth from 1950 to 1975. They discovered that Party secretaries who were promoted came from regions that maintained or improved economic growth (and that also had strong patronage ties to Moscow officials).

These conclusions are not as pertinent to the present study as is Reisinger's and Willerton's classification and rank ordering of regions. Although their results must be treated circumspectly (because only forty-four of fifty-five regions were ranked, excluding Moscow and Leningrad), Reisinger and Willerton report that the Party organization in Nizhnii Novgorod (then Gor'kii) consistently achieved economic growth and timely plan fulfillment and was ranked third overall on their scale of political prominence and performance. While this may provide tentative support for the argument that regions which were politically prominent and well governed under communism are similarly well governed in the post-Soviet era, it is important to note that Reisinger and Willerton rank Saratov's Party organization sixth highest, whereas Party organizations in Yaroslavl' and Tiumen' ranked twenty-fourth and twenty-sixth, respectively.

In this admittedly rough comparison of the performance between old and new regional government institutions, there is not all that much con-

---

[9] Cf. Table 1.2, ch. 1.

[10] William Reisinger and John Willerton, "Elite Mobility in the Locales: Toward a Modified Patronage Model," in David Lane, ed., *Elites and Political Power in the USSR* (London: Edward Elger, 1988), pp. 104–24.

sistency in the regional governments' accomplishments during and after the Soviet era. Whereas the Party organization in Nizhnii Novgorod rated high, just as its new regional government was a high achiever, Saratov's Party organization achieved almost as much historically, yet its new regional government performed quite poorly relative to Nizhnii Novgorod from 1990 on. This is particularly interesting since Saratov and Nizhnii Novgorod had the highest rates of deputy incumbency of the four oblasts in this study. Further, under communism, Tiumen' ranked far lower than one might have expected given that it had a relatively high ranking in the post-Soviet era.

Another measure of the possible link between regional government performance and the regional government's relationships with the center is anecdotal. After 1990–91, when Boris Yeltsin was ascendant at the national level, some argued that the center was giving preferential treatment to certain regions—decided largely on the basis of regional governors' loyalty to the president. These regions allegedly included Nizhnii Novgorod. If one spent any time at all in Nizhnii Novgorod, however, it would be difficult to see how this alleged favoritism translated into concrete assistance at the regional government level. For example, Nizhnii Novgorod was reputed to be the flagship of Russian privatization, but this was accomplished by the regional government *in spite* of Moscow's interference, not because of it.

Indeed Nizhnii Novgorod's governor, Boris Nemtsov, had a poor relationship with the Russian Property Committee (Goskomimushchesvto) and its chairman at the time, Anatolii Chubais. Nemtsov resented the center's attempts to interfere in the region's privatization program and in changes made to Russian privatization legislation after the process had begun in Nizhnii Novgorod.[11] In addition, Nizhnii Novgorod was one of many provinces that the central government effectively punished in 1992 and 1993 for balancing its regional budget. The central government allotted greater proportions of tax revenues to regions that ran deficits in order to cover their deficits, while regions with balanced budgets were allotted no budgetary increase.[12] This generated considerable resentment

[11] Information on relations between Nemtsov and Chubais is from interviews with officials in Nizhnii Novgorod from the International Finance Corporation, November 1992. Governor Nemtsov expressed considerable ill will toward central authorities regarding privatization at a meeting that the author was permitted to attend between representatives from Nizhnii Novgorod and members of the Yeltsin/Gaidar government (including Anatolii Chubais) in Nizhnii Novgorod, November 25, 1992.

[12] For a summary of how central tax receipts were distributed to provincial governments, see Darrell Slider, "Federalism, Discord, and Accommodation: Intergovernmental

in Nizhnii Novgorod toward both the legislative and executive branches of government in Moscow.

Finally, area specialists might also argue that foreign interest in Nizhnii Novgorod increased regional governing capacities. This argument, however, mixes cause and effect. In interviews with the International Finance Corporation in Nizhnii Novgorod, officials explained that they selected Nizhnii Novgorod over other oblasts as a region in which to consult on privatization *because* the regional government appeared competent (and also because Nizhnii was relatively close to Moscow and was a large industrial center).[13] Further, it is important to note that Saratov also had its share of foreign consultants, yet its regional government performance was remarkably lower than Nizhnii Novgorod's. Saratov, in fact, was the base of operations for the United States Peace Corps in Russia, and there was also a great deal of German and French investment interest there.

In sum, these explanations of performance variations proved unsatisfying. Although relatively little variation existed along measures of wealth among the oblasts, where variation did exist, the pattern could not, in particular, account for Nizhnii Novgorod's high level of regional government performance. Moreover, an examination of economic and political relationships between these oblasts and the central government also failed to explain performance variations observed in chapter 4.

The next section therefore examines the possible relationships between regional government performance and variations in degrees of real and potential social conflict within each region.

Social Conflict and Performance

G. Bingham Powell observed that "if everyone had the same political preferences, the task of making policy would be much easier."[14] Similarly, the issue of social stability has long been thought a central variable in explaining the performance capabilities of well-governed states. Samuel Huntington, for example, in his classic analysis of political development and change, argued that rapid social change leads to increased so-

---

Relations in Post-Soviet Russia," in Jeffry Hahn and Theodore Friedgut, eds., *Local Power and Post-Soviet Politics* (Armonk, N.Y: M. E. Sharpe, 1994).

[13] Author's interviews with representatives from the International Finance Corporation, Nizhnii Novgorod, November 1992.

[14] G. Bingham Powell, *Contemporary Democracies: Participation, Stability, and Violence* (Cambridge, Mass.: Harvard University Press, 1982), p. 41.

cial strain which in turn dissolves social and political stability.[15] Conflictual and unstable societies would understandably be more difficult to govern than those unmarked by deep social, political, and economic cleavages.

If, for example, in the provinces examined here, change were taking place faster in one region than in the others, we might expect more social instability that might in turn negatively affect the new regional governments' performance. Certainly instability was rampant across transitional Russia from at least 1990 on as a result of the sudden and rapid economic and political changes. This section compares a variety of potential causes of social conflict in each of the four oblasts examined here.

Specifically, I compare (1) the extent of social division during the post-Soviet transition period on especially important social and economic issues—for example, the distribution of attitudes toward privatization of property, the market, and minorities; (2) disparities in economic development within regions—specifically, divisions between rural and urban sectors—and rates of potentially destabilizing economic change—for example, privatization and unemployment; and (3) as a measure of ideological polarization, I examine variation in patterns of support for political parties in the December 1993 elections.

Because the regional authorities in Nizhnii Novgorod were often considered politically progressive, and because regional government performance was highest there, I expected to observe some variation along ideological and attitudinal measures between the populations there and Saratov, where performance was far lower. Also, since one of the salient differences between regions was in fact the degree of conflict within regional government organs (between soviets and administrations and within soviets) and between levels of government (oblast, city, and raion), I expected to observe similar variation along measures of social conflict. To my surprise, however, I generally found little to no variation. Where slight variation existed, it did not follow the performance pattern demonstrated in chapter 4.

Attitudes toward Key Social and Economic Issues

I begin testing for possible sources of instability by examining attitudes toward several policy areas that were especially contentious in the early 1990s—privatization and the transition from a planned economy to a market economy. If respondents in Saratov, the region with the poorest

---

[15] Samuel P. Huntington, *Political Order In Changing Societies* (New Haven, Conn.: Yale University Press, 1968).

TABLE 5.2
Attitudes toward Private Property: "Private property will ruin Russia."

	Fully Agree (%) (1)	Sooner Agree Than Disagree (%) (2)	Sooner Disagree Than Agree (%) (3)	Fully Disagree (%) (4)	Standard Deviation	N[a]
Nizhnii Novgorod	15.0	9.7	26.9	48.4	1.08	754
Tiumen'	15.4	10.5	25.1	49.1	1.10	650
Yaroslavl'	12.9	12.5	31.3	43.5	1.03	833
Saratov	15.7	9.9	23.5	50.9	1.11	841

[a]Respondents were given four options: "fully agree" (1); "sooner agree than disagree" (2); "sooner disagree than agree" (3); and "fully disagree" (4). I discarded option 5—"difficult to answer"—and recalculated standard deviations and the number of observations appropriately.

performing regional government, expressed a great deal of division on these issues, then we might conclude that social division was having a negative impact on government capabilities. In short, if social divisions explained performance variations, then the deepest cleavages should appear in Saratov, whereas Nizhnii would be virtually undivided compared to Saratov, with Tiumen' and Yaroslavl' falling somewhere in between.

Yet across these issues, no oblast appeared particularly more divided than another. Table 5.2 demonstrates that virtually no difference exists among the oblasts in the extent to which popular opinion was for or against private property. Indeed differences between standard deviations are small.

Looking to the next potentially divisive issue of support for free markets, the results are similar. In all four oblasts, at least 85 percent of respondents agreed fully with the statement that people should have the right to earn as much money as they can as long as they can do so legally. The differences between standard deviations are again quite small (Table 5.3).

Finally, I asked respondents in each region to what degree they felt that people of the hundred or so nationalities within the Russian Federation should be able to live and work together. As Table 5.4 demonstrates, Tiumen' had a far more diversified population (only 72.6 percent are Russians), followed by Saratov (85.6 percent Russian), then Nizhnii

TABLE 5.3

Support for Free Markets: "People should have the right to earn as much money as they can as long as they do so legally."

	Fully Agree (%) (1)	Sooner Agree Than Disagree (%) (2)	Sooner Disagree Than Agree (%) (3)	Fully Disagree (%) (4)	Standard Deviation	N[a]
Nizhnii Novgorad	87.1	8.5	2.3	2.0	0.57	946
Tiumen'	87.6	9.2	1.5	1.5	0.52	759
Yaroslavl'	85.5	7.9	4.7	1.9	0.62	984
Saratov	85.4	9.0	3.5	2.1	0.61	980

[a]Respondents were given four options: "fully agree" (1); "sooner agree than disagree" (2); "sooner disagree than agree" (3); and "fully disagree" (4). I discarded option 5—"difficult to answer"—so as not to bias standard deviations and have recalculated N appropriately.

(94.7 percent Russian), and Yaroslavl' (96.4 percent Russian).[16] At the time of the survey, ethnic issues played an important role at the national level. Many ethnic republics and autonomous oblasts and okrugs were declaring themselves sovereign from the Russian Federation. In addition, in some oblasts ethnic tensions ran high.

I expected that ethnic division would possibly explain Saratov's low level of regional government performance. In Saratov, the long-standing issue of the reestablishment of a homeland for ethnic Germans was a contentious issue and received wide press coverage, particularly in 1991–92.[17] To my surprise, however, attitudes toward ethnic diversity in Saratov were among the most tolerant of the four oblasts. Saratov was a close second to Nizhnii Novgorod, and Yaroslavl' and Tiumen' proved far less tolerant.[18] In sum, divisions over this issue, just as with attitudes toward

[16] *First Book of Demographics for the Republics of the Former Soviet Union: 1951–1990* (Shady Side, Md.: New World Demographics, 1992), p. 89.

[17] Ethnic Germans had settled along the Volga from the time of Peter the Great on. Stalin expelled most from the area during World War II, although a few still remained in Saratov. German architectural influences are still visible throughout the city of Saratov, and a train traveler will frequently hear German spoken by fellow passengers carrying Russian passports.

[18] Strains between northern peoples in the far northern region of Tiumen' persistently keep ethnic issues alive in Tiumen'. In Yaroslavl' the issue of ethnicity had become salient by

TABLE 5.4

Toleration of Ethnic Diversity: "People of all nationalities can live and work together for the good of Russia."

	Fully Agree (%) (1)	Sooner Agree Than Disagree (%) (2)	Sooner Disagree Than Agree (%) (3)	Fully Disagree (%) (4)	Standard Deviation	N[a]
Nizhnii Novgorod	88.4	8.0	2.4	1.2	0.51	954
Tiumen'	79.4	16.7	2.0	1.9	0.59	743
Yaroslavl'	82.0	12.1	5.0	1.9	0.65	953
Saratov	87.3	9.5	1.7	1.5	0.52	980

[a]See note to Table 5.3.

private property and earning power, did not fit the pattern of regional government performance. Indeed, none of these oblasts was significantly more divided than the others along these attitudinal measures of potential social conflict. These measures of social division, then, are not a reliable explanation of the observed variations in regional government performance.

Rural/Urban Developmental Disparities and the Influence of Economic Changes

Another indication of possible polarization is relative urban/rural developmental disparities. If, for example, salary differences between urban and rural areas were great in one oblast, we might expect that the region was more polarized and harder to govern. Similarly, if the disparities between rich and poor were significant, we might also assume that the polity was more unruly and difficult to govern.

I expected that this might be a plausible explanation for Saratov's lower performance given that Saratov, of these four oblasts, had the largest agricultural sector and the largest proportion of its population living in agricultural settlements (26 percent). However, although there may have been tension between urban and rural regions, Table 5.5 demon-

1993 because of an influx of merchants from the Caucusus whom locals accused of being linked to the Mafia.

TABLE 5.5
Salary per Month in April 1993 in Four Regions

Monthly Salary (in Rubles)	Nizhnii Novgorod		Tiumen'		Yaroslavl'		Saratov	
	Urban	Rural	Urban	Rural	Urban	Rural	Urban	Rural
Lower Percentage	78.5	89.9	28.5	50.4	77.6	84.5	85.4	94.9
0–10,000	23.4	47.2	5.3	5.7	25.5	29.6	45.7	60.6
10,001–20,000	35.4	29.0	12.2	19.5	34.2	37.4	27.0	28.3
20,001–30,000	19.7	13.7	11.0	25.2	17.9	17.5	12.7	6.0
Middle Percentage	17.8	9.2	19.7	39.0	19.2	13.15	12.7	3.3
30,001–40,000	8.9	4.4	6.7	18.7	10.8	7.3	7.8	2.3
40,001–60,000	8.9	4.8	13.0	20.3	8.4	5.8	4.9	1.0
Higher Percentage	3.5	0.8	51.7	10.5	3.2	2.4	1.8	1.6
60,001–80,000	2.5	0.4	11.8	7.3	1.7	1.9	1.2	1.3
80,001–100,000	0.4	0.4	11.0	2.4	0.9	0.5	0.4	0.3
Over 100,000	0.6	0.0	28.9	0.8	0.6	0	0.2	0.0

Source: These data come from the 1993 survey. Respondents were asked to indicate their monthly household income from all sources.

strates that variations in the relative incomes of city and country dwellers were not significant between oblasts. In all four regions rural residents earned less than urbanites. The highest proportions of poor rural dwellers (earning 10,000 rubles or less) were in Nizhnii Novgorod and Saratov—the two regions at opposite ends of the performance scale. In Nizhnii Novgorod, Saratov, and Yaroslavl', the majority of both urban and rural dwellers earned less than 30,000 rubles per month.

In the middle-range category (30,000 to 60,000 rubles per month), urbanites in Nizhnii Novgorod, Saratov, and Yaroslavl' earned more than rural dwellers. Indeed, the contrast here was greatest in Saratov where urban salaries exceeded those in rural areas by a ratio of about 4:1. Although this might suggest potential for more urban/rural conflict in Saratov, in Nizhnii Novgorod (the region with the highest-performance regional government) the urban/rural salary ratio was 2:1. In Yaroslavl' the salary ratio was even smaller, suggesting that Nizhnii Novgorod had more cause for urban/rural conflict than Yaroslavl', a region with a lower-performance regional government. In Tiumen' the urban/rural salary ratio at the middle range was reversed (1:2), with fewer urban dwellers than ruralites in the middle-income range. In contrast, however, at the very highest income levels, divisions between urban and rural areas were highest in Tiumen' (5:1), while differences in Yaroslavl' and Saratov were minuscule. In Nizhnii Novgorod, urban/rural disparities in income were larger at the highest-income level, but, as in Yaroslavl' and Saratov, the number of survey respondents claiming this level of monthly income was minute compared to the number of high-wage earners in Tiumen'.

In summary, if performance was explicable by the potential conflict caused by great income differentials between urban and rural sectors and between rich and poor, we would have expected these contrasts to be greatest in Yaroslavl' and especially in Saratov. Yet contrasts between urban and rural areas at the lowest- and highest-income levels were greatest in Tiumen'—the region with the second highest level of regional government performance. Further, little difference in income proportions was evident in Nizhnii Novgorod and Saratov despite the rather large variation in the performance of their regional governments.

As another measure of potential conflict, I examined rates of economic change. Although destabilizing change in the former Soviet Union began in earnest in the late 1980s, in 1992 prices were freed and privatization programs were initiated. These dramatic economic changes precipitated widespread social dislocation. The transition to a market economy brought about positive and negative economic and social changes. For the first time in seventy years, Russians were permitted to own property through the sale of shares to private individuals. But while more goods were suddenly available in stores, prices were much higher. Moreover, with Russians now free to earn as much money as they could, meaningful income differentials arose along with new classes of haves and have-nots. Finally, the command economy's collapse also meant the end of guaranteed employment.

Thus high rates of privatization and other indicators of rapid change might have been socially destabilizing forces that had a negative impact on constituent evaluations of regional government. This in turn might account for the lower levels of regional government performance reported in chapter 4. If this hypothesis were true, we should expect higher rates of privatization and unemployment in Saratov and proportionately smaller rates in each of the higher-performance cases. In fact, however, as shown in Table 5.6, rates of privatization and unemployment in Saratov were only slightly higher than in Tiumen', whereas Yaroslavl' and Nizhnii Novgorod both had considerably higher rates of potentially destabilizing change. This is particularly noteworthy given the significant

TABLE 5.6
Rates of Unemployment and Privatization in Four Regions

Measures of Economic Change	Nizhnii Novgorod	Tiumen'	Yaroslavl'	Saratov
Unemployment (%) (December 1993)	1.10	0.20	4.50	0.90
Enterprises Privatized (%) (December 1993)	70.0	35.0	72.0	49.0

Source: Goskomstat as reported by Vladimir Gimpelson, Darrell Slider, and Sergei Chrugov, "Political Tendencies in Russia's Regions: Evidence from the 1993 Parliamentary Elections," *Slavic Review* (Fall 1994): 711–32.

differences in the regional government performances of Nizhnii Novgorod and Saratov.

Ideological Divisions

The 1993 national legislative elections and the new system of party list voting provided the opportunity to test for possible ideological divisions among residents of the four regions. Table 5.7 reports results of party list voting for the ten largest registered parties in each region.

Voting data reveal two different pieces of information. The first demonstrates variations among regions in support for each party. If, for example, voters in Nizhnii Novgorod were more concentrated in their support for a single party than voters in Saratov, one might be justified in arguing that ideological cleavages in Nizhnii Novgorod were less severe and therefore the business of governing was easier there than in Saratov. A second way of interpreting these results is to analyze differences in voter partisanship. If, for example, those oblasts registering higher government performance in the first years of representative government proved to be the homes of more "progressive" voters in December 1993, then one might draw the conclusion that there was a better "fit" between residents there and a democratic form of government. Results in Table 5.7 reveal, however, that no significant variations existed among regions in terms of the degree of ideological fragmentation within each region. Further, the ideological variation between regions in terms of the proportion of votes each party received (reformist versus conservative) was not as the performance ranking in chapter 4 would have predicted.

TABLE 5.7
December 1993 Electoral List Voting Results in Four Regions

	Percentages Supporting the Party				
	Russian Federation	Nizhnii Novgorod	Tiumen'	Yaroslavl'	Saratov
Reformist Parties					
Russia's Choice					
(Y. Gaidar)	15.5	14.0	13.4	22.3	12.3
Yabloko (G. Yavlinsky)	7.9	12.2	5.9	7.3	8.6
Party of Democratic					
Reform (A. Sobchak)	4.1	4.4	4.6	4.0	2.5
Party of Unity and Accord					
(S. Shakrai)	6.7	5.7	6.7	6.3	5.7
REFORMIST SUBTOTAL	34.2	36.3	30.6	39.9	29.1
Centrist Parties					
Democratic Party of					
Russia (N. Travkin)	5.5	7.1	6.3	5.7	6.5
Civic Union (A. Volski)	1.9	3.2	2.1	2.5	2.7
Women of Russia					
(A. Fedulova)	8.1	9.7	14.8	1.0	9.9
CENTRIST SUBTOTAL	15.5	20.0	23.2	9.2	19.1
Rightist/Conservative Parties					
Liberal Democratic Party					
of Russia (V. Zhirinovsky)	22.9	19.9	21.0	21.7	26.6
Communist Party of the					
Russian Federation					
(G. Zyuganov)	12.4	11.6	11.0	8.1	15.3
Agrarian Party of Russia					
(M. Lapshin)	7.9	9.1	10.6	7.5	7.6
RIGHTIST SUBTOTAL	43.2	40.6	42.6	37.3	49.5

Source: Election results are from *Biulleten'* of the Central Election Commission of the Russian Federation, issue 12, March 1994. The remaining small proportions of the votes in each region went to the Future of Russia Party, Constructive Ecological Movement, and the Dignity and Charity Movement.

First, the distribution of voters demonstrates that in all four regions the majority of voters were grouped at one of the ends of the ideological spectrum (reformist or conservative), with a smaller number of voters grouped in the middle. Of the four regions, the greatest number of voters supporting a single party was in Saratov, with 26 percent supporting the

Liberal Democratic Party of Russia. Indeed, almost 50 percent of voters in Saratov supported right-wing parties. This demonstrates that the region with the most ideological consensus among citizens was Saratov—where government performance was lowest.[19]

It is noteworthy, of course, that the Liberal Democratic Party of Russia, under Vladimir Zhirinovsky, is one of the more extreme right-wing parties. Throughout the December 1993 elections, Zhirinovsky effectively threatened to end democratic rule in Russia. The high proportion of voters in Saratov supporting right-wing elements might therefore indicate that voters there were conservative and perhaps less suited to and less supportive of representative regional government. This might have had a negative effect on new representative regional government performance there.[20]

Significantly, however, in Nizhnii Novgorod, the largest proportion of voters (19.9 percent) also supported Zhirinovsky's party, and 42 percent of voters in Tiumen' (the region where regional government performance was second highest) supported right-wing parties. Furthermore, Yaroslavl', not Nizhnii Novgorod, was the most "reformist" oriented of the four oblasts—with 39.9 percent supporting reformist parties and 37.3 percent supporting more traditional ideological elements—yet regional government performance there was well below that in both Nizhnii Novgorod and Tiumen'.

The evidence here indicates that ideological polarization in the 1993 elections did not reflect the variations in regional government performance observed in chapter 4. The highest degree of ideological consensus was in Saratov, the region with the lowest level of regional government performance. Moreover, the greatest proportion of voters supporting "reformist" parties was not in Nizhnii Novgorod, but in Yaroslavl'

[19] This should not be confused with elite consensus discussed in chapters 2 and 6.

[20] Alternatively, if one considers a vote for Zhirinovsky to be a protest vote, the high proportion of votes for him could be construed as a consequence of low performance rather than a cause of it. Evidence is mounting, however, that the vote for Zhirinovsky was not merely a protest vote, but a rational calculation on the part of voters who strongly supported many of Zhirinovsky's policy views. He promised, for example, to bring law and order to Russian communities while still continuing economic reform. Examples of this argument can be found in the analysis of electoral results and policy preferences of Russian voters in Jerry F. Hough, "Public Attitudes toward Economic Reform and Democratization," *Post-Soviet Affairs* 10, no. 1 (Spring 1994): 1–37; and Josephine Andrews and Kathryn Stoner-Weiss, "Regionalism and Reform: Evidence from the Russian Provinces," *Post-Soviet Affairs* 11, no. 4 (October–December 1995): 384–406.

where regional government performance was relatively low. Moreover, neither ideological polarization nor political orientation explained the observed performance pattern.

CULTURAL AND SOCIAL-STRUCTURAL HYPOTHESES

To test more comprehensively the impact that residents' political attitudes and behavior have on government performance in the four regions, this section examines possible cultural and social-structural explanations of performance variations. I begin by testing for evidence of what Gabriel Almond and Sidney Verba refer to as "civic culture." These are attitudes that are supportive of democratic forms of government. If these are present in Nizhnii Novgorod and Tiumen', we might expect a positive correlation between performance and a "democratic" political culture.

The second part of this section tests a compelling social-structural argument put forward in Robert Putnam's formidable study of institutional performance—*Making Democracy Work*. In explaining performance variations among Italy's twenty regional governments over a twenty-year period, Putnam uncovers an enduring social-structural phenomenon that he calls the "civic community." Its theoretical roots lie in republicanism and the notion that the success of representative political institutions depends on the character of citizens, that is, their civic virtue.

Putnam's theory is more appropriately categorized as social-structural rather than cultural because it focuses on the behavior of societal actors rather than their beliefs and attitudes alone. As a result, Putnam's theory is treated here as distinct from works such as Almond and Verba's *The Civic Culture*.

In fact, the evidence demonstrates that little variation exists among the four oblasts along political cultural and social-structural lines. This does not, of course, provide conclusive evidence that the cultural hypotheses might not explain performance if there were variation in these areas. It indicates, however, that neither a democratic political culture nor a civic community plays a role in explaining higher regional government performance in these Russian oblasts. As with measures of socioeconomic modernity, a lack of variation in sociocultural explanations would be the likely result regardless of the regions one chose to examine in post-Soviet Russia. I discuss the historical reasons why this is so at the end of this chapter.

151

TABLE 5.8

Citizen Support of Freedom of Association: "Any person has the right to form a social or political organization regardless of how extreme its program."

	Agree (%) (1 and 2)	Disagree (%) (3 and 4)	Mean Score[a]	N[b]
Nizhnii Novgorod	35.0	65.0	2.86	692
Tiumen'	32.1	67.9	2.97	656
Yaroslavl'	29.5	70.5	2.93	818
Saratov	26.0	74.0	3.02	799

[a]A higher mean score indicates greater disagreement.

[b]Respondents were given four options: "fully agree" (1); "sooner agree than disagree" (2); "sooner disagree than agree" (3); and "fully disagree" (4). I discarded option 5— "difficult to answer"—so as not to bias mean scores and recalculated N appropriately.

A Democratic Political Culture?

Because the 1990 election installed genuine representative government at the regional level for the first time in Russia, testing for traditionally "democratic" values seemed reasonable. In the spring 1993 survey, therefore, interviewers asked respondents in each of the four oblasts the extent to which they supported some of the bulwarks of democratic society— freedom of association, the right of voters to choose freely between several candidates in any election, and the right to unlimited freedom of speech. Little statistically significant variation was evident, however, among these regions in the degree to which respondents professed to believe in these aspects of a "democratic" political culture.

Regarding freedom of association (Table 5.8), there is some evidence of a positive correlation between performance and belief in this democratic value. Respondents from Nizhnii and Tiumen' were slightly more supportive than those from either Saratov or Yaroslavl'. The statistically significant variation among oblasts was small, however. The difference between the mean scores of Nizhnii and Saratov—the highest- and lowest-performance cases—was significant at the .01 level, although the differences between all other paired means were not statistically significant at .05 or greater.

Although some evidence at the extreme ends of the performance scale supports the influence of political culture, the overall data only weakly suggests that respondents from Nizhnii Novgorod and Tiumen' were more supportive of freedom of association than were those from the other two regions. Indeed, little variation among regions existed.

TABLE 5.9

Citizen Support of Free Elections: "Voters should have the right to choose freely from among several candidates in any election."

	Agree (%) (1 and 2)	Disagree (%) (3 and 4)	Mean Score[a]	N[b]
Nizhnii Novgorod	97.3	2.7	1.13	901
Tiumen'	97.3	2.7	1.19	737
Yaroslavl'	99.0	1.0	1.08	953
Saratov	99.2	0.8	1.05	992

[a]A higher mean score indicates greater disagreement.

[b]Respondents were given four options: "fully agree" (1); "sooner agree than disagree" (2); "sooner disagree than agree" (3); "fully disagree" (4). I discarded option 5—"difficult to answer"—so as not to bias mean scores and recalculated N appropriately. The means of Nizhnii and Tiumen' differ although the percentages agreeing and disagreeing are the same because the percentage of respondents answering 1 versus 2 differ. Differences between means are all statistically significant at .05 or better except for the difference between the means of Saratov and Yaroslavl'.

This outcome is supported by the data in Table 5.9 regarding citizen support for freedom of choice between candidates. Again, the four cases exhibited little variation. The proportion of respondents agreeing with the statement that "voters should have the right to choose freely from among several candidates in any election" was over 97 percent in all four oblasts. Further, the proportion agreeing was even slightly higher in Saratov and Yaroslavl' than in Tiumen' and Nizhnii. The lack of variation among provinces, therefore, does not support the notion that democratic political culture has a positive effect on performance.

Finally, interviewers asked respondents the extent to which they supported an unlimited right to freedom of speech (Table 5.10). The argument that a democratic political culture leads to higher government performance would lead us to expect that respondents from Nizhnii Novgorod and Tiumen' should be more supportive of this quintessential democratic value. Yet the data in Table 5.10 reveal that respondents from Saratov (67.6 percent in favor versus 59.6 percent in Nizhnii and 51.0 percent in Tiumen') were more supportive of an unrestricted right to freedom of speech than in any of the three higher-performance cases. Differences between the means of Nizhnii and Saratov were statistically significant at greater than the .05 level, as were the differences between the means of Saratov and Tiumen' and of Saratov and Yaroslavl'. The differ-

TABLE 5.10

Citizen Support of Free Speech: "People have the right to free speech even if they exercise this right unreasonably."

	Agree (%) (1 and 2)	Disagree (%) (3 and 4)	Mean Score[a]	N[b]
Nizhnii Novgorod	59.6	40.4	2.22	832
Tiumen'	61.0	39.0	2.18	701
Yaroslavl'	57.0	43.0	2.23	897
Saratov	67.6	32.4	2.01	850

[a] A higher mean score indicates greater disagreement.

[b] Respondents were given four options: "fully agree" (1); "sooner agree than disagree" (2); "sooner disagree than agree" (3); "fully disagree" (4). I discarded option 5—"difficult to answer"—so as not to bias mean scores and recalculated N appropriately.

ences between the means of all other pairs were not statistically significant.

Across all three key questions, there was little variation among provinces and thus virtually no evidence to support the argument that a democratic political culture somehow arose in Nizhnii Novgorod or Tiumen', but not in Yaroslavl' or Saratov. I test this preliminary conclusion further in a search for Robert Putnam's "civic community" in Russia.

In Search of the Civic Community

The idea that the character of a political community depended on the relative virtue of its citizens is an idea put forward in Plato's *Republic* and then developed further by Nicolo Machiavelli. It was later disputed by classical liberals who followed them: "Whereas the republicans had emphasized community and the obligations of citizenship, liberals stressed individualism and individual rights."[21] Although communitarian theorists like Michael Walzer and Michael Sandel have resurrected the republican idea, one of the many contributions of Putnam's study of Italy is to test empirically the link between civic virtue and the performance of democratic government. While this approach was in part inspired by Almond and Verba's *The Civic Culture*, Putnam's study departs from the political culture tradition in that he examines not just attitudes toward government but also citizen behavior in what he calls a "civic community."

[21] Putnam, *Making Democracy Work*, p. 87.

One of the defining characteristics of a civic community is a rich tradition of associationalism and civic engagement. Citizens in a civic community, however, are not required to behave altruistically. Rather, Putnam acknowledges that no society can eradicate self-interested motivations. Drawing from de Tocqueville's observations of associational life in America, Putnam argues that within a civic community, citizens practice "self-interest properly understood"—or self-interest that is "alive to the interests of others."[22] The opposite of this is what Edward Banfield called "amoral familism," where community members "maximize the material, short-run advantage of the nuclear family; [and] assume that all others will do likewise."[23]

The civic community also incorporates equal rights and interpersonal trust among the citizenry. Says Putnam, "Such a community is bound together by horizontal relations of reciprocity and cooperation, not by vertical relations of authority and dependency. Citizens interact as equals, not as patrons and clients nor as governors and petitioners."[24]

The civic community is marked by norms of solidarity, interpersonal trust, and tolerance. Trust is a particularly important characteristic of a civic community because it enables a community to overcome problems of collective action where "shared interests are unrealized because each individual, acting in wary isolation, has an incentive to defect from collective action."[25]

Associational membership creates structures of cooperation and public spiritedness even if the clubs and societies to which citizens belong do not have a political purpose. Following Almond and Verba, Putnam argues that "participation in civic organizations inculcates skills of cooperation as well as a sense of shared responsibility for collective endeavors. Moreover, when individuals belong to 'cross-cutting' groups with diverse goals and members, their attitudes will tend to moderate as a result of group interaction and cross-cutting pressures."[26] In short:

> Some regions of Italy have many choral societies and soccer teams and bird-watching clubs and Rotary clubs. Most citizens in those regions read eagerly about community affairs in the daily press. They are en-

[22] Alexis de Tocqueville, *Democracy in America*, trans. J. P. Mayer, ed. G. Lawrence (Garden City, N.Y.: Anchor, 1969), as cited in Putnam, *Making Democracy Work*, p. 88.

[23] Edward Banfield, *The Moral Basis of a Backward Society* (Chicago: The Free Press, 1958), p. 85, as cited in Putnam, *Making Democracy Work*, p. 87.

[24] Putnam, *Making Democracy Work*, p. 88.

[25] Ibid., p. 89.

[26] Ibid., p. 90.

gaged by public issues, but not by personalistic or patron-client politics. Inhabitants trust one another to act fairly and to obey the law. Leaders in these regions are relatively honest. They believe in popular government, and they are predisposed to compromise with their political adversaries. Both citizens and leaders here find equality congenial. Social and political networks are organized horizontally, not hierarchically. The community values solidarity, civic engagement, cooperation, and honesty.[27]

Putnam finds that these attributes are strikingly well correlated to high democratic performance in the regions of Italy. He traces the origin of networks of civic engagement in Italy to as far back as the twelfth century and discovers that traditions of civic engagement endured through Italian unification, the industrial revolution, fascism, and into the late twentieth century. In contrast, less civic regions never adopted cooperative behavior or became engaged in community affairs, and this has meant the persistence of inequality, mistrust, and instability. This lack of trust in uncivic communities has meant that they have had no accumulation of "social capital"—a combination of social features (trust, engagement, and networks) that can improve a community's ability to overcome collective action dilemmas and enables their governments to build records of accomplishment.

Although Putnam's work is a compelling explanation of differences in regional government performance in Italy, a systematic analysis demonstrates that the civic community does not fare well on a conceptual trek eastward to Russia. In each of the four regions of this study, I tested for the presence of the key characteristics of the civic community. I attempted to replicate many of the same measures that Putnam employed in Italy. These can be grouped in three categories: measures of political involvement and mobilization, trust, and readership levels of the daily press.

If Putnam's theory were a convincing explanation of government performance in provincial Russia, then some approximation of the civic community should have been apparent in Nizhnii Novgorod but not in Saratov, with Yaroslavl' and Tiumen' falling between these two extremes. Instead, there was little variation across provinces. Further, along some measures, in all four of these communities it was easier to spot attributes more akin to Banfield's "amoral familism" than to Putnam's civic community.

---

[27] Ibid., p. 115.

TABLE 5.11
Electoral Turnout

	1989 USSR (% voted)	1990 Regional/ RSFSR (% voted)	1991 March Referenda (% voted)	1991 RSFSR Presidential (% voted)	1993 National Elections[a]
Nizhnii Novgorod	78.7	76.0	74.0	75.0	52.0
Tiumen'	64.2	68.9	*74.0	72.0	49.0
Yaroslavl'	84.8	70.0	74.8	75.0	56.0
Saratov	80.5	80.8	71.0	*89.0	59.0

Source: All figures from 1989 come from a question on our 1993 survey and are not official. The pattern, however, is in line with the official figures from other elections shown here. The asterisk (*) indicates that these two figures are also from the 1993 survey, as official figures were not available in regional newspapers.

[a]Electoral turnout figures from the 1993 national legislature elections come from *Biulleten'* of the Central Election Commission.

POLITICAL INVOLVEMENT AND MOBILIZATION

As a measure of political involvement and mobilization, I compared electoral turnout for several elections: the 1989 USSR Congress of People's Deputies election, the 1990 regional government elections, the March 1991 referenda, the June 1991 presidential elections, and the December 1993 national elections to the State Duma and Federation Council. As a second measure of mobilization, I compared the frequency with which respondents wrote letters to local newspapers or contacted local television and radio stations regarding political issues. As a final measure of involvement, I compared the levels of membership in voluntary associations across the four oblasts.

Looking first to voter turnout, in both Saratov and Yaroslavl' participation levels were not significantly lower than in Nizhnii Novgorod across four elections. Indeed, voter turnout in both Saratov and Yaroslavl' was almost always consistently higher than in Tiumen'. Moreover, except for the 1991 March referenda, Saratov's electoral turnout rate was consistently higher than that of Nizhnii Novgorod (Table 5.11).

Because electoral turnout may be influenced by patron-client relationships rather than an actual propensity for political mobilization (perhaps, for example, voter turnout was high in Saratov and Yaroslavl' because political patrons mobilized their clients to vote), I employed another measure of mobilization: in the 1993 survey respondents were asked if

157

TABLE 5.12

Citizens' Political Mobilization: "Have you ever written a letter or contacted a local radio or television station about an issue that bothered you?"

	Yes (%)	No (%)	Mean Scores	N
Nizhnii Novgorod	8.7	91.3	1.91	978
Tiumen'	9.8	90.2	1.90	774
Yaroslavl'	5.5	94.5	1.95	990
Saratov	5.3	94.7	1.95	996

ᵃA lower mean score indicates greater mobilization. Differences between mean scores were statistically significant at the .01 level except the differences between Nizhnii and Tiumen' and between Yaroslavl' and Saratov which were not significant at the .05 level or better.

they had ever written letters to local newspapers or contacted local radio or television stations shows about an issue they found bothersome (Table 5.12).

Table 5.12 demonstrates first that very little variation exists among the four regions in the extent to which respondents reported themselves willing to mobilize enough to contact the local press on bothersome issues. Indeed, in all four oblasts greater than 90 percent of respondents reported that they had never done so. What little variation there is shows Tiumen' with a slightly more mobilized population—9.8 percent of respondents reported that they had made the effort to contact the local press on an issue. Nizhnii's level of mobilization was somewhat lower than that in Tiumen', but the differences between means were not statistically significant at .05. Similarly, there was no difference between the means in Yaroslavl' and Saratov. The limited variation here, therefore, provides weak evidence at best in support of the argument that regions where government performance was higher were those where the general population was more politically mobilized.

Yet when comparing levels of membership in voluntary organizations, Nizhnii Novgorod and Tiumen' maintained significantly higher levels of civic engagement than did Yaroslavl' and Saratov. In the 1993 survey interviewers asked respondents to indicate to which social organizations they belonged, including political parties, informal associations, religious organizations, sports clubs, cultural societies, philanthropic organizations, parents' associations, and neighborhood clubs. In Nizhnii Novgorod there were 243 memberships per thousand respondents; in Tiu-

TABLE 5.13

Interpersonal Trust among Citizens: "In general, no one cares what happens to their neighbor."

	Agree (%) (1 and 2)	Disagree (%) (3 and 4)	Mean Score[a]	N[b]
Nizhnii Novgorod	55.7	44.3	2.28	933
Tiumen'	67.3	32.7	2.05	734
Yaroslavl'	50.4	49.6	2.37	970
Saratov	49.2	50.8	2.48	971

[a]A higher mean score indicates greater trust.

[b]Respondents were given four options: "fully agree" (1); "sooner agree than disagree" (2); "sooner disagree than agree" (3); "fully disagree" (4). I discarded option 5—"difficult to answer"—so as not to bias mean scores and recalculated N appropriately. The difference between the means of Yaroslavl' and Nizhnii Novgorod was not significant at the .05 level. All other differences were statistically significant at the .05 level or better.

men' the number was even greater—285 memberships per thousand. Yaroslavl' ranked third with 152 memberships, and Saratov registered 136 per thousand. Residents of Nizhnii and Tiumen', therefore, appeared to be more willing to join organizations. Although it is difficult to distinguish the direction of causality here (Did more people belong to social organizations because performance was higher, or did their tendencies to be joiners lead to higher performance?), this result contradicts the level of voter turnout and provides some support for the weakly positive findings in Table 5.12. It also indicates that the horizontal linkages within Nizhnii and Tiumen' were perhaps stronger than in Yaroslavl' and particularly Saratov.

Although this measure may be encouraging for the civic community hypothesis, an integral component of Putnam's argument is that associational membership encourages trust among citizens. Tables 5.13 and 5.14, however, indicate strikingly low levels of interpersonal trust among respondents in all four regions.

TRUST

The 1993 survey included several questions designed to assess relative levels of interpersonal trust among respondents. Undeniably, trust is often a difficult concept to measure. I therefore attempted to replicate as many of Putnam's measures as possible, while including some of my own.

159

TABLE 5.14

Level of Suspicion among Citizens: "If you aren't careful, someone will take advantage of you."

	Agree (%) (1 and 2)	Disagree (%) (3 and 4)	Mean Score[a]	N[b]
Nizhnii Novgorod	79.5	20.5	1.77	829
Tiumen'	78.2	21.6	1.79	675
Yaroslavl'	79.3	20.7	1.76	830
Saratov	84.3	15.7	1.63	878

[a]A higher mean score indicates greater trust.

[b]Respondents were given four options: "fully agree" (1); "sooner agree than disagree" (2); "sooner disagree than agree" (3); "fully disagree" (4). I discarded option 5—"difficult to answer"—so as not to bias mean scores and have recalculated N appropriately.

Although Putnam found high levels of trust in regions with correspondingly high levels of associational membership and high regional government performance, in the Russian provinces similarly strong correlations did not appear. Indeed, the differences among respondents in the four regions were so slight that levels of interpersonal trust cannot be used as variables to help explain differences in government performance.

In the first measure of relative levels of interpersonal trust, there was some variation in the extent to which respondents from each oblast agreed with the statement, "In general, no one cares what happens to their neighbor" (Table 5.13). The variation, however, was not what we might expect given the performance pattern observed in chapter 4. According to this measure of interpersonal trust, respondents from Saratov and Yaroslavl' appeared to trust their neighbors' good intentions more than did respondents from Tiumen' and Nizhnii Novgorod.

A second question measures the level of suspicion respondents held for their neighbors (Table 5.14). Although a slightly greater proportion of residents in Saratov expressed more suspicion than those in the other oblasts, there is little evidence of the high levels of trust necessary to argue that Nizhnii and Tiumen' had a civic community. More than 75 percent of the population in all four oblasts agreed with the statement that "if you aren't careful, someone will take advantage of you," indicating that in provincial Russia suspicion generally ran high. Although there were statistically significant differences between the means of Nizhnii and Saratov (at .01), Yaroslavl' and Saratov, and Tiumen' and Saratov,

TABLE 5.15

Newspaper Readership as a Measure of Civic Interest

	Percentage of Total N of Respondents[a]			
	Nizhnii Novgorod	Tiumen'	Yaroslavl'	Saratov
Central Papers	60.5	63.3	56.4	59.5
Oblast Papers	38.6	43.0	42.7	38.2
City Papers	33.0	46.7	32.1	21.6
Raion Papers	30.5	18.0	16.8	29.8
Factory or Other	5.7	3.9	9.1	2.8
Average Readership across Five Categories Above	32.5	35.0	31.4	30.4
Do Not Read the Paper	10.3	7.4	11.8	13.2

[a]Numbers do not add up to 100 percent because respondents were asked to indicate all the papers they read regularly.

the difference between the means of Yaroslavl' and Nizhnii and that of Tiumen' and Nizhnii was not significant at the .05 level. As with the first measure of interpersonal trust within these four communities, then, relatively little variation existed among the provinces on this important aspect of the civic community. Again, this indicates that trust was not really a variable in explaining differences in regional government performance in these four regions.

NEWSPAPER READERSHIP

Finally, Putnam also identifies knowledge of and interest in the polity through newspaper readership as another attribute of residents of a civic community. The 1993 survey explored this in each of these four oblasts (Table 5.15). Average levels of newspaper readership across all five categories of newspapers (central, oblast, city, raion, and factory) were slightly higher in the higher-performance cases, but the differences were rather slight—less than 5 percent across all four regions. Similarly, the differences between oblasts in those who do not read the newspaper included a narrow range of 7.4 percent in Tiumen' and 13.2 percent in Saratov.

In sum, on these aspects of the civic community index, we have somewhat contradictory results. Saratov had high levels of political mobilization as measured by electoral turnout, but lower levels of contact with the media regarding bothersome issues. Further, Tiumen' and Nizhnii Novgorod had slightly higher levels of membership in voluntary organizations. Significantly, however, although associational membership was marginally higher in Nizhnii Novgorod and Tiumen', this did not translate into the horizontal networks of interpersonal civic trust that are essential to building social capital and a civic community. Indeed, in all four of these communities, mistrust and mutual suspicion was so rampant that trust did not really vary among the oblasts.

Nor were there any striking variations in the extent to which people in these four oblasts liked to stay informed about politics as measured by newspaper readership. There is little evidence, therefore, that the civic virtue of residents of regions with higher-performance governments accounted for performance differences. In general, no significant variation existed among these four provinces along most measures of the civic community. Although the data do not prove that if there had been variation, the civic community would not have played a role in determining levels of performance, where there was slight variation on measures of the civic community, the data only weakly corresponded to the performance pattern observed in chapter 4.

Historically there are good reasons why a democratic political culture and a civic community should generally be absent in Russia. Indeed, given that none of the Russian provinces experienced a Western-style industrial revolution or significant historical variation in the rise of a middle class (as required by Barrington Moore, for example[28]) before (or after) the revolution of 1917, the absence of a civic or democratic consciousness across oblasts should not be surprising. Although the city of Nizhnii Novgorod was a trading center before the revolution (earning the name *"karman Rossii"*—the pocket of Russia) and its architecture reveals an abundance of pre-revolutionary wealth, the same is true for Saratov and Yaroslavl'. Of the four oblasts, Tiumen' was historically the poorest until oil and gas were discovered in the region in the 1950s and 1960s. Further, the pre-revolutionary historical record strongly suggests that of the four provinces Saratov appeared to be the most politically radical and might have held the most democratic promise. Oliver Radkey reports that because of the degree to which Russia's political future was

---

[28] Barrington Moore, Jr., *Social Origins of Dictatorship and Democracy: Lord and Peasant in the Making of the Modern World* (Boston: Beacon, 1967). The essence of Moore's theoretical formulation is that in countries where there was no bourgeoisie, there was ultimately no democracy.

debated, "the city of Saratov [was] sometimes called the 'Athens on the Volga.'"[29] Similarly, Donald Raleigh notes that "well before the Revolution of 1917, Saratov had acquired a reputation as one of the most radical Volga provinces."[30]

Finally, the relatively uniform levels of mistrust across these regions is a testament to the effectiveness of totalitarianism's atomization of Soviet society. There is little reason to believe, therefore, that democrats have somehow sprung up in Nizhnii Novgorod but not in Saratov. Nor is there reason to think that variations in levels of relative modernity accounted for performance differences. Finally, there was little evidence of the influence of democratic social structures on regional government performance.

Given the importance that Robert Putnam attaches to social capital and the civic community in making democracy work, the growth and functioning of representative government in the Russian provinces may by ultimately faltering and unsuccessful. In examining political and economic elite relationships, however, chapter 6 offers an alternative to this discouraging conclusion.

[29] Oliver Henry Radkey, *The Election to the Russian Constituent Assembly of 1917* (Cambridge, Mass.: Harvard University Press, 1950), p. 9.

[30] Donald Raleigh, *Revolution on the Volga: 1917 in Saratov* (Ithaca, N.Y.: Cornell University Press, 1986), p. 23.

* CHAPTER 6 *

The Political Economy of Government
Performance: Testing the Theory

In Nizhnii Novgorod and Tiumen', the two highest-performance cases, political actors, when asked in interviews what they viewed as their most significant accomplishment in such turbulent times in Russia, almost invariably responded "consensus" or "stability."[1] In Saratov, in contrast, government suffered deadlock and repeated conflict between the legislative and executive branches, within the legislature itself, and between the capital city government and the oblast. The Saratov newspapers were routinely filled with articles concerning the latest blowout between the governor and the head of the oblast legislature. This included systematic opposition to gubernatorial appointments to executive posts and the threatened resignation of the chairman of the oblast soviet over various similar conflicts no less than three times in fourteen months.[2] Deputy interviews also revealed instability within the Saratov oblast soviet itself. In Yaroslavl' there were routine disagreements between city- and oblast-level governments, and clear divisions within the legislature as well as sporadic disputes between legislative and executive branches.

I begin with the assumption that because regional legislatures and executives represented societal interests, instability within and among political institutions reflected broader conflicts among societal actors within each region. While chapter 5 addressed a range of hypotheses focusing on possible variations among mass attitudes or social structures that may have explained why one region might have been more unstable than another, the evidence cast serious doubt on that line of analysis.

Instead of pervasive conflict at the societal level giving rise to instability within and between levels of government, this chapter provides

---

[1] For example, author's interviews with Vasilii Kozlov, chair of the Economic Prognosis Department, Nizhnii Novgorod Oblast Administration, May 10, 1993; Vitali Romanov, People's Deputy, Tiumen' Oblast Soviet, July 22, 1993; Boris Nemtsov, Governor, Nizhnii Novgorod Oblast Administration, December 17, 1992, Nizhnii Novgorod Conference on Regional Aspects of Economic Reform. Nemtsov explained, "Nizhnii Novgorod works well because of political agreement on big questions."

[2] See, for example, *Saratovskie Vesti* (20 June 1992) and (24 June 1992), regarding conflicts over Governor Belikh's appointments.

extensive empirical evidence that the labor, asset, and output concentration of the regional economy in a particular sector or among a few particularly large enterprises conditioned the degree to which economic actors competed for access to political resources. Thus this chapter explicitly and rigorously tests the theoretical claims introduced in chapter 2 and demonstrates that the more concentrated the regional economy, the more cooperative were economic and political elites, and the higher was regional government performance as a result.

The empirical data in this chapter show that not all economic interests had the same concerns, and support the argument that in regions where labor, assets, and productive output were concentrated in a particular sector, or among a few large enterprises, competition between economic actors for access to scarce political resources was reduced. Economic concentration therefore enabled political and economic actors to overcome the two collective action dilemmas described initially in chapter 2: (i) the formation of economic interest groups, and (ii) cooperation between these key economic interests and regional governments for the benefit of both.[3] Economic concentration also promoted interdependency between economic and political actors and an exchange of one type of political power in return for another. Cooperation between economic and political actors fostered higher levels of institutional performance by enabling the state to call upon the political authority of key groups of economic actors in return for granting them systematic access to state resources. The result, at least in the short term, was consensus and relative stability in a highly transitional political and economic environment, leading in turn to higher regional government performance.

In illustrating the argument that economic concentration fostered collective action between and among economic and political actors, leading to consensus and higher regional government performance, I use three types of evidence: measures of regional economic concentration; evidence of economic interest group formation and business-government collective action; and examples of the impact of collective action on regional government performance.

COMPARATIVE REGIONAL ECONOMIC CONCENTRATION

The first task is to arrive at measures of economic concentration. This aggregate measure is made up of three important components: concen-

---

[3] Mancur Olson, *The Logic of Collective Action: Public Goods and the Theory of Groups* (Cambridge, Mass.: Harvard University Press, 1965; reprinted 1971).

tration of the economy in particularly large enterprises (high labor concentration); concentration of enterprise assets and output (concentration of capital and productive capacity); and concentration of enterprises within a single economic sector (sectoral concentration). Comparisons among the four regions are shown in Table 6.1.[4] I use the three categories of economic concentration named above to account for the likelihood that some sectors of industry are more capital-intensive than they are labor-intensive. Using measures that only demonstrate the degree to which the regional labor force was concentrated in several enterprises would overlook the fact that Tiumen's economy, for example, is highly concentrated sectorally and the dominant sector of the economy (oil and gas extraction) is asset- and capital-intensive, not labor-intensive. The key indicator of concentration is the aggregate concentration score shown in the bottom row of Table 6.1. Generally, the measures of concentration consistently followed the expected pattern of regional government performance, thus limiting the opportunity for the ranking system, collinearity, or weighting to play a role in biasing the composite index. In short, the findings here are quite robust.

Nizhnii Novgorod

Overall, the aggregate concentration data are striking. Nizhnii Novgorod, the region with the highest-performing regional government, had the most concentrated regional economy across all three types of measures. It ranks highest—with a score of 1.6 (where 1 is most concentrated and 4 is least concentrated) in aggregate economic concentration. Nizhnii Novgorod clearly had a core group of twenty or so very large factories. Indeed, twenty-three of the twenty-five largest factories had more than five thousand workers, whereas only fifteen of the hundred largest factories in Nizhnii had one thousand or fewer workers. Perhaps most significant, the twenty largest enterprises in Nizhnii Novgorod employed more than 15 percent of the total oblast working population (in industry and agriculture). This made those enterprise directors quite powerful vis-à-vis the regional government, and it established the regional government's potential dependency on them.

---

[4] Gross regional product statistics and measures more commonly used in the West are not yet reliably available at the oblast level in Russia. Some regions do calculate their own economic statistics, but there is little consistency in the methodology used across oblasts. As a result, I have used central State Committee on Statistics (Goskomstat/Roskomstat) figures.

TABLE 6.1
Comparative Economic Concentration, 1989–1990

	Nizhnii Novgorod	Tiumen'	Yaroslavl'	Saratov
A. LABOR FORCE CONCENTRATION[a]				
Average Number of Employees per Firm (in 100 largest firms)	4,769 (1)	1,340 (4)	3,786 (2)	2,226 (3)
Percentage of the Total Oblast Labor Force Employed in 20 Largest Firms	15.5 (1)	4.1 (4)	15.0 (2)	7.1 (3)
Of 100 Largest Firms per Oblast				
Firms with 1,000 or Fewer Workers (%)	15	61[b]	56	47
1,001–5,000 Workers (%)	63	36	37	42
5,001–100,000 Workers (%)	23 (1)	3 (4)	7 (3)	11 (2)
B. CONCENTRATION OF INDUSTRIAL ASSETS AND OUTPUT[c]				
Asset Concentration (%)	60 (2)	69.9 (1)	53.6 (3)	50.6 (4)
Output Concentration (%)	63 (2)	68.7 (1)	52 (3)	44 (4)
C. SECTORAL CONCENTRATION				
Of 20 Largest Firms, Percentage Concentrated in a Single Industrial Sector	60 (1)	60 (1)	30 (4)	40 (3)
In the Industrial Branch Structure of the Economy, Percentage Output Concentrated in Single Largest Industrial Branch[d]	45.0 (2)	70.2 (1)	32.2 (3)	30.9 (4)
Agricultural Sectoral Output[e]	Highly dispersed (1)	Highly dispersed (1)	Concentrated in meat and vegetables (2)	Concentrated in wheat (3)

(continued)

TABLE 6.1 (*Continued*)

	Nizhnii Novgorod	Tiumen'	Yaroslavl'	Saratov
Proportion of Agro-Industrial Production as a Proportion of All Industrial Production[f]	2.5 (2)	3.0 (1)	2.0 (3)	1.5 (4)
Number of Collective/State Farms per 1,000 Population[g]	0.30 (2)	0.18 (1)	0.40 (3)	0.48 (4)
Number of Private Farms per 1,000 Population (as of January 1, 1992)[h]	0.20 (1)	0.37 (2)	0.40 (3)	0.60 (4)
Aggregate Concentration Score[i]	1.6	2.2	2.9	3.8

[a]Data come from the Office of Foreign Availability and the Bureau of Export Administration, United States Department of Commerce. Supplementary data on the larger defense plants in Saratov and Nizhnii Novgorod are from the United States Department of Commerce, U.S.-Russia Defense Conversion Subcommittee, 1993. Some material was also made available separately in Saratov and Tiumen'. Kornai uses a similar method for measuring industrial firm size distribution (*The Socialist System*, pp. 400–401).

[b]As indicated in the text, most of these enterprises were in the oil and gas sector and were largely interdependent.

[c]Regarding methods of defining market structure, see James L. Pappas and Mark Hirschey, *Managerial Economics*, 5th ed. (New York: Dryden, 1987), pp. 399–401. Asset concentration is a measure of assets of the ten largest firms divided by the assets of the hundred largest firms. Output concentration is a measure of total output of the ten largest firms as a proportion of total output of the hundred largest firms. A few defense enterprises in Saratov and Nizhnii Novgorod did not list their output or asset levels. These were calculated using industry standards and averages of those that were reported. This practice is a common methodology used to calculate enterprise structure in the West. See, for example, Robert C. Higgins, *Analysis for Financial Management*, 2d ed. (Homewood, Ill.: Robert D. Irwin, 1989), pp. 291–93.

[d]*Pokazateli ekonomicheskogo razvitiia respublik, kraev, oblastei Rossiiskogo federatsii* (Moskva: Respublikanskii informatsionno-izdatelski tsentr, 1992), pp. 133–213.

[e]I arrived at these classifications by examining the total number of agricultural products produced in each region as published by Goskomstat (see ibid., pp. 133–213).

[f]A lower number means a higher proportion. These numbers are a composite ranking of 1 through 4 of the specific share of the agro-industrial complex as a percentage of a region's total industrial production. Four measures are published by the State Committee on Statistics: number of enterprises, volume of production, number of employees, and percentage of value of industrial-production resources (see ibid., pp. 212–13). The composite scores were produced by assigning a 1 to 4 ranking along each of these four measures for each oblast where 1 is highest of the four oblasts and 4 is lowest.

[g]Ibid., p. 13.

[h]Ibid., p. 141.

[i]A lower score indicates greater concentration. This is a composite score along eleven measures of concentration. Only the largest firms were included for the measure of the hundred largest firms. Each oblast was ranked from 1 to 4, where 1 is most concentrated and 4 is least concentrated. Ranks appear in brackets in Table 6.1. These rank scores were summed and divided by 11 to gain the aggregate concentration score.

Second, Nizhnii Novgorod's market structure was highly concentrated in terms of the region's industrial asset and output concentration proportions (60 percent and 63 percent, respectively). Third, Nizhnii Novgorod's economy was also highly sectorally concentrated. Sixty percent of the region's twenty largest enterprises were largely devoted to military equipment production before the end of the Cold War.[5]

Finally, Nizhnii Novgorod's agricultural sector was dispersed and relatively weak in comparison to Saratov and Yaroslavl', the two lower-performance cases (although stronger than the agricultural sector in Tiumen'). That Nizhnii Novgorod's agricultural sector was weak indicates that the economy was industrially concentrated. In short, of the four oblasts examined in this study, Nizhnii Novgorod, where regional government performance was highest, had the most concentrated economy in the aggregate across all three types of measures.

Tiumen'

Although Tiumen' had a relatively larger proportion of smaller enterprises than the other three oblasts (61 percent of the largest hundred firms had one thousand or fewer employees), these firms were highly concentrated within a single sector and were largely interdependent. Most were almost exclusively extractors of raw materials (specifically oil, gas, and timber) and were located within a single geographic region of the oblast (the central to extreme northern areas). Although a relatively small percentage (4 percent) of the industrial labor force worked in the ten largest enterprises in Tiumen', regional economic officials estimated in 1993 that perhaps as many as half the region's working-age inhabitants were in some way employed by the oil and gas industry—either in a geological research institute, at a drilling site, or in a refinery.[6] The strength of the oil and gas sector in Tiumen' is reflected best in the regional asset concentration ratio of 69.9 percent and the output concentration ratio of 68.7 percent. These figures indicate a highly concentrated regional market structure.

Finally, of the four oblasts, Tiumen' was the most sectorally concen-

---

[5] In interviews with the author, officials in the region's Economic Prognosis Department estimated the region's total defense industrial production to have been as high as 85 percent of total industrial output before the end of the Cold War.

[6] Author's interviews with officials in the Economic Prognosis Department, Tiumen' Oblast Administration, August 1993.

trated. It had a small agricultural sector (with only 0.18 collective/state farms per 1,000 population and 0.37 private farms per 1,000), but 70.2 percent of all industrial output was concentrated in a single lucrative sector—oil and gas. Concentration of the regional economy in a single sector should have encouraged collective action, and the economy of Tiumen' was especially highly sectorally concentrated as well as being highly concentrated in terms of assets and output. The aggregate concentration score for Tiumen' was 2.2, only slightly lower than that for Nizhnii Novgorod.

Yaroslavl'

Yaroslavl' and Saratov, the two regions where regional government performance was third and fourth lowest, respectively, were certainly less economically concentrated than either Tiumen' or Nizhnii Novgorod. In particular contrast to Nizhnii Novgorod, 56 percent of the hundred largest firms in Yaroslavl' had one thousand or fewer workers, and seven firms there had more than five thousand workers. As in its performance ranking, Yaroslavl' ranks third, behind Nizhnii and Tiumen', in terms of concentrated market structure, with asset and output concentration ratios of 53.6 percent and 52 percent, respectively.

Further, Yaroslavl' ranks far lower in measures of sectoral concentration than either Nizhnii or Tiumen', with only 30 percent of the twenty largest firms concentrated in a single economic sector (heavy industry—nondefense) and only 32.2 percent of regional economic output concentrated in a single industrial branch. Although Yaroslavl' did have seven large firms, it is significant that, in contrast to Nizhnii, the top twenty-five industrial firms in Yaroslavl' were dispersed across several sectors that included diesel engines, consumer goods (like watches and clocks as well as photographic equipment and textiles), petroleum refining, synthetic rubbers and chemical products.

Although the region's agriculture was weak relative to the Black Earth agricultural areas of southern Russia that border Saratov, the number of collective/state farms per 1,000 population in Yaroslavl' was significantly greater than in either Nizhnii Novgorod or Tiumen', as was the number of private farms per 1,000 by 1992. Thus Yaroslavl' had a stronger agricultural sector, and this proved to be the source of intersectoral conflict. As with the performance of its regional government, Yaroslavl' ranked third (2.9) in aggregate economic concentration, behind Nizhnii Novgorod and Tiumen'.

Saratov

Finally Saratov, the oblast with the lowest performing regional government, consistently rated as the most dispersed economy of the four provinces. First, 47 percent of Saratov's hundred largest firms had one thousand or fewer workers. Eleven enterprises in Saratov had between five thousand and fifteen thousand workers, but in contrast to Nizhnii Novgorod in particular, where GAZ (Gor'kovskii Avtomobilnyi Zavod) had more than one hundred thousand workers, Saratov had only one gigantic enterprise (Saratov Electromechanical Production Organization, or SEPO) having more than fifteen thousand workers. The percentage of the total oblast labor force employed in the region's twenty largest firms was only 7.1 percent compared to 15.5 percent in Nizhnii Novgorod and 15 percent in Yaroslavl'.

Second, Saratov's asset and output concentration measures were the lowest of all four oblasts, trailing both Nizhnii Novgorod and Tiumen' significantly although, as we would expect from its relative regional government performance, closer to Yaroslavl'.

In addition, of the four oblasts, Saratov was the least sectorally concentrated. While Saratov, like Nizhnii Novgorod, had several important defense firms,[7] only 40 percent of the twenty largest firms (compared to 60 percent in Nizhnii Novgorod) had a clear defense orientation, with the balance comprised of chemical, agro-industrial, and consumer products plants.

Of the four oblasts examined here, Saratov was also the most agricultural. It had the highest proportion of collective/state farms per 1,000 population and the highest proportion of private farmers per 1,000 population. As with Yaroslavl', therefore, Saratov had a strong agricultural lobby. This was in no small part due to the fact that Saratov was one of Russia's most important wheat-producing provinces.[8] An especially high quality strain of wheat was the basis of Saratov's agricultural sector, and it was a crop of considerable importance to the Russian Federation as a whole. Because the agricultural sector in Saratov was strong and concen-

---

[7] Indeed, because of the importance of some of their defense plants, both Saratov and Nizhnii Novgorod were closed to foreigners until 1990–91. Nizhnii Novgorod's city of Arzamas was home to a significant portion of the Soviet nuclear defense industry (specializing in missile warhead assembly) and was closed not only to foreigners but to Soviet citizens from outside the area as well.

[8] *Pokazateli sotsial'nogo razvitiia respublik, kraev i oblastei Rossiiskoi federatsii* (Moskva: Respublikanskii informatsionno-izdatel'skii tsentr, 1992), p. 217.

trated in wheat production, the powerful agricultural lobby played an important and divisive role in Saratov politics. This will be discussed in greater detail below. As with its regional government performance, Saratov ranked last in economic concentration, with an aggregate score of 3.8.

In sum, there is a good match in the aggregate between economic concentration and performance. As with institutional performance, the aggregate economic concentration pattern showed Nizhnii Novgorod ranking ahead of Tiumen', with Yaroslavl' ranking third and Saratov consistently trailing. Thus the provinces with the two highest-performance governments had the most concentrated regional economies. Nizhnii Novgorod had not only a high degree of labor force concentration but also a high degree of concentration of industrial output and assets. Finally, its economy was also highly sectorally concentrated. In the aggregate, Nizhnii proved to be the most economically concentrated.

Although Tiumen' was less concentrated economically in terms of labor, of the four oblasts it had the highest asset and output concentration and the highest sectoral concentration; as a result, its aggregate concentration score was slightly lower than Nizhnii Novgorod's. Of these oblasts, then, Nizhnii Novgorod and (to a slightly lesser degree) Tiumen' most resembled "company towns." The high degree of concentration in the regional economy led to the formation of key economic interest groups. Even more important, it led to collective action between political and economic actors.

ECONOMIC CONCENTRATION AND COLLECTIVE ACTION

The high degree of economic concentration in Tiumen' and Nizhnii Novgorod facilitated the collective action of economic interest groups as well as the collective action of political and economic actors. Table 6.2 summarizes the evidence and illustrates the causal chain in the figure above the table. Numbers appearing above the explanatory diagram correspond to the indicators shown in table 6.2.

Nizhnii Novgorod

In Nizhnii Novgorod the presence of a core group of about twenty directors of particularly large and economically important defense enterprises

TABLE 6.2

Summary of Measures of Economic Concentration Correlated with Higher Government Performance

1 Economic Concentration →	2 Collective action of economic actors →	3 Collective action between political and economic actors →	4 Consensus →	5 Higher Performance
Measures	*Nizhnii Novgorod*	*Tiumen'*	*Yaroslavl'*	*Saratov*
1a. Areas of Concentration of Regional Economy	—labor —assets/output —sectoral	—assets/output —sectoral	—labor	None: —highly dispersed
1b. Economic Concentration Index[a]	1.6	2.2	2.9	3.8
2. Formation of Economic Interest Groups	—enterprise associations —large, cohesive block of seats in soviet	—enterprise associations —block of seats in soviet	—no formal organizations —small agricultural lobby versus splintered industrial interests	—no formal organizations —agricultural interests versus splintered industrial interests
3a. Elite Pool	Narrow: —strong political links to key industrial sectors	Narrow: —strong political links to key industrial sectors	Wide: —weak political links to conflicting and numerous industrial and agricultural sectors	Wide: —weak political links to conflicting and numerous industrial and agricultural sectors

(*continued*)

TABLE 6.2 (*Continued*)

Measures	Nizhnii Novgorod	Tiumen'	Yaroslavl'	Saratov
3b. Collective Action	—systematic meetings between economic groups and political actors —formal statements of collaboration —incorporation of economic actors into state structures	—systematic meetings between economic groups and political actors —formal statements of collaboration —incorporation of economic actors into state structures	—no systematic meetings —no formal agreements —pervasive patron-client networks; no horizontal integration between political and economic actors	—no systematic meetings —no formal agreements —pervasive patron-client networks; no horizontal integration between political and economic actors
4. Consensus between and among Political and Economic Actors over Political Goals	High: —limited and fluid factionalization in soviet —no conflict between legislature and executive —no conflict between oblast and city governments	Medium-High: —fluid factions moderated by overlapping memberships —limited conflict between legislature and executive —no conflict between oblast and city governments	Medium-Low: —factionalization within soviet —some legislative and executive conflict —some conflict between city and oblast governments	Low: —strong factionalization within soviet —sharp legislative and executive conflict —sharp conflict between oblast and city governments
5. Performance	High	Medium-High	Medium-Low	Low

[a]From Table 6.1. Again, a lower score indicates greater concentration.

174

quickly crystallized as a formidable political force. In 1990 they were able to gain almost 30 percent of the seats in the oblast soviet, and they were among the first group of industrialists in Russia to form an enterprise association.[9]

Indeed, a pattern of broad consultation began relatively early. Shortly after taking office, Governor Nemtsov and oblast soviet chair Krestianinov, recognizing the importance of opening a dialogue with this group of economic actors, cruised for a few hours down the Volga on a river boat with the region's leading industrial enterprise directors. Their purpose was to present their policy platforms and to convince this core group of enterprise directors that only through collective action could they achieve these goals.[10] In return, this core group of regional employers was assured access to regional policy instruments and resources—specifically, relief from the burden of social welfare requirements that diverted scarce defense enterprise resources from investment in conversion to civilian products; development of foreign and domestic trade ties to sell enterprise products; and worker retraining programs. Although many of these enterprises were to be privatized, and some enterprise directors saw this as a threat to their control, in fact privatization in the region was conducted in such a way that political authorities were able to steer enough shares to labor collectives and enterprise directors so that most were able to retain their positions. Moreover, political actors were able to rely on the authority of enterprise directors in implementing some key policy initiatives (and at election time) in return for giving business actors privileged and systematic inclusion in the policy process.

Evidence of the cooperative relationship between political and economic actors in Nizhnii Novgorod is significant. In late 1991 and early 1992 the political leadership began negotiating semiformal agreements for cooperation. These documents were referred to as "social guaran-

[9] Irina Starodubrovskaia, in her "Attitudes of Enterprise Managers toward Market Transitions," in Michael McFaul and Tova Perlmutter, eds., *Privatization, Conversion, and Enterprise Reform in Russia* (Stanford, Calif.: Center for International Security and Arms Control, 1993), p. 62, indicates that there is a misconception that most Russian enterprises were members of such associations. In a survey of enterprise managers, she notes that slightly more than 50 percent of respondents belonged to these associations. In some cases, the associations were local branches of the old Soviet industrial ministries and their departments. Although they no longer had any official governmental authority, they were in some cases effective lobby groups.

[10] Author's conversation with Evgenii Gorkov, Vice Governor, Department of International Relations, Nizhnii Novgorod Oblast Administration, May 1994.

tees."[11] Some of these were specifically designed to soften the burdens of key economic actors. In return, these economic actors were to provide political support and legitimacy to the political leadership.

Further evidence of the cooperative relationship in Nizhnii Novgorod can be found in the formal incorporation of enterprise interests into oblast political organs. For example, to address the enterprise need for increased trade and access to foreign markets for local products, Nemtsov appointed one of the assistant directors of Gor'kovskii Avtomobilnyi Zavod (GAZ), the single largest employer in the region (with more than one hundred thousand workers) as deputy governor in charge of foreign economic relations.

Evidence also suggests that collective action between economic and political actors in Nizhnii Novgorod and Tiumen' was further undergirded by the company town effect. As noted earlier, in Nizhnii Novgorod and Tiumen', political actors were drawn from a narrower elite pool. Many had strong professional links to the key sectors of the regional economy. In Nizhnii Novgorod, for example, not only were the governor and the chair of the oblast soviet graduates of the Nizhnii Novgorod Radio Physics Institute (a VUZ, or *vysshee uchebnoe zavedenie*—an institute of higher learning and roughly the equivalent of a technical specialty university), but so too were both the chair of the oblast soviet Committee on the Economy and the chair of the oblast administration's Department of Economic Prognosis. In addition, a more recent graduate of the Institute was the chair of the Nizhnii Novgorod Banking House. This is significant because virtually all the founding members of the Banking House were the largest defense enterprises of the region. The Bank itself, as the brainchild of the region's political actors, was intended expressly to assist them in funding defense conversion.[12] Finally, that the region's economy was concentrated in a declining sector may also have served to enhance business/government interdependence in Nizhnii Novgorod. The decline of the defense sector following the end of the Cold War meant that orders for defense products were falling, and these cutbacks meant possible factory closures.

Political actors' links to the radio-physics industry—which produced electronic communications and measurement technology with defense

[11] *Nizhegorodskaia pravda* January 25, 1992; see also ibid., March 5, 1992, regarding the governor and the chair of the oblast soviet meeting with representatives of trade organizations and unions about the privatization of retail trade.

[12] Author's interview with Boris Brevnov, Director of the Nizhnii Novgorod Banking House, November 22, 1992.

applications—is particularly significant considering that at least ten of the hundred largest enterprises in the oblast were devoted to producing radio-communications and electronic measurement systems. These included Nitel, a defense enterprise employing 13,000 workers that was the world's leading producer of VHF air surveillance missile systems during the Cold War; Krasnoe Sormovo Shipyard, a submarine plant and the second largest employer in the region (with 19,600 workers); and Popov Communications Equipment, employing 8,000 workers and producing aviation communications equipment.[13]

Although direct evidence is scarce, indirect evidence indicates that these links supported collective action between political and economic interests in Nizhnii Novgorod. One example of this was privatization of enterprises. While many enterprise directors were hesitant initially to implement the region's aggressive privatization scheme because they feared a loss of control over their enterprises, through ongoing negotiations the political leadership was able to promise various forms of compensation in return for privatization. One observer from the International Finance Corporation revealed that in negotiations with enterprise directors, Governor Nemtsov had certainly "played to his economic constituency" in promising to limit access to the bidding for shares of privatizing enterprises in return for the cooperation of enterprise directors and work collectives.[14]

Tiumen'

Like Nizhnii Novgorod, in Tiumen' the concentration of the regional economy had a positive effect on the resolution of collective action dilemmas. In Tiumen' a coalition of economic interests formed naturally in

[13] U.S.-Russia Defense Conversion Subcommittee, U.S. Department of Commerce, November 1992 and September 1993. Documents PB93–101509, PB93–18366, and PB94–100211.

[14] Author's interview with International Finance Corporation representative in Nizhnii Novgorod who preferred not to be identified, Nizhnii Novgorod, November 1992. Sometimes promises made by the political leadership were not always enough to reassure enterprise directors. The most striking example of (illegal) resistance to privatization was at GAZ—the Gor'kii Automobile Factory. In this case the enterprise director, Boris Vidaev, feared that he would not receive enough shares in the enterprise; he therefore appropriated funds intended for the development of a new product in order to purchase shares in the enterprise. Governor Nemtsov succeeded in having Vidaev removed as director, but Vidaev retained a seat on the new corporation's Board of Directors by a vote of the labor collective (see *Nezavisimaia gazeta*, January 21, 1994, p. 1).

the oil and gas industries.[15] This group represented oil and gas enterprises that were largely concentrated in the north of the oblast in two autonomous okrugs (Khanty-Mansi and Yamal-Nenets). They participated directly in promoting candidates in the oblast soviet. For example, one oil and gas enterprise reportedly sponsored twenty-eight employee candidates in the 1990 elections to the raion, city, and oblast soviets. The enterprise extended a paid leave to the candidates to pursue their campaigns. Fourteen of the candidates won seats, six of whom were elected to the oblast soviet.[16] Although the percentage of seats in the legislature won by enterprise directors (11 percent) was not as great as that of economic interests in the Nizhnii Novgorod oblast soviet, thirty-two directors were still elected to the soviet and, because of the overarching influence of oil and gas in the region's economy, they retained considerable influence.

Second, just as in Nizhnii, in Tiumen' a pattern of consultation between economic and political actors began relatively early. Local and national newspapers report relatively frequent meetings between oblast political actors and the key group of oil and gas enterprise directors.[17]

Indeed, the economy's extreme concentration in the oil and gas industries heightened the interdependence of political and economic actors. That the economy in Tiumen' was sectorally concentrated in the oil and gas industry is also notable because of the way the region had been treated in the Soviet period. Under the formerly hypercentralized economy, proceeds from the vast oil and gas reserves of Tiumen' went directly to Moscow and almost nothing was left in the oblast for reinvestment in regional infrastructure and social services. The result was that Tiumen' was one of the primary sources of hard currency earnings for the Soviet Union, but the region's inhabitants lived in relative poverty. Before the 1990 regional soviet elections, Tiumen' was distinguishable from other provinces not so much by its wealth of oil and gas, but by the depth of its economic crisis. One local observer noted, "The causes

[15] An enterprise association, as well as the Association of Entrepreneurs, had formed by 1991 in Tiumen' oblast.

[16] Author's interview with Vitalii Romanov, People's Deputy, Tiumen' Oblast Soviet, July 22, 1993. Deputy Romanov was one of the six elected to the oblast soviet from this enterprise.

[17] See, for example, *Tiumenskie izvestiia*, November 29, 1991, and *Izvestiia*, January 9, 1992, as summarized in the *Current Digest of the Post-Soviet Press* 44, no.1 (1992): 25. The *Izvestiia* article refers to this group of directors as oil and gas "barons."

of this crisis were clear—we were in effect in the situation of a colony having no rights whatsoever to the riches of our land and the products of our labor."[18]

As a result, when the veil of central control was lifted and a regional government was elected in Tiumen', groups that were previously subordinated to separate central government ministries were able to join together. Local journalists immediately reported on the oil (in the south-central part of the region) and gas (in the extreme north) alliance that formed in the 1990 election: "Earlier we had no such alliance of the North and the South and neither the North or the South ever got anything."[19] Further, as the central ministries pulled back and the Soviet Union collapsed, oil and gas production dropped as needed funds for capital investment in oil and gas extraction and geological research dried up.[20] The shortage of investment capital for oil and gas enterprises, the rapid deterioration of drilling equipment in the harsh climate coupled with the dependence of the regional economy on oil and gas, and the depressed state of social services in the oblast served to heighten the interdependence between political and economic actors in Tiumen'.

The regional economy's dependency on the oil and gas sector meant that collective action in Tiumen' focused on the regional political leadership's attempts to revive it in return for oil and gas enterprise assistance in implementing regional government social policy. As part of this, economic and political actors in Tiumen' began a cooperative effort to wrestle more authority over the proceeds from the region's oil and gas extraction away from the central government. This resulted in a presidential decree—"On the Development of Tiumen' Oblast"—that was signed in September 1991. It allowed the regional government to sell or trade 10 percent of the oil and gas extracted in the province, and it laid the groundwork for further reinvestment in oil and gas capital equipment. [21]

Collective action between business and government, as in Nizhnii

---

[18] *Tiumenskaia pravda*, September 24, 1991, p. 1. For a comprehensive study of the oil and gas industry under the Soviet regime, see Thane Gustafson, *Crisis amid Plenty: The Politics of Soviet Energy under Brezhnev and Gorbachev* (Princeton, N.J.: Princeton University Press, 1989).

[19] *Tiumenskaia pravda*, April 15, 1990, p. 1.

[20] *Izvestiia*, January 9, 1992, reports that oil production dropped from 389 million tons in 1987 to 309 million tons in 1992. The extraction of natural gas increased in the same period, but growth in the rate of extraction fell by 50 percent.

[21] Cf. chapter 4.

Novgorod, was promoted by the concentration of the economy in Tiumen' which produced a narrower elite pool from which to draw political actors. As mentioned above, some thirty oil and gas enterprise directors were elected to the oblast soviet, including the head of Surgutneftgaz, the region's third largest oil and gas extraction enterprise. Further, of those directors elected to the soviet, several were reportedly heads of regional soviet commissions. It did not seem unusual, therefore, that the first governor of the oblast, Iurii Shafranik, was the head of one of the largest crude oil extraction enterprises in the oblast—Langepas. As part of the network of oil and gas enterprise directors, Shafranik was able to draw on his professional ties in negotiating with the region's key economic group.

As in Nizhnii Novgorod, overlapping ties in Tiumen' promoted credible commitments between political and economic actors. The web of horizontal professional ties also more easily facilitated cooperation among political groups and between them and economic actors. As early as May 1990, only two months after the regional soviet was elected in Tiumen, the region's representatives in the USSR and RSFSR Supreme Soviets (elected in 1989 and 1990, respectively) signed a joint declaration of cooperation with the deputies in the oblast soviet.[22] There were also formal statements of collaboration between political and economic actors in the region. For example, the Tiumen' Congress of Entrepreneurs declared it a "civic duty" to ensure the implementation of the decree on the oblast's economic development.[23] Similarly, Governor Shafranik stressed that in order for the oblast's economic and social recovery to be successful, the government "must lean on all productive and professional associations."[24]

It is important to note, though, that Tiumen' has experienced some friction between economic and political interests. The tradition of ongoing negotiation and accommodation in the oblast has, however, mediated conflict such that overall stability is more or less maintained. The source of the problem—the attempted separation of the two northern autonomous okrugs—was in effect retaliation on the part of oil and gas enterprises (in the two autonomous okrugs) against the central government in Moscow for reneging on the promises made to the region in the 1991 Decree. Although this was initially couched in terms of ethnic self-

---

[22] The declaration is published in *Tiumenskaia pravda*, May 16, 1990, p. 1.
[23] Ibid., October 16, 1991.
[24] Ibid., October 17, 1991.

determination of the autonomous okrugs' titular populations (the Khanty, Mansi, Yamal, and Nenets peoples), there was no doubt that control over natural resources was the central issue.[25] By late 1992 the autonomous okrugs had declared themselves republics in order to increase their control over their natural resources. Although their demands effectively split the oblast budget into three parts (one for the oblast and one for each of the two autonomous okrugs), cooperative arrangements with the oblast persisted through the establishment of joint governing bodies (for example, a council of the autonomous okrug leaderships and the oblast soviet to coordinate policy). Indeed, a considerable accomplishment of collective action in Tiumen' was maintaining the integrity of the oblast's borders in the face of mounting centrifugal pressures. This example also serves to illustrate the transactional nature of business-government cooperation in Tiumen'. The cooperative relationship is threatened if one side or the other does not see concrete benefits flowing from it. Thus, while there was some conflict in Tiumen', collective action wrought by the concentration of the economy in the oil and gas sector persisted.

In both Nizhnii and Tiumen', then, the embeddedness of political behavior in highly concentrated regional economies promoted the formation of organized business interests capable of lobbying government; the interdependence of business and government; and collective action of key economic and political actors. Although disputes occurred, they were mediated by the general consensus that pervaded political and economic interaction in these two oblasts, which, as I will demonstrate later in this chapter, promoted higher government performance.

Yaroslavl'

The evidence demonstrates that in Yaroslavl' and Saratov, the two regions with lower government performance, the trends observed in Nizhnii Novgorod and Tiumen' were not present. As Table 6.1 noted, in

[25] This is because Yamal and Nenets peoples make up less than 4 percent of the population of the autonomous okrug that bears their name, whereas the Khanty and Mansi population in the autonomous okrug to which their names are given comprised 0.9 percent and 0.5 percent, respectively. The majority population group in the Yamal-Nenets area is 20 percent Ukrainian (giving the okrug the nickname "Yamal-Donetsk") and 79 percent Russian. Similarly, Khanty-Mansi autonomous okrug is 60 percent Russian, 11.5 percent Ukrainian, and 7.6 percent Tatar, with the remaining population comprised of several small ethnic groups. These figures come from research completed by Eduard Bagramov, Director of Ethnic Studies, Russian Institute of Social and National Problems, 1992.

Yaroslavl' and Saratov the regional economies were more dispersed among sectors and among enterprises within various sectors. Dispersed economic power led to dispersed political power and conflict. In Yaroslavl' and especially Saratov, at the oblast level, there was little evidence of cooperative economic interest group behavior. Further, conflict rather than collective action characterized many aspects of business and government interaction. The extent of the divisions within these oblasts was reflected in conflict between and within branches and levels of government. The result was lower regional government performance.

Despite the industrially dominated economy in Yaroslavl', because industry was dispersed among sectors and enterprises, no strong industrial lobby formed and a smaller agricultural lobby was able to wield political influence out of proportion to the size of the region's agricultural sector. This raised the specter of conflict within the region between agricultural and industrial interests.

The agricultural lobby had strong ties to the old Communist Party organization in the region. In a comprehensive analysis of the 1990 regional soviet elections in Yaroslavl', Jeffrey Hahn and Gavin Helf discovered that the Party had allied itself with agricultural elites: "There were clear signals that this [group] could now deliver a most precious resource in the new political environment: it could generate support, most clearly in the countryside. It was among members of this group and in the electoral districts that they could deliver that the apparat looked for votes."[26]

Helf and Hahn rather curiously attribute the Party organization with a victory in the 1990 regional soviet elections in Yaroslavl'. In fact, it was but the first in a string of victories by the agrarian lobby in Yaroslavl' oblast in the competition between economic sectors and enterprises for access to political resources.

First, agrarians were able to influence some elite selection within the oblast that became a further source of conflict. For example, the agrarian lobby had a client in the chairman of the oblast soviet, Aleskandr Veselov. He had been the Party first secretary of the Pereslavl'-Zalessko gorkom and had direct professional ties to the agricultural sector. Unfortunately for the political process in Yaroslavl', he had no ties to the strong industrial sector in the province. He was, instead, part of a narrow net-

---

[26] Gavin Helf and Jeffrey Hahn, "Old Dogs and New Tricks: Party Elites in the Russian Regional Elections of 1990," *Slavic Review* 51, no. 3 (Fall 1992): 520.

work of agrarian elites that attempted to subdue and control industrial interests in favor of agriculture. This gave political voice to the agrarian/industrialist conflict.

The agrarian lobby was not so powerful, however, that it was able to claim a victory in the appointment of other regional political actors. For example, the deputy chair of the oblast soviet, Iulius Kolbovksii, was a candidate from the self-styled "democratic" faction within the soviet, and oblast soviet commissions were headed by members of different factions—agrarians and democrats (more or less pro-industry).[27] Further, the appointment of Anatolii Lisitsyn as regional governor was a hollow victory for both ends of the political spectrum in Yaroslavl'. Although the agrarian lobby succeeded in preventing the industrialist reform-oriented candidate from gaining a victory, their own candidate, the former ispolkom chair, was also ultimately rejected by the soviet. Moreover, a dispersed economy produced factionalization within government organs and a more dispersed elite pool from which to choose political actors. These factors contributed to conflict within the oblast.[28]

Second, the agrarian elite's attempts to exercise control over policy in the region produced conflict with other economic actors. In interviews, members of the oblast administration and the oblast soviet explained the demand in the soviet from some corners to "turn upside down" (razviazat') the province's agriculture rather than to direct scarce resources into industrial upgrading to make Yaroslavl' products competitive with imports.[29] One of the schemes favored by the agricultural lobby and their clients in the soviet was to reclaim land flooded by a water reservoir in the northern region of the oblast to grow flax. Plans such as this, and the large proportion of the oblast budget allotted to agricultural subsidies, caused considerable upset and conflict within the soviet (producing factions).[30] It also sustained conflict between the soviet and the

[27] Author's interviews with deputies in Yaroslavl' Oblast Soviet, particularly Vladimir Borisov, April 14, 1993.

[28] For more on conflict within and between political institutions, see Blair A. Ruble, *Money Sings: The Changing Politics of Urban Space in Post-Soviet Yaroslavl'* (Washington, D.C.: Woodrow Wilson Center Press with Cambridge University Press, 1995), especially pp. 7–13.

[29] The word *razviazat'* was used by Aleksandr Veselov, chairman of the Yaroslavl' Oblast Soviet of People's Deputies, in an interview with the author, January 6, 1993.

[30] Almost 50 percent of the 1993 budget was allotted to agricultural subsidies, up from 40 percent in 1992.

administration and between the oblast and the capital city government of Yaroslavl'.[31]

Some of the larger industrial enterprises objected individually to the disproportionate political influence yielded to agricultural elites, but this only served to promote conflict within and between regional political structures. This conflict often played out not only as intra-legislature and legislative-executive conflict at the oblast level but also conflict between the city government and the oblast—particularly over budgetary allocations and policy priorities. This was because the largest and most vocal enterprises were located in the city of Yaroslavl', and one or two enterprise directors had strong professional connections to city-level officials (the first deputy chairman of the Yaroslavl' city soviet, for example, formerly worked in management at one of the largest plants in the city— Yaroslavl' Motor Works Avtodizel').

As a result of the struggle between sectors and little collective action within the industrial sector as a whole, cooperation between government and economic interest groups was narrow. Often, major economic interests (the bulk of the industrial sector) were overlooked in favor of a minority group. One result of this was what might be termed the *political defection* of individual industrial concerns to a political opposition—the city-level government and a faction within the oblast soviet representing industrial interests. In contrast to Nizhnii Novgorod and Tiumen', dispersed economic power precipitated dispersed political power— divergent and often conflicting interests in the economic community produced conflict within and among branches and levels of government. This lowered relative government performance.

Saratov

While a dispersed economy in Yaroslavl' produced conflict within and between political and economic interests, in Saratov this effect was magnified. As in Yaroslavl', in Saratov there was little evidence of economic interest group formation and concerted collaboration.[32] Economic inter-

---

[31] Author's interviews with Anatolii Lisitsyn, Head of Administration, Yaroslavl' oblast, April 15, 1993, and Vladimir Bakaev, first deputy chairman of the Yaroslavl' city soviet, April 13, 1993.

[32] At the end of 1993 evidence suggested modest collaboration on the part of a group of several defense enterprises to lobby regional government, but their efforts met with mixed results. In addition, a group of private entrepreneurs, the so-called Group of Thirteen, formed before the December 12, 1993, election, but their candidates did not do well. (I am

ests that did collaborate found themselves competing with other industries and sectors. In short, the dispersion of the economy across sectors, industries, and smaller enterprises promoted competition for access to political resources rather than collective action.

With respect to formal economic interest group collaboration, deputies in the oblast soviet elected from large enterprises complained in interviews that competition between enterprises for political resources was the norm.[33] Further, in contrast to the horizontal consultations between enterprises and political actors in Nizhnii Novgorod, in Saratov vertical patron-client ties (*sviazi*) between enterprises and political actors (specifically, the governor and the presidential representative) decided which enterprises would get policy aid and which would not. Although one of the key enterprise directors persistently worked on his own rather than in conjunction with others, several other directors allied themselves with the presidential representative or the deputy mayor of the city of Saratov. Of course Vladimir Golovachev, the presidential representative, was not officially supposed to play a role in policy making, but in this case he was able to interfere in the processes of government. Because he had formerly been the Saratov city (*gorkom*) chair before the Party organization was abolished and he was named presidential representative, Golovachev was able to build the position of presidential representative into an independent seat of power through old patron-client ties.

A split between industrial and agricultural interests was also discernible. As in Yaroslavl', these competing factions produced divisions between branches and levels of government (the city versus the oblast) and contributed to factionalization within the oblast soviet. Of the four ob-

indebted to Regina Smyth of Pennsylvania State University for relaying this information while observing the 1993 national elections in Saratov oblast.) Indeed, the December 1993 election results in Saratov reveal how dispersed political power in the region remained. Of four deputies (in single-member districts) elected from Saratov to the State Duma, two were nationalists, one was a Communist, and the fourth was a member of Russia's Choice. Saratov also elected one of five successful candidates in single-member districts from Vladimir Zhirinovsky's Liberal Democratic Party (LDPR). In the party list voting, the vote was split among the LDPR (26.6 percent), the Communist Party (15.3 percent), and Russia's Choice (12.3 percent)—all of whom had relatively different programs. Electoral results are reported in *Biulleten'* of the Central Electoral Commission, issue 12, March 1994. For more on the December 1993 national elections in Saratov, see Regina Smith, "Political Strategy in the Transition: The Case of Saratov," in Timothy Colton and Jerry Hough, eds., *The Russian Elections of 1993* (Brookings Institution, forthcoming).

[33] Author's interviews with deputies of Saratov Oblast Soviet of People's Deputies, April 1993.

lasts included in this study Saratov, even more than Yaroslavl', witnessed strong factionalization within the regional legislature (the soviet actually insisted that factions register themselves and declare their members) and suffered most from divided government.

Divisions within the soviet and between legislative and executive branches of government reflected deep divisions between economic interests in the oblast. The agricultural lobby, for example, was at least partially responsible for the appointment of Iurii Belikh as governor of the oblast in February 1992. Belikh had been the director of a poultry factory and had no real political experience. Perhaps more important, he had no strong professional ties to actors in the region's other key economic sectors.[34] The chair of the oblast soviet, Nikolai Makarevich, was similarly politically inexperienced and, as a lawyer, had no strong formal ties to the region's disparate economic interests. In short, the divergent professional experiences of Makarevich and Belikh attest to the diverse pool from which political elites were drawn in Saratov.

Makarevich bitterly opposed Belikh's appointments to the departments of the administration, complaining that a few were too strongly linked to the old Communist Party apparatus and that others were corrupt.[35] Conflict between and within branches of government in Saratov was so intense that Makarevich threatened to resign three times in fourteen months.

Thus, whereas in Nizhnii Novgorod and Tiumen' commitments between economic and political actors were upheld by overlapping professional horizontal networks, in Saratov this pattern of interaction was absent. Instead, just as in Yaroslavl', competing economic actors were vertically linked to different factions and particular actors within regional government institutions.

As a result, access to political resources were distributed as a reward for political support on a more personalistic, patron-client footing. In interviews, many deputies accused Saratov's governor of selling favors and subsidies to individuals on a particularistic basis.[36] Moreover, broad

---

[34] Iurii Belikh's biography appears in *Saratovskie vesti*, February 28, 1992.

[35] See *Saratovskie vesti*, July 16–20, 1992, for examples. Belikh was dismissed from his post as governor by President Yeltsin in February 1996, having been accused of mismanaging oblast funds.

[36] In one case, for example, Governor Belikh ordered regional banks to pay credits to one factory to pay employee wages. Belikh was then allowed to campaign in the factory during the December 1993 election when he ran for (and won) a seat in the Federal Assembly.

cooperation between economic and political interests was inhibited by pervasive suspicion between competing interests. Any collaboration that did take place was narrow and personalistic. As a result, those interests left out of these narrow relationships defected to the political opposition (either another faction in the soviet or a different branch or level of government), thereby condemning the political process to an ongoing cycle of sharp conflict. This had a negative effect on regional government performance.

THE POLITICAL ECONOMY OF REGIONAL GOVERNMENT PERFORMANCE: LINKING THEORY TO PRACTICE

The argument so far has been that in regions where economies were concentrated, as in Nizhnii Novgorod and Tiumen', collective action between organized economic interests and political actors took place. The embeddedness of social interactions in an atmosphere that resembled a "company town" helped focus societal interests and heightened the interdependence of economic and political actors. It also narrowed the pool from which political elites were drawn such that horizontal (preexisting) professional networks helped to sustain credible commitments between political and economic actors.

Collective action between political and economic interests meant that the state included economic interests in the policy process (in policy formation and implementation) and economic interests gained material advantages from the state. In return, economic interests lent the state some of their political power by guaranteeing consensus and using their resources to promote government efficacy and legitimacy within civil society. This relationship therefore sustained consensus and higher regional government performance.

Chapter 4 provided a variety of performance measures that ranked the four regions consistently in roughly the same pattern such that Nizhnii Novgorod rated highest followed by Tiumen' and Yaroslavl' with Saratov trailing. The reader will recall that these measures included (1) the policy process (How smoothly does government run?); (2) policy output and implementation (Is government prompt in identifying and addressing important issues?); and (3) responsiveness (How well do constituents rank their governments?). Where collective action between business and government was pervasive, performance was improved along all these dimensions.

With respect to the policy process, the evidence indicated that the concentration of the economy in a particular sector narrowed the elite pool in both Nizhnii Novgorod and Tiumen'. As a result, the internal allocation of authority (measured by selection of leaders within the soviet) was consensual rather than conflictual as in Saratov in particular. We would expect this because the effect of economic concentration increased industry's capture of government. This should promote consensus regarding the skills leaders need because the pool from which leaders are drawn was linked to essential economic groups.

Further, concentration of the economy should also have had the effect of limiting the degree of factionalization and conflict within the regional legislature and between branches and levels of government. In Saratov and Yaroslavl', factionalization within the regional soviets proved to be an ongoing problem. Factions ran deep, and conflict between them was especially sharp in Saratov. In contrast, Nizhnii Novgorod evinced little evidence of factionalization within the regional soviet. The small factions that did exist within the Tiumen' soviet had cross-cutting and fluid memberships. In interviews, deputies in the soviet noted that members of one lobby group were also members of another, and they freely attended meetings of different groups. Further, the factions seldom voted together and, to an outside observer, appeared to be little more than discussion groups.

As a result of the consensus in Nizhnii Novgorod and Tiumen' over political goals, achieving a quorum in the regional soviet was not as persistent a problem as in Yaroslavl' and Saratov. Deputies in Nizhnii Novgorod and Tiumen' attended meetings of the soviet because conflict was minimal and their time was not wasted on repeated argument. Further, consensus on political goals that stemmed from the concentration of the economy meant that the soviet spent less time on organizational matters in Nizhnii Novgorod than on policy issues. In contrast to the attitude of deputies in Nizhnii Novgorod, in Saratov, for example, deputies repeatedly expressed their disgust with soviet sessions and many preferred to spend their time in wage-paying jobs rather than attending meetings of the soviet.[37]

Finally, cooperation between political and economic interests facilitated the government's ability to gather sociological and economic data.

---

[37] This sentiment was expressed repeatedly in the author's interviews with deputies from the Saratov Oblast Soviet and was also noted by the First Deputy Chair of the Saratov Oblast Soviet, Viktor Ukhaniov, April 28, 1993.

Enterprises provided economic data—including industrial output, profits, and losses—trusting that the regional government would not use this information to tax the enterprise indiscriminately. Further, the more information the regional government had about economic and social hardships, the better it could respond by relieving enterprises of their heavy social welfare burdens.

In terms of policy output and implementation, Nizhnii Novgorod and Tiumen' were shown in chapter 4 to be far more proactive regarding regional economic development programs. Both oblasts had coherent and broad economic development plans that included extensive inter-regional (and foreign) trade initiatives and economic development policies. In Nizhnii Novgorod, this encompassed rapid privatization and defense conversion. This was also a result of the concentration of their regional economies and the resulting consensus over political goals. Concentration of the economy facilitated cooperative relations such that key organized economic interests participated in policy formation and used their authority to ensure the implementation of economic development programs. Further, educational policy (and other forms of social welfare policy) in both Nizhnii Novgorod and Tiumen' benefited from the incorporation of economic interests into policy output and implementation. Not only did educational reform begin to relieve overburdened enterprises from heavy financial responsibilities, it also served enterprises longer-term interests in training workers for a new social and economic environment.

In contrast, Yaroslavl' and particularly Saratov were unable to match Nizhnii Novgorod and Tiumen' in the scope of their policy output and the degree to which policy was implemented. This was a result of the conflict between competing economic interests regarding allocation and implementation priorities. Even if the different interests could agree objectively that economic development and educational policy were important to the oblast as a whole, no one appeared willing to play political entrepreneur or act collectively to achieve these goals. Thus conflict between competing interests continued, and assistance was distributed preferentially, thereby perpetuating conflict.

The clash of demands on these governments merely served to increase their policy loads and, as a result, they were able to accomplish little relative to Nizhnii Novgorod and Tiumen'. Some evidence of government overload in Saratov was the rapid dramatic increase in the size of government following Governor Belikh's appointment (within a year the bureaucratic apparatus on the executive side of government went from

1,082 people to 1,802). As Anthony King has argued in the British case, "If the demands are greater, the size of the machine needed to deal with them is likely to be greater. If the problems are more intractable, the machine needed to deal with them is likely to be more complex. Complexity added to scale yields further complexity."[38] This likely had a negative effect on government performance in Saratov.

Responsiveness, the third category of performance, was measured primarily by the degree of constituent satisfaction with the government. Again, across almost all these measures, Nizhnii Novgorod rated highest, Tiumen' second, Yaroslavl' third, and Saratov was a consistent laggard. This pattern can be explained by the concentration of the regional economy and the resulting cooperative relationships between economic and political actors in Nizhnii and Tiumen'. Given the smooth policy process and the regional government's ability both to produce and implement policies with the aid of organized economic interests, it is perhaps not surprising that constituent approval of government was high in Nizhnii and Tiumen'. But it is also noteworthy that part of the relationship between business and government involved business interests using their resources to promote government support within civil society more broadly. The Russian worker's continued dependence on the workplace, and the ongoing influence of enterprise directors over their workers, meant that the inclusion of the enterprise director in a cooperative arrangement with government promoted the support and approval of regional government actors among the enterprise's employees. Thus constituent approval of government should have been higher.

In contrast, in Yaroslavl' and Saratov, where economic power was relatively dispersed, conflict rather than consensus was the result. In the face of this relative immobilism, it is not surprising that constituent satisfaction with government in these two oblasts, and especially in Saratov, was low.

In regions with lower-performance governments, therefore, political and economic actors did not overcome crucial collective action dilemmas. As a result of the dispersion of economic power, political power was similarly dispersed. Different parts of government in these regions appealed to divergent and conflicting interests. Those interests that did not find their needs satisfied by regional government defected to the

[38] Anthony King, "Overload: Problems of Governing in the 1970s," *Political Studies* 23, nos. 2–3 (September 1975): 295. Information on the growth in government size in the other three provinces is incomplete, but it is safe to assert that increases, where they occurred, were far more modest.

political opposition, perpetuating further conflict.[39] Representative government for these disaffected groups meant excessively narrow representation. Those individuals whose narrow interests were served by regional government were not interested in maintaining broadly representative government. They received their particularized benefits from regional government in the absence of collective action. Unfortunately, this meant that overall regional government effectiveness and responsiveness were low.

CONCLUSION

This chapter traced the differences in regional government performance to collective action between economic and political interests that arose in regions where the assets, output, and labor force of the area were concentrated within a few enterprises and sectors. In addition, the embeddedness of elite interactions in a concentrated economic community heightened the interdependence of economic and political actors. This cooperation was further upheld by horizontal professional networks among political and economic actors. The consensus over political goals that resulted brought about relatively higher regional government performance.

[39] Jeffry Frieden makes a similar point in *Debt, Development, and Democracy: Modern Political Economy and Latin America* (Princeton, N.J.: Princeton University Press, 1991), p. 6.

Democracy and the Market at Risk?

SAMUEL HUNTINGTON argued that regardless of their shortcomings, the one thing communist governments could do was govern.[1] In the post-communist context, however, this study has demonstrated that there was considerable variation in the efficacy of the first successor governments. Although the pace of institution building is perhaps better measured in decades, clearly the reform of regional political institutions in 1990 fundamentally altered the political process in provincial Russia. The popular election of regional governments succeeded in changing regional leaders' political point of reference from Moscow to local constituencies throughout the Russian provinces. Yet despite the fact that institutional change was uniform at the oblast level, some regional governments proved better able to formulate and implement policies and were more successful in satisfying their constituents.

Not surprisingly, context played a decisive role in determining the relative capabilities of the new regional government institutions. What *is* perhaps surprising is that where Robert Putnam found that history and social context mattered most in the Italian provinces, against the background of rapid economic and political change in post-Soviet Russia, economic context proved to be the salient difference in explaining variations in regional government performance. In the Russian case, the more concentrated the regional economy, the higher was regional government performance.

In contrast to Western Europe and North America, the social legacy of Soviet communism is the absence of an ordered and organized Russian civil society. Coupled with simultaneous and massive economic and political change, the underdevelopment of civil society has meant that economic interests had the most potential to influence regional government performance. As chapters 2 and 6 argued, the lack of strong social and political institutions (especially political parties) capable of representing mass interests generally meant that societal interests were instead still represented largely through the workplace. As a result, the cooperation

---

[1] Samuel P. Huntington, *Political Order in Changing Societies* (New Haven, Conn.: Yale University Press, 1968), p. 1.

of powerful economic actors became crucial to the successful operation of new political institutions.

The residue of the old institutional framework, and the behavioral norms stemming from it, clearly influenced elite behavior and political outcomes in reformed institutions. Concentrated regional economies—described metaphorically as "company towns"—facilitated the organization and packaging of social demands and promoted collective action between organized economic interests and regional governments. The stability and consensus over political goals that resulted from the company town effect resulted in higher regional government performance.

ELITE CONSENSUS: EFFECTIVENESS AT THE EXPENSE OF RESPONSIVENESS?

At least two troubling normative implications arise from this theory. The immediate concerns of the conscientious reader undoubtedly are (1) the relationship between economic concentration and effective and responsive representative government; and (2) the tension between elite integration and the development of responsive democratic government.

First, the conclusion that economic concentration gave rise to consensual relationships between political and economic actors which in turn led to effective and responsive representative institutions is perhaps counter-intuitive and surprising to social science theorists of democracy and the market. The economic concentration aspect is counter-intuitive especially to Americans because their own economy is probably the most diverse in the world. This is a legitimate concern. It should be remembered, however, that the United States is, of course, at a very advanced stage of political and economic development compared to transitional Russia. The United States is full of diverse and divergent interests, but it also has a strong tradition of interest group formation and lobbying.

Russia, in contrast, has a weak civil society and virtually no tradition of interest group formation. Further, under the Soviet system, inter-enterprise contact was limited because control was vertically established through the domineering central ministries in Moscow. The collapse of this system of vertical integration therefore fostered the rise of the company town phenomenon in regions where economies were concentrated. Thus, although the atomization of Soviet society may have impeded spontaneous collective action at the level of civil society in the post-Soviet period, the Soviet system's effective establishment of "company towns" appears to have provided a natural impetus for collective action in some regions once the command economy collapsed.

Second, that collective action between political and business actors should lead to effective and responsive *representative* government is also perhaps counter-intuitive. Too much elite integration, while bringing higher levels of government efficiency and stability, may imperil government responsiveness. How much elite integration is permissible before a democratic government loses its capacity to respond to a more general constituency? In short, is elite integration a desirable equilibrium from the point of view of stable, effective, *and* responsive democratic government in the long term? Robert Dahl noted that "these questions demand nothing less than a complicated assessment of democracy itself."[2]

The comparative politics literature of the postwar period through the 1970s outlined the elitist-pluralist debate on this issue. Elite theorists and authors of work on consociational democracy pointed to the need for, at the very least, procedural consensus among elites.[3] Further, there is little controversy regarding the need for consensus to strengthen a government's stability and effectiveness. Indeed, "political elites in the stable pluralist democracies of the West typically display high levels of consensus on . . . 'codes of conduct.'" In addition, "commitments to the politics of bargaining and compromise, tolerance for political opponents, and a willingness to abide by parliamentary and electoral decisions are widely shared norms."[4]

This ethos of bargaining and norms of compromise render every successful democratic government in some sense consensual.[5] Indeed, theorists of corporatism and consociationalism have demonstrated that often consensus and accommodation between the state and social interests is of prime importance in enabling democratic governments to govern effectively—particularly in times of crisis as in post-Soviet Russia.[6]

---

[2] Robert A. Dahl, ed., *Political Opposition in Western Democracies* (New Haven, Conn.: Yale University Press, 1966), p. 387.

[3] For example, Arend Lijphart, *The Politics of Accommodation: Pluralism and Democracy in the Netherlands* (Berkeley: University of California Press, 1968); Hans Daalder, "On Building Consociational Nations: The Cases of The Netherlands and Switzerland," *International Social Science Journal* 23 (1971).

[4] Robert D. Putnam, *The Comparative Study of Political Elites* (Englewood Cliffs, N.J.: Prentice-Hall, 1976), p. 116.

[5] Ibid., p. 128.

[6] A classic example is Lijphart, *The Politics of Accommodation*.

Arguing against this, pluralists maintain that too much consensus and elite integration is a danger to democracy. Highly integrated elites are likely to be or become oligarchic.[7] This prohibits ordinary citizens from being addressed by and involved in the political system. As a result, democracy may only be able to survive if elites are heterogeneous. If pluralists are correct, then the consensual elite needed to maintain government efficiency and stability comes at the expense of responsiveness.

Dahl has posited that there may in fact be a trade-off between the seemingly contradictory goals of efficiency and stability versus responsiveness. Regimes may not be able to maximize both goals beyond some ideal point before an increase in one results in a decrease in the other.[8] Similarly, although arguing that "for a lasting democratic transition to occur, the . . . elite must be transformed from disunity to consensual unity,"[9] John Higley with Lowell Field also have argued that no government can be fully democratic and fully responsive.[10]

Certainly this study of Russian regional government is not arguing that higher-performance governments were fully democratic and fully responsive. None of the four oblasts examined here reached this standard, and it is probably fair to assert that few governments anywhere are likely to do so. Several important issues, however, may nuance the more extreme claims of the elitist-pluralist debate.

First, the debate does not take into account the importance of a regime's stage of political development. A regime in transition from authoritarianism or totalitarianism to a more democratic form of government may actually be responsive to citizens if it provides stability and effective government through some measure of elite integration. Undeniably, ten years of perestroika in Russia exacted a substantial toll on the average citizen's quality of life. The dramatic political and economic changes that have transpired over the past decade brought enormous social instability

---

[7] This is the argument in Robert Michels's *Political Parties: A Sociological Study of the Oligarchical Tendencies of Modern Democracy* (New York: Dover, 1959; orig. 1911). Michels's work is a study of oligarchical tendencies in an institution ostensibly committed to democratic goals—the German Social Democratic Party.

[8] Dahl, *Political Oppositions in Western Democracies*, p. 388.

[9] John Higley and Michael Burton, *Democratic Transitions and Democratic Breakdowns: The Elite Variable* (Texas Papers on Latin America: Working Papers of the Institute of Latin American Studies, University of Texas at Austin, paper 88–03, 1988), p. 9.

[10] Lowell Field and John Higley, "Elites and Non-Elites: The Possibilities and Their Side Effects" (Andover, Mass.: Warner Modular Publications, 1973), as cited in Putnam, *Elites*.

and unpredictability to daily life. For the first time in at least a generation, Russians were exposed to the possibility of unemployment and significant drops in living standards and buying power. Traditional career paths changed, and the future was generally uncertain.

As a result, consensual political and economic elites and the stability that this consensus brought in Russia were arguably a response to a desire among the citizenry for calm. Further, the absence of well-organized interest associations at the level of civil society meant that often citizen interests were represented by their employers—economic actors in the regional economy. Significantly, there was little evidence of conflict between capital and labor. Indeed, in work stoppages in the summer of 1993, labor and management voiced virtually identical demands to Moscow.[11] Thus, since 1990, societal interests were represented not only through their elected representatives in the regional government but also, in many cases, through the manager of their workplace.

In addition, given the volatility and instability of transitional Russia, the stability that cooperation between economic and political elites brought allowed governments to accomplish things. A record of achievement under the auspices of representative institutions may actually build popular support for democratic government in the future rather than leading to further disillusionment with the transition and the adoption of a more authoritarian system. Gabriel Almond and Sidney Verba noted in their study of democracy in five countries that "the development of stable political commitment may hinge upon the ability of the political system, especially in its formative stages, to produce output that satisfies the expectations of the members of the system. Only in this way can a stable and balanced commitment to the system be created and maintained."[12]

A second reason why the stage of political development is particularly important in informing the traditional elitist-pluralist debate concerns the establishment of institutions, rules, and behavioral norms. A transition from a nondemocratic to a democratic system requires that new

---

[11] Sheila Marnie, "Warning Strike at Defense Industrial Plants," *Radio Free Europe/Radio Liberty Daily Report*, July 30, 1993; and Iurii Konorov, "The Defense Sector Has Stopped Work," *Rossiiskaia gazeta*, September 17, 1993, reported in *Foreign Broadcast Information Service Daily Report*, September 22, 1993, pp. 19–20, as cited in Kimberly Marten Zisk, "The Foreign Policy Preferences of Russian Defense Industrialists: Integration or Isolation?" in Celeste A. Wallander, ed., *The Sources of Russian Conduct after the Cold War* (Boulder, Colo.: Westview, 1996), pp. 95–120.

[12] Gabriel Almond and Sidney Verba, *The Civic Culture: Political Attitudes and Democracy in Five Nations* (Newbury Park, Calif.: Sage, 1989), p. 372.

norms of behavior—rules—be established and new institutions formed. Rules, according to James March and Johan Olson, are:

> The routines, procedures, conventions, roles, strategies, organizational forms and technologies around which political activity is constructed. We also mean the beliefs, paradigms, codes, cultures, and knowledge that surround, support, elaborate and contradict those roles and routines. It is a commonplace observation in empirical social science that behavior is constrained or dictated by such cultural dicta and social norms. Action is more often based on identifying the normatively appropriate behavior than on calculating the return expected from alternative choices. *Routines are independent of the individual actors who execute them; [and] are capable of surviving considerable turnover in individuals.*[13]

In order for government to work effectively during a transitional period, there must be minimal agreement on the legitimacy of the new system. The development of norms of bargaining and negotiation are integral to the transition from communist authoritarianism—where this behavior was far more limited and closed—to a more pluralist and democratic form of government.[14] Elite cooperation in Russia's regions was achieved through a process of negotiation and bargaining. Further, continued collective action can establish and strengthen pervasive norms of reciprocity and trust that are integral to the functioning of democratic regimes. These behavioral norms also constitute a crucial variable in a transitional political period—a fundamental understanding of the new rules of the game.

Elite cooperation observed at this stage, then, actually may be positive

---

[13] James G. March and Johan P. Olson, *Rediscovering Institutions: The Organizational Basis of Politics*, (New York: Free Press, 1989), p. 22; emphasis added.

[14] The sovietological literature of the 1970s and early 1980s argued that there was evidence of what Jerry Hough termed *institutional pluralism* within the Soviet bureaucracy, but this behavior was limited to the bureaucratic level alone (Jerry F. Hough, "The Soviet System: Petrification or Pluralism?" in Jerry F. Hough, *The Soviet Union and Social Science Theory* [Cambridge, Mass.: Harvard University Press, 1977], pp. 19–48). An attempt to apply group theory to Soviet politics was also made in Gordon Skilling and Franklyn Griffiths, eds., *Interest Groups in Soviet Politics* (Princeton, N.J.: Princeton University Press, 1971). This was followed by an influx of work on interest group activity in the Soviet system (including Hough, above). Skilling then published a rejoinder article noting that he had not intended to suggest in the edited volume that the Soviet system was in any way truly pluralist (see Gordon Skilling, "Interest Groups and Communist Politics Revisited," *World Politics* 36, no. 1 (1983): 1–27.

not only for institutional performance but also for the growth of democracy. Conflict could and did occur, but it was not irresolvable because of the establishment and acceptance of the rules by which the political game was played. It was exactly this that made the behavior of economic and political elites in "company towns" predictable. In turn, it was this predictability that was absent in the lowest-performing governments.

A third and related point regarding the influence of elite cooperation on civil society and responsiveness concerns the accumulation of social capital. In his comprehensive study of Italian regional government performance, Robert Putnam concludes that social capital, although not easy to build, "is the key to making democracy work."[15] In chapter 5, this study of Russian provincial government systematically tested for social-structural and cultural variations between provinces that might indicate the influence of an accumulation of social capital. Few differences, however, appeared among the four regions.

If the positive influence of social capital is limited to the societal level, then Putnam's is a discouraging prediction for the future functioning of democracy in post-Soviet Russia. If, however, social capital is not conceptually restricted to the societal level, then we may have reason to believe that it was accumulating at the *elite level* in regions where regional government performance was higher.[16] The horizontal networks of communication, and the chains of obligation necessary for the accumulation of social capital that Putnam observed at the societal level in Italy, appeared among political and economic elites in the higher-performance regions of provincial Russia. Just as Putnam argued that this behavior at the societal level positively influenced government performance (and elite behavior), it is possible in Russia that the reverse might eventually be true—that social capital among elites may precipitate the accumulation of social capital among society more generally in Russia's future.

One preliminary indicator of this may be the number of voluntary or-

[15] Robert Putnam, *Making Democracy Work: Civic Traditions in Modern Italy* (Princeton, N.J.: Princeton University Press, 1993), p. 185.

[16] Indeed Putnam, in *Making Democracy Work*, does not indicate that social capital is applicable only to civil society. Significantly, other analysts of social capital also do not specifically limit its accumulation to the societal level. See, for example, James S. Coleman, *Foundations of Social Theory* (Cambridge, Mass.: Belknap Press of Harvard University Press, 1990), esp. pp. 302–9; and Elinor Ostrom "Constituting Social Capital and Collective Action," Indiana University Workshop in Political Theory and Policy Analysis, 1993, pp. 1–2.

ganizations to which respondents in Nizhnii Novgorod and Tiumen' belonged relative to Saratov and Yaroslavl' (reported in chapter 5). Although the density of associational membership was higher in the two higher-performance regions, the reader will recall that societal-level trust was universally low across regions. If social capital was accumulating among elites in Nizhnii Novgorod and Tiumen' and this had some influence on social structures and behavior in civil society, we would expect to see a greater number of voluntary organizations in the higher-performance cases (as we did), as well as a possible increase in the levels of interpersonal trust in future analyses. A longer observation time, however, would be required to enable a proper assessment of this hypothesis.

Regrettably, it is also possible that in the long term and in the absence of mediating factors (as, for example, the accumulation of social capital and norms of reciprocity and trust at the level of civil society), the effect of extended business-government cooperation on the growth of democracy and the market will be negative. It may freeze state-nonstate relationships, precluding the inclusion of new economic and societal interests in government and therefore limiting government responsiveness while perhaps maintaining only some of its effectiveness. As a result, government performance would decline over the long term.

Economically, excessive business-government cooperation in transitional Russia may encourage support for what are often gigantic and inefficient enterprises where their fate may have been better decided by market forces. *The lesson of this study, then, may well be that not all good things go together.* Higher regional government performance during the First Russian Republic may not necessarily mean higher regional government performance in the future.

Regional governments and observers of Russia should not give up hope, however. Aside from the possibility of the accumulation of social capital, certain mitigating factors may help provincial governments in Russia overcome the possibility of a slide toward oligarchy and further economic inefficiency.

From an economic point of view, however, one important factor in discouraging continued support for inefficient industries may be the importance of international trade to some regions' economies. An international trade orientation might encourage an acceptance of market principles. This may in turn convince the directors of inefficient enterprises of the need to strive to produce higher-quality, competitive goods and may encourage further integration into the world economic system and mar-

TABLE 7.1

Export Structure of Products from Regional Enterprises and Organizations

	Nizhnii Novgorod	Tiumen'	Yaroslavl'	Saratov
Total Exports 1990 (millions of rubles in 1990 rubles)	591	4,807	242	317
Total Exports 1989 (millions of rubles in 1989 rubles)	554	5,627	304	303
Total Exports 1988 (millions of rubles in 1988 rubles)	905	4,704	299	296

Source: Data drawn from *Vneshneekonomicheskie sviazi RSFSR* (Moskva: Goskomstat Respublikanskii informatsionno-izdatel'skii tsentr, 1991).

ketization. Kimberly Zisk has made a similar argument in explaining the trade policy preferences of some defense enterprise directors.[17]

The key variable here is the proportion of the regional economy that was devoted to foreign trade under the Soviet system. Table 7.1 demonstrates that in both Nizhnii Novgorod and Tiumen', for example, in comparison with Yaroslavl' and Saratov, high proportions of the regional economy were devoted to exports. In the case of Tiumen' these were primarily raw materials, and in Nizhnii Novgorod they were largely high-tech defense goods and some consumer goods. The bulk of these exports would have gone to Eastern Europe through central authorities in Moscow. But with the collapse of the Soviet Union and the disintegration of old trade ties, economic and political actors in these regions would likely be anxious to become integrated into the world economy—trade or perish. This inclination may in turn explain favorable orientations toward Western investment and market reform now and in the future.

Politically, competitive elections at the local level will continue to pressure ambitious regional government actors seeking reelection to be responsive to voter concerns. As noted by Gabriel Almond and Sidney Verba:

[17] Zisk, "The Foreign Policy Preferences of Russian Defense Industrialists."

An electoral system, designed to turn power over to a particular elite for a limited period of time, can achieve a balance between power [i.e., the ability to take decisions] and responsiveness: the elites obtain power, yet this power is limited by the periodic elections themselves, by the concern for future elections during the interelection period, and by a variety of other formal and informal checks.[18]

In short, regular competitive elections render political actors directly accountable to their electorate. In addition, if civil society is gradually resurrected, the development of political parties in Russia will promote the further systematization of voter choice between elites and will enhance accountability.

All this, however, still leaves the problem of those regional governments that operate in the context of dispersed economies and no strong international trade orientation. What can regional governments in these situations do to improve their performance? This study suggests that somehow these governments need to take measures to impose an organization on the demands placed upon them. Governments that can create an environment of political organization and inclusion (regardless of the degree to which their economies are concentrated) of major economic and societal interests are more likely to be effective and responsive governments in the future.

The difficulty is, of course, that governments operating within the context of a dispersed economy face dilemmas of collective action. This problem suggests a foreign policy implication for Western governments bent on assisting Russia in its transition to democracy. Western countries that have rational foreign policy interests in encouraging democratization and marketization in Russia should act as political entrepreneurs in assisting in the development of organized interest groups (including, for example, chambers of commerce) throughout Russia.

LESSONS FROM THE RUSSIAN EXPERIENCE

This study traced the effects of formal institutional change on political behavior. The reform of regional government institutions, beginning with their popular election in 1990, did in fact change political behavior in the Russian provinces, although not uniformly.

---

[18] Almond and Verba, *The Civic Culture*, p. 342.

In chapter 1, I began by asking why, even in the face of identical institutional reform, some newly elected oblast-level governments performed better in their first few years of operation than others. Chapter 2 previewed the central argument of this book—that civil society in the post-Soviet context is poorly organized and that coterminous political and economic change made economic actors particularly important to the functioning of regional governments. Chapter 2 also stressed that the behavior established by the former institutional framework influenced individual and collective outcomes in the new institutional context.

Chapter 3 discussed the nature of the regional government reform and described the first popular elections of regional governments in 1990. Chapter 4 then provided a systematic test of regional government performance that revealed significant variation among the four provincial governments examined in this study.

Chapters 5 and 6 tested hypotheses that might explain these variations. Chapter 5 searched the comparative politics literature for plausible explanations of these performance differences, but they proved to be unsatisfactory. There was generally little variation among regions on the variables identified by the comparative politics literature, and, where variation did occur, it did not fit the performance pattern established in chapter 4.

Chapter 6 therefore empirically tested the theory introduced in chapter 2. The conclusion that the more highly concentrated the regional economy, the more political and economic elites acted collectively and the higher was regional government performance was based on newly available evidence from four of fifty-five regions (oblast- and krai-level governments) of Russia. The robustness of this analysis depends on the degree to which the theory is generalizable to other provinces in post-Soviet Russia. From an examination of Nizhnii Novgorod, Tiumen', Yaroslavl', and Saratov, this study should facilitate generalizations applicable to politics in all fifty-five oblast-level governments in the Russian Federation. We should expect to see collective action, consensus, and higher regional government performance (at least in the short term) in oblasts with highly concentrated regional economies.

Further, this analysis of regional government performance has a general practical application. If the findings here are correct, this study has uncovered a political-economic dynamic of "good" or at least "better" government in the regions of post-Soviet Russia. For Western decision makers and potential investors, locating regions in Russia where regional economic and political actors work together constructively is helpful in that these regions may provide a more stable investment environment for foreign financial and intellectual capital.

For regional government actors, the primary lesson of this study points to the need for negotiated compromise in keeping government running well—especially during the early stages of an economic and political transition. This can be more easily facilitated by the formation of formalized societal and economic interest groups.

Finally, these findings resonate well with the comparative politics literature on business-government relations and interest intermediation which demonstrates the interdependence between economic and political actors—especially in times of crisis. However, the argument presented here specifically uses the language of collective action to capture the give-and-take of politics which is often overlooked in corporatist and elite pacting analyses. Further, this study bridges earlier corporatist analysis and the more recent political economy literature that focuses on how economic factor endowments can structure politics.

In the end, however, the conclusions here provide a potentially unsettling prediction for the future of Russian democracy. If cooperative business-government relationships persist in the very long term, there is a risk that democratic responsiveness will be sacrificed in the interest of stability and government effectiveness. Although systematic exploration of this conclusion is beyond the scope of this study, it is possible that the careful balance between democratic responsiveness and government stability and effectiveness may be jeopardized should political parties, after several more electoral cycles at both the local and national levels, continue to be relatively powerless as entities representing collective interests, and if new economic interests (that are not descendants of Soviet industry) are prevented from joining actively in the political process. The "local heroes" of today, therefore, must take care to ensure that they do not become impediments to higher regional government performance and democratic governance in the future.

Regional Government Structures

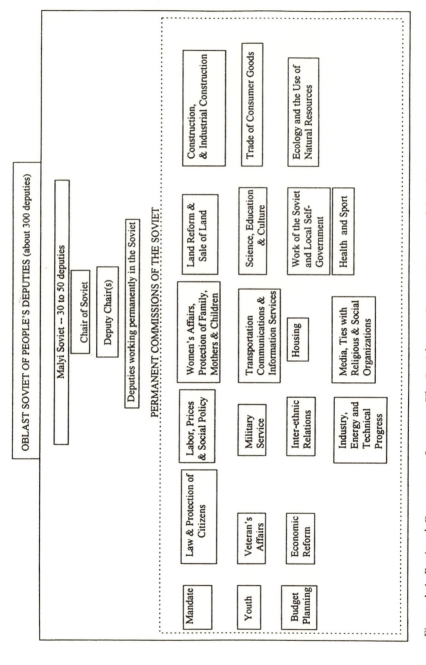

OBLAST SOVIET OF PEOPLE'S DEPUTIES (about 300 deputies)

Malyi Soviet -- 30 to 50 deputies

Chair of Soviet

Deputy Chair(s)

Deputies working permanently in the Soviet

PERMANENT COMMISSIONS OF THE SOVIET

Mandate	Law & Protection of Citizens	Labor, Prices & Social Policy	Women's Affairs, Protection of Family, Mothers & Children	Land Reform & Sale of Land	Construction, & Industrial Construction
Youth	Veteran's Affairs	Military Service	Transportation Communications & Information Services	Science, Education & Culture	Trade of Consumer Goods
Budget Planning	Economic Reform	Inter-ethnic Relations	Housing	Work of the Soviet and Local Self-Government	Ecology and the Use of Natural Resources
		Industry, Energy and Technical Progress	Media, Ties with Religious & Social Organizations	Health and Sport	

Figure A.1. Regional Government Structure: The Legislature. *Source:* Diagram of the oblast soviet provided by the Saratov oblast soviet.

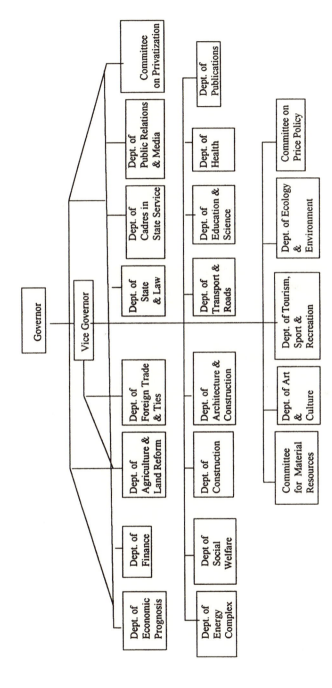

Figure A.2. Regional Government Structure: The Executive. *Source:* Diagram of the oblast administration provided by the Nizhnii Novgorod oblast administration.

207

Cross-Tabulations of Constituent Satisfaction with Regional Government by Urban and Rural Dwellers and by Levels of Education

As noted in chapter 4, footnote 66, this appendix displays cross-tabulations of respondents in rural and urban settings and those with high and low educational levels in each of the four oblasts. The evidence here demonstrates that urbanites were generally more satisfied with government performance than ruralites and the better educated were more satisfied than the poorly educated. However, levels of satisfaction among urban and rural dwellers varied across oblasts. Urbanites in regions that scored high on the "objective" measures of performance were more satisfied with government than were urbanites in regions with objectively lower-performance governments. Similarly, the well educated in high-performance cases were happier with government performance than the well educated in lower-performance cases. What mattered, then, regarding levels of constituent satisfaction, was in which oblast respondents lived and not their level of education or whether they were city or country dwellers.

TABLE B.1

Approval of Leadership by Urban versus Rural Dwellers: "How satisfied are you with the activities of the leadership of this oblast?"

	Satisfied (%)		Dissatisfied (%)	
	Urban	Rural	Urban	Rural
Nizhnii Novgorod	47.6	48.1	52.4	51.7
Tiumen'	34.1	19.4	66.1	80.6
Yaroslavl'	31.9	43.8	68.1	56.2
Saratov	12.0	19.0	88.0	81.0

TABLE B.2

Alienation from Leadership by Urban versus Rural Dwellers: "In this oblast, political leaders are so distant from regular people that they do not understand what people want."

	Alienated (agree) (%)		Not Alienated (disagree) (%)	
	Urban	Rural	Urban	Rural
Nizhnii Novgorod	61.3	78.0	38.7	21.9
Tiumen'	88.8	76.8	23.1	23.1
Yaroslavl'	81.9	85.3	18.07	14.7
Saratov	84.1	77.8	15.9	22.2

TABLE B.3

Urban versus Rural Satisfaction with Regional Government across Eight Policy Areas:
How satisfied are you with the way the leadership of this oblast is resolving the following
problems? (%)

	Nizhnii		Tiumen'		Yaroslavl'		Saratov	
	Urban	Rural	Urban	Rural	Urban	Rural	Urban	Rural
Housing								
Dissatisfied (1–4)	64.7	49.8	62.3	65.9	67.2	57.4	84.8	86.6
Satisfied (6–9)	18.6	21.1	18.0	12.9	16.7	11.5	4.2	6.1
Neither Dissatisfied								
nor Satisfied (5)	16.7	29.1	19.7	21.1	16.1	31.1	11.0	7.3
Transport								
Dissatisfied	57.0	34.1	49.9	60.7	56.6	56.5	66.6	67.5
Satisfied	18.7	28.2	28.3	15.9	16.2	16.4	10.1	12.5
Neither Dissatisfied								
nor Satisfied	24.2	37.8	21.8	23.4	27.2	27.1	23.3	20.0
Unemployment								
Dissatisfied	43.6	35.7	34.0	52.4	52.5	51.8	59.1	63.4
Satisfied	26.9	22.1	32.8	20.0	14.8	10.9	12.8	15.5
Neither Dissatisfied								
nor Satisfied	29.5	42.1	33.2	27.6	32.7	37.3	28.1	21.1
Wages								
Dissatisfied	70.7	71.0	60.7	68.3	76.3	82.8	80.8	85.6
Satisfied	14.1	11.6	14.3	10.4	8.7	4.5	5.0	5.4
Neither Dissatisfied								
nor Satisfied	15.2	17.3	25.0	21.3	15.0	12.7	14.2	9.0
Prices								
Dissatisfied	76.8	79.3	69.8	82.0	83.3	84.1	90.0	88.8
Satisfied	12.4	8.9	12.2	8.3	7.8	4.3	2.4	4.5
Neither Dissatisfied								
nor Satisfied	10.8	11.8	18.0	9.7	8.9	11.6	7.6	6.7
Provision of Food Products								
Dissatisfied	44.4	49.7	57.2	68.5	48.0	56.0	73.1	71.3
Satisfied	29.1	18.3	16.6	13.0	22.7	11.0	10.9	13.8
Neither Dissatisfied								
nor Satisfied	26.5	32.0	26.2	18.5	29.3	33.0	16.0	14.9

(continued)

TABLE B.3 (*Continued*)

	Nizhnii		Tiumen'		Yaroslavl'		Saratov	
	Urban	Rural	Urban	Rural	Urban	Rural	Urban	Rural
Industrial Stagnation								
Dissatisfied	51.9	48.4	60.5	70.6	65.4	63.8	77.4	69.9
Satisfied	18.9	10.5	13.2	8.3	10.1	6.2	5.2	13.0
Neither Dissatisfied								
nor Satisfied	29.2	41.1	26.3	21.1	24.5	30.0	17.4	17.1
Environment								
Dissatisfied	72.6	56.4	71.0	71.1	67.7	63.8	73.2	70.2
Satisfied	15.1	15.3	12.5	11.0	13.8	11.0	11.8	18.0
Neither Dissatisfied								
nor Satisfied	12.2	28.4	16.5	17.9	18.5	25.2	15.0	11.8

TABLE B.4

Satisfaction with Pace of Economic Reform by Urban versus Rural Dwellers:
"Do you think that economic reform in this oblast is going too quickly,
too slowly, or at the correct tempo?

	Satisfied (at the Right Pace) (%)		Dissatisfied (Too Quickly or Too Slowly) (%)	
	Urban	Rural	Urban	Rural
Nizhnii Novgorod	43.0	39.8	57.0	58.1
Tiumen'	35.2	22.6	64.8	77.4
Yaroslavl'	24.5	14.0	75.5	86.0
Saratov	14.4	14.9	85.6	85.1

TABLE B.5

Satisfaction with Governor and Oblast Soviet by Urban versus Rural Dwellers:
"Do you believe that the following political actors and organizations are
capable of solving the concrete problems of your region?"

	Satisfied (Yes) (%)		Dissatisfied (No) (%)	
	Urban	Rural	Urban	Rural
Governor				
Nizhnii Novgorod	81.2	75.7	19.0	24.3
Tiumen'	64.1	61.8	35.9	38.2
Yaroslavl'	72.0	75.4	28.0	24.6
Saratov	58.0	60.2	42.0	39.8
Soviet				
Nizhnii Novgorod	67.6	64.3	32.2	35.7
Tiumen'	48.6	50.8	51.4	36.5
Yaroslavl'	67.4	69.0	32.6	31.0
Saratov	44.0	47.3	56.0	52.7

TABLE B.6

Approval of Oblast Leadership by Level of Education: "How satisfied are you
with the activities of the leadership of this oblast?" (%)

	Nizhnii Novgorod	Tiumen'	Yaroslavl'	Saratov
Satisfied				
Unfinished High School/Primary School	44.3	35.3	39.1	18.2
High School	47.0	29.1	30.3	13.5
Higher/Unfinished Higher	53.0	34.5	41.0	12.3
Dissatisfied				
Unfinished High School/Primary School	55.7	64.7	60.8	81.8
High School	53.0	69.1	69.7	86.5
Higher/Unfinished Higher	47.0	53.0	59.0	87.7

TABLE B.7

Alienation from Oblast Leadership by Level of Education: "In this oblast, political leaders are so distant from regular people that they do not understand what people want." (%)

	Nizhnii Novgorod	Tiumen'	Yaroslavl'	Saratov
Alienated (Agree)				
Unfinished High School/Primary School	80.3	76.4	89.5	84.5
High School	67.0	81.0	83.2	80.8
Higher/Unfinished Higher	49.1	70.8	73.7	81.5
Not Alienated (Disagree)				
Unfinished High School/Primary School	19.7	23.6	10.5	15.5
High School	33.9	19.0	16.8	19.2
Higher/Unfinished Higher	50.9	29.2	26.3	18.5

213

Table B.8a

Satisfaction with Oblast Government across Eight Policy Areas by Level of Education in Nizhnii Novgorod and Tiumen': "How satisfied are you with the way the leadership of this oblast is resolving the following problems?" (%)

	Nizhnii Novgorod			Tiumen'		
	Primary/ Unfinished High School	High School	Postsecondary/ Unfinished Postsecondary	Primary/ Unfinished High School	High School	Postsecondary/ Unfinished Postsecondary
Housing						
Dissatisfied (1–4)	61.2	61.6	59.1	60.3	62.9	62.9
Satisfied (6–9)	22.0	19.0	17.6	23.5	15.8	17.8
Neither Dissatisfied nor Satisfied (5)	16.8	19.4	23.3	16.2	21.3	19.3
Transport						
Dissatisfied	52.2	49.7	53.4	55.9	52.2	49.5
Satisfied	22.5	20.5	22.8	20.5	25.9	27.5
Neither Dissatisfied nor Satisfied	25.4	29.8	23.8	23.5	22.0	23.1
Unemployment						
Dissatisfied	47.9	41.5	35.0	46.9	36.7	35.4
Satisfied	25.0	24.1	30.1	30.4	29.1	32.9
Neither Dissatisfied nor Satisfied	27.1	34.4	34.9	22.7	34.2	31.7

Wages						
Dissatisfied	54.1	65.7	67.7	64.8	71.9	74.6
Satisfied	17.4	11.7	11.7	13.8	13.2	13.2
Neither Dissatisfied nor Satisfied	28.5	22.6	20.6	21.4	14.9	12.2
Prices						
Dissatisfied	69.6	70.6	86.5	70.8	79.1	79.7
Satisfied	13.6	11.0	9.0	11.6	13.2	9.7
Neither Dissatisfied nor Satisfied	16.8	18.4	4.5	17.6	8.7	10.6
Provision of Food Products						
Dissatisfied	60.4	56.9	67.1	40.6	46.9	47.2
Satisfied	15.9	17.7	7.5	28.9	25.6	26.4
Neither Dissatisfied nor Satisfied	23.7	25.4	25.4	30.5	27.5	26.4
Industrial Stagnation						
Dissatisfied	64.4	59.0	73.2	50.0	52.8	47.0
Satisfied	13.9	12.0	9.0	19.1	15.6	18.4
Neither Dissatisfied nor Satisfied	21.7	29.0	17.8	30.8	31.5	34.6
Environment						
Dissatisfied	72.6	70.8	62.2	70.0	70.5	60.5
Satisfied	12.2	11.6	16.6	15.0	13.9	19.0
Neither Dissatisfied nor Satisfied	15.2	17.6	21.2	15.0	15.6	20.5

Table B.8b

Satisfaction with Oblast Government across Eight Policy Areas by Level of Education in Yaroslavl' and Saratov (%)

	Yaroslavl'			Saratov		
	Primary/ Unfinished High School	High School	Higher/ Unfinished Higher	Primary/ Unfinished High School	High School	Higher/ Unfinished Higher
Housing						
Dissatisfied	54.9	69.6	63.5	88.0	85.0	84.0
Satisfied	17.9	14.1	15.5	4.9	5.6	3.3
Neither Dissatisfied nor Satisfied	27.2	16.3	21.0	7.1	9.4	12.7
Transport						
Dissatisfied	53.6	58.1	56.2	70.0	64.2	70.6
Satisfied	15.8	14.2	20.3	11.6	11.1	9.3
Neither Dissatisfied nor Satisfied	30.6	27.7	23.5	18.4	24.7	20.1
Unemployment						
Dissatisfied	58.3	52.1	45.8	66.8	61.5	53.3
Satisfied	8.0	14.2	19.8	10.8	14.2	15.0
Neither Dissatisfied nor Satisfied	33.7	33.7	34.4	22.4	24.3	31.7

Wages						
Dissatisfied	82.9	78.7	69.1	87.6	83.9	74.9
Satisfied	6.8	6.8	11.2	3.0	5.2	6.6
Neither Dissatisfied nor Satisfied	10.3	14.5	19.7	9.4	10.9	18.5
Prices						
Dissatisfied	91.9	71.0	71.0	91.5	91.0	84.4
Satisfied	4.5	6.8	9.7	3.5	2.6	4.1
Neither Dissatisfied nor Satisfied	3.6	19.3	19.3	5.0	6.4	11.5
Provision of Food Products						
Dissatisfied	51.8	50.9	45.1	77.8	73.0	67.3
Satisfied	12.6	22.0	22.4	9.3	11.5	14.5
Neither Dissatisfied nor Satisfied	35.6	27.3	32.5	12.9	15.4	18.2
Industrial Stagnation						
Dissatisfied	70.4	65.5	57.3	76.7	74.7	73.3
Satisfied	5.8	9.9	10.8	5.1	9.6	7.2
Neither Dissatisfied nor Satisfied	23.8	24.6	31.9	18.2	15.7	19.5
Environment						
Dissatisfied	59.2	69.1	70.5	69.6	69.1	80.5
Satisfied	13.5	13.3	11.2	15.2	15.9	9.1
Neither Dissatisfied nor Satisfied	27.3	17.6	18.3	15.2	14.9	10.3

TABLE B.9
Satisfaction with the Pace of Economic Reform by Level of Education:
"Do you think that economic reform in this oblast is going too quickly,
too slowly, or at the correct tempo?" (%)

	Nizhnii Novgorod	Tiumen'	Yaroslavl'	Saratov
Satisfied (at the Right Pace)				
Unfinished High School/Primary School	33.6	25.6	20.7	13.0
High School	43.0	32.0	22.0	15.7
Higher/Unfinished Higher	48.2	34.8	24.5	13.6
Dissatisfied (Too Quickly or Too Slowly)				
Unfinished High School/Primary School	66.4	74.4	79.3	87.0
High School	57.0	68.0	78.0	84.3
Higher/Unfinished Higher	51.8	65.1	75.5	86.4

TABLE B.10
Satisfaction with Governor by Level of Education: "Do you believe that
the following political actors and organizations are capable of solving
the concrete problems of your region?" (%)

	Nizhnii Novgorod	Tiumen'	Yaroslavl'	Saratov
Satisfied (Yes)				
Unfinished High School/Primary School	76.3	53.5	70.5	58.0
High School	80.1	61.2	72.0	56.7
Higher/Unfinished Higher	82.1	70.2	79.0	64.4
Dissatisfied (No)				
Unfinished High School/Primary School	23.7	46.5	29.5	42.0
High School	19.9	38.8	28.0	43.3
Higher/Unfinished Higher	17.9	29.8	21.0	35.6

TABLE B.11

Satisfaction with the Oblast Soviet by Level of Education: "Do you believe that the following political actors and organizations are capable of solving the concrete problems of your region?" (%)

	Nizhnii Novgorod	Tiumen'	Yaroslavl'	Saratov
Satisfied (Yes)				
Unfinished High School/Primary School	69.6	51.9	63.5	47.0
High School	64.2	49.2	68.8	43.0
Higher/Unfinished Higher	70.9	54.7	69.1	48.2
Dissatisfied (No)				
Unfinished High School/Primary School	30.4	48.1	36.5	53.0
High School	35.8	50.8	31.2	57.0
Higher/Unfinished Higher	29.1	45.3	30.9	51.8

* Bibliography *

CDPSP   *Current Digest of the Post-Soviet Press*
CDSP   *Current Digest of the Soviet Press*
FBIS   *Foreign Broadcast Information Services*
RFE/RL   *Radio Free Europe/Radio Liberty Reports*
RSFSR   Russian Socialist Federated Soviet Republic

Abdulatipov, Ramazan Gadzhimuradovich (chairman of the Council of Nationalities of the Supreme Soviet of Russia). "Kuda nesiesh'sia, Rus'? Ne daet otveta." *Pravda*, 19 February 1992.

Aliushin, Aleksei. "Constitutional Reform, Goals, Tasks, Problems." *Rossiiskaia gazeta*, 2 March 1992.

Almond, Gabriel A., and G. B. Powell. *Comparative Politics: A Developmental Approach*. Boston: Little, Brown, 1966.

Almond, Gabriel A., and Sidney Verba. *The Civic Culture: Political Attitudes and Democracy in Five Nations*. Princeton, N.J.: Princeton University Press, 1963. Reprint: Newbury Park, Calif.: Sage, 1989.

Amsden, Alice. *Asia's Next Giant: South Korea and Late Industrialization*. New York: Oxford University Press, 1989.

Andrews, Josephine, and Kathryn Stoner-Weiss. "Regionalism and Reform: Evidence from the Russian Provinces." *Post-Soviet Affairs* 11, no. 4 (October–December 1995): 384–406.

Andrle, Vladimir. *Managerial Power in the Soviet Union*. Lexington, Mass.: Lexington Books, 1976.

Antonchenko, Valentina (head of Department of Education, Saratov Oblast Administration). Interview with the author, Saratov, 20 April 1993.

Aristotle. *The Politics*. Edited and translated by Edward Barker. New York: Oxford University Press, 1981.

Aspaturian, Vernon. "The Theory and Practice of Soviet Federalism." *Journal of Politics* 12, no. 1 (1950): 20–51.

Atkinson, Michael, and William D. Coleman. "Strong States and Weak States: Sectoral Policy Networks in Advanced Capitalist Economies." *British Journal of Political Science* 19 (1989): 47–67.

Axelrod, Robert. *The Evolution of Cooperation*. New York: Basic Books, 1984.

Bahry, Donna. *Outside Moscow*. New York: Columbia University Press, 1987.

Bakaev, Vladimir (first deputy chair of the Yaroslavl' city soviet). Interview with the author, Yaroslavl', 13 April 1993.

Banfield, Edward. *The Moral Basis of a Backward Society*. Chicago: The Free Press, 1958.

Barabashev, Georgii (Faculty of Law, Moscow State University). Interview with the author, Moscow, 19 March 1992.

Bates, Robert H., "Contra Contractarianism: Some Reflections on the New Institutionalism." *Politics and Society* 16, nos. 2–3 (1988): 387–401.

Beer, Samuel H. In "Federalism and the National Idea: The Uses of Diversity." *Harvard Graduate Society Newsletter*, Harvard University, Cambridge, Mass., Fall 1991.

Beer, Samuel H. *To Make a Nation: The Rediscovery of American Federalism.* Cambridge, Mass.: Harvard University Press, Belknap Press, 1993.

Beldor, Lev (Foreign Economic Ties and Trade Department, Nizhnii Novgorod oblast administration). Interview with the author, Nizhnii Novgorod, 5 January 1993.

Berliner, Joseph. *Factory and Manager in the USSR.* Cambridge, Mass.: Harvard University Press, 1957.

Bialer, Seweryn. "The Changing Soviet Political System: The 19th Party Conference and After." In Seweryn Bialer, ed., *Politics, Society, and Nationality inside Gorbachev's Russia*, 193–241. Boulder, Colo.: Westview, 1989.

Biddulph, Howard. "Local Interest Articulation at CPSU Congresses." *World Politics* 36, no. 1 (1983): 28–52.

Biulleten' Nizhegorodskogo oblastnogo soveta narodnykh deputatov. Nizhnii Novgorod: Nizhegorodskaia oblastnaia tipografiia, February–December 1992.

Biulleten' of the Central Election Commission of the Russian Federation. Issue 12, March 1994.

Blalock, Hubert M., Jr. *Conceptualization in the Social Sciences.* Beverly Hills, Calif.: Sage, 1982.

Borisov, Vladimir (deputy in Yaroslavl' Oblast Soviet). Interview with the author, Yaroslavl', 14 April 1993.

Brevnov, Boris (chairman of the Nizhegorodskii bankerskii dom). Interview with the author, Nizhnii Novgorod, 22 November 1992.

Bunce, Valerie, and John Echolls. "Soviet Politics in the Brezhnev Era: Pluralism or Corporatism?" In Donald R. Kelley, ed., *Soviet Politics in the Brezhnev Era*, 1–26. New York: Viking, 1980.

CDPSP 4, no. 9 (1992).

Chotiner, Barbara. *Dismantling an Innovation: The 1964 Decision Reunifying Industrial and Agricultural Organs of the CPSU.* Pittsburgh, Pa.: Center for Russian and East European Studies, 1985.

———. *Khrushchev's Party Reform: Coalition Building and Institutional Innovation.* Westport, Conn.: Greenwood, 1984.

Coleman, James S. *Foundations of Social Theory.* Cambridge, Mass.: Harvard University Press, Belknap Press, 1990.

Colton, Timothy. *Moscow: Governing the Socialist Metropolis.* Cambridge, Mass.: Harvard University Press, Belknap Press, 1995.

———. "The Politics of Democratization: The Moscow Election of 1990." *Soviet Economy* 6, no. 4 (October–December 1990): 285–344.

Daalder, Hans. "On Building Consociational Nations: The Cases of the Netherlands and Switzerland." *International Social Science Journal* 23, no. 3 (1971): 355–70.

Dahl, Robert A. *Democracy and Its Critics.* New Haven, Conn.: Yale University Press, 1989.

———. "The Evaluation of Political Systems." In Ithiel de Sola Pool, ed., *Contemporary Political Science: Toward Empirical Theory*, 166–181. New York: McGraw-Hill, 1967.

———. *Polyarchy: Participation and Opposition.* New Haven, Conn.: Yale University Press, 1971.

———. *A Preface to Democratic Theory.* Chicago: University of Chicago Press, 1956.

———, ed. *Political Opposition in Western Democracies.* New Haven, Conn.: Yale University Press, 1966.

Deev, Nikolai (chief researcher, Institute of State and Law, Russian Federation Academy of Sciences). Interview with the author, Moscow, 20 February 1992.

Eckstein, Harry. "The Evaluation of Political Performance: Problems and Dimensions." *Sage Professional Papers in Comparative Politics* 2, no. 1–17. Beverly Hills, Calif.: Sage, 1971.

Ekonomika i politika v Rossii: Nizhegorodskii prolog. Epitsentr: Nizhnii Novgorod, June–September 1992.

Ershov, Vladimir. *Ia vizhu tsel': Zapiski deputata.* GIPP Nizhpoligraf: Nizhnii Novgorod, 1992.

Evans, Peter. *Embedded Autonomy: States and Industrial Transformation.* Princeton, N.J.: Princeton University Press, 1995.

Fainsod, Merle. *Smolensk under Soviet Rule.* Boston: Unwin Hyman, 1958. Reprint, 1989.

FBIS, 12 August 1991.

FBIS, 4 November 1993.

Field, G. Lowell, and John Higley. *Elitism.* Boston: Routledge and Kegan Paul, 1980.

———. "Elites and Non-Elites: The Possibilities and Their Side Effects." Andover, Mass.: Warner Modular, 1973.

Filipov, Vladimir A. (chairman, Info-Tsentr, Department of the Activities of the Soviet, Tiumen' Oblast Soviet of People's Deputies). Interview with the author, Tiumen', 26 July 1993.

First Book of Demographics for the Republics of the Former Soviet Union: 1951–1990. Shady Side, Md.: New World Demographics, 1992.

Fried, Robert C., and Francine F. Rabinovitz. *Comparative Urban Politics: A Performance Approach.* Englewood Cliffs, N.J.: Prentice-Hall, 1980.

Frieden, Jeffry. *Debt, Development, and Democracy: Modern Political Economy and Latin America, 1965–1985.* Princeton, N.J.: Princeton University Press, 1991.

Friedgut, Theodore. *Political Participation in the USSR*. Princeton, N.J.: Princeton University Press, 1979.

Gabrichidze, B. N. "Sovet, presidium, ispolkom: sootnoshenie i razgranichenie funktsii." *Sovetskoe gosudarstvo i pravo*, no. 3 (1991): 77–86.

Gaddy, Clifford. "Economic Performance and Policies in the Defense Industrial Regions of Russia." In Michael McFaul and Tova Perlmutter, eds., *Privatization, Conversion, and Enterprise Reform in Russia*, 103–36. Stanford, Calif.: Stanford University Center for International Security and Arms Control, 1994.

Geertz, Clifford. "Thick Description: Toward an Interpretive Theory of Culture." In Clifford Geertz, *The Interpretation of Cultures*, 3–30. New York: Basic Books, 1973.

Gimpelson, Vladimir, Darrell Slider, and Sergei Chrugov. "Political Tendencies in Russia's Regions: Evidence from the 1993 Parliamentary Elections." *Slavic Review* (Fall 1994): 711–32.

Gleason, Gregory. *Federalism and Nationalism: The Struggle for Republican Rights in the USSR*. Boulder, Colo.: Westview, 1990.

Gor'kovskaia pravda, Nizhnii Novgorod, 20 March 1990.

Gorbachev, Mikhail S. Speech to the Central Committee, 25 February 1986, as reported in *FBIS Daily Report*, 1–25.

"Gorbachev Sizes Up Restructuring." *CDSP* 40, no. 26 (27 July 1988): 7–11.

Gorkov, Evgenii (deputy-governor, Department of International Relations, Nizhnii Novgorod Oblast Administration). Interview with the author, Cambridge, Mass., May 1994.

Gorodetskaia, Natalia. "Irkutsk Refuses to Pay Taxes into the Federal Budget." *Nezavisimaia gazeta*, 22 May 1992, 2.

"Government Reorganization Plan Cited." *FBIS*, 10 July 1991.

Gourevitch, Peter. "International Trade, Domestic Coalitions, and Liberty: Comparative Responses to the Crisis of 1873–1896." *Journal of Interdisciplinary History* 8, no. 2 (1977): 281–313.

Granberg, Anatolii G. *Intensifikatsia ekonomicheskoi i mezhregional'noi integratsii*. Chetvertoe sovetsko-bolgarskoe rabochee soveshchanie. "Sovershenstvovanie form territorial'noi organizatsii proizvodstva." Novosibirsk, 1984.

———. *Sintez regional'nykh i narodnokhoziastvennykh modelei i zadach territorial'nogo sotsialno-ekonomicheskogo razvitiia*. Doklad, vtoroi sovetsko-zapadnogermanskii seminar. "Modelirovanie razvitiia territorial'nikh sotsialno-ekonomicheskikh sistem." Novosibirsk, 1983.

Granovetter, Mark. "Economic Action and Social Structure: The Problem of Embeddedness." *American Journal of Sociology* 91 (1985): 481–510.

Gurr, Tedd Robert, and M. McClelland. "Political Performance: A Twelve Nation Study." *Sage Professional Papers in Comparative Politics* 2, no. 1–18. Beverly Hills, Calif.: Sage, 1971.

Gustafson, Thane. *Crisis amid Plenty: The Politics of Soviet Energy under*

Brezhnev and Gorbachev. Princeton, N.J.: Princeton University Press, 1989.

Hahn, Jeffrey W. *Soviet Grassroots: Citizen Participation in Local Soviet Government.* Princeton, N.J.: Princeton University Press, 1988.

————. "Counter-Reformation in the Provinces: How Monolithic?" Paper prepared for the Annual Meeting of the American Association for the Advancement of Slavic Studies, Phoenix, Ariz., 19–22 November 1992.

————. "The Development of Local Legislatures in Russia: The Case of Yaroslavl'." Paper delivered at Conference on Democratization in Russia: The Development of Legislative Institutions. Harvard University, 29–31 October 1993.

————. "Local Politics and Political Power in Russia: The Case of Yaroslavl'." *Soviet Economy* 7, no. 4 (1991): 322–41.

Hall, Peter, and Rosemary Taylor. "Political Science and the Four New Institutionalisms." Paper presented at the Annual Meeting of the American Political Science Association, New York, September 1994.

Hardin, Russell. *Collective Action.* Baltimore, Md.: The Johns Hopkins University Press, 1982.

Helf, Gavin, and Jeffrey W. Hahn. "Old Dogs and New Tricks: Party Elites in the Russian Regional Elections of 1990." *Slavic Review* 51, no. 3 (Fall 1992): 511–30.

Higgins, Robert C. *Analysis for Financial Management.* 2d ed. Homewood, Ill.: Robert D. Irwin, 1989.

Higley, John, and Michael G. Burton. *Democratic Transitions and Democratic Breakdowns: The Elite Variable.* Austin: Texas Papers on Latin America, Working Papers of the Institute of Latin American Studies, University of Texas at Austin, Paper 88–103, 1988.

Higley, John, and Richard Gunther, eds. *Elites and Democratic Consolidation in Latin America and Southern Europe.* New York: Cambridge University Press, 1992.

Higley, John, G. Lowell Field, and Knut Groholt. *Elite Structure and Ideology: A Theory with Applications to Norway.* New York: Columbia University Press, 1976.

Hill, Ronald J. "The Development of Soviet Local Government Since Stalin's Death." In Everett M. Jacobs, ed., *Soviet Local Politics and Government,* 18–33. Boston: George Allen and Unwin, 1983.

Horne, Mari. "Political Origins of Corporatist Order: The Politics of Enterprise Reform." In Michael McFaul and Tova Perlmutter, eds., *Privatization, Conversion, and Enterprise Reform in Russia,* 85–102. Stanford, Calif.: Center for International Security and Arms Control, 1993.

Hough, Jerry F. "Public Attitudes toward Economic Reform and Democratization." *Post-Soviet Affairs* 10, no. 1 (Spring 1994): 1–37.

————. *The Soviet Prefects: The Local Party Organs in Industrial Decision-Making.* Cambridge, Mass.: Harvard University Press, 1969.

———. *The Soviet Union and Social Science Theory*. Cambridge, Mass.: Harvard University Press, 1977.

Hough, Jerry F., and Merle Fainsod. *How the Soviet Union Is Governed*. Cambridge, Mass.: Harvard University Press, 1979.

"How Close is Russia to Breaking Up?" *CDPSP* 44, no. 8 (25 March 1992): 1.

Hughes, James. "Regionalism in Russia: The Rise and Fall of Siberian Agreement," *Europe-Asia Studies* 46, no. 7 (1994): 1133–61.

Hunter, Floyd. *Community Power Structure*. Chapel Hill: North Carolina University Press, 1953.

Huntington, Samuel P. "The Goals of Development." In Samuel P. Huntington and Myron Weiner, eds., *Understanding Political Development*, 3–32. Boston: Little, Brown, 1987.

———. *Political Order in Changing Societies*. New Haven, Conn.: Yale University Press, 1968.

———. *The Third Wave: Democratization in the Late Twentieth Century*. Norman, Okla.: University of Oklahoma Press, 1991.

Informatsionnyi biulleten' Saratovskii oblastnoi sovet narodnykh deputatov. Saratov: Saratovskaia oblastnaia tipografiia, December 1991–December 1992.

Inkeles, Alex, and Raymond A. Bauer. *The Soviet Citizen*. Cambridge, Mass.: Harvard University Press, 1959.

Interview by the author with deputies from the Saratov Oblast Soviet of People's Deputies, April 1993.

Interview by the author with the Economic Prognosis Department, Tiumen' Oblast Administration. Tiumen', August 1993.

Interview by the author with the Head of Finance Department, Saratov Oblast Administration, Saratov, 23 April 1993.

Interview by the author with the International Finance Corporation representative in Nizhnii Novgorod who preferred not to be identified. Nizhnii Novgorod, November 1992.

Izvestiia, 9 January 1992.

K soiuzu suverennykh narodov: sbornik dokumentov KPSS, zakonodatel'nykh aktov, deklaratsii, obrashchenii i prezidentskikh ukazov, posviashchenykh probleme natsional'no-gosudarstvennogo suvereniteta. Moskva: Institut teorii i istorii sotsializma TsK KPSS, 1991.

Karl, Terry Lynn. "Dilemmas of Democratization in Latin America." *Comparative Politics* 23 (1990): 1–21.

Kasoff, Allen. "The Administered Society: Totalitarianism without Terror." *World Politics* 16, no. 4 (1964): 558–75.

Katzenstein, Peter J. *Corporatism and Change: Austria, Switzerland, and the Politics of Industy*. Ithaca, N.Y.: Cornell University Press, 1984.

———. *Small States in World Markets: Industrial Policy in Europe*. Ithaca, N.Y.: Cornell University Press, 1985.

226

Kibirskii, Dimitri (Department for Social and Economic Problems and International Relations, Saratov Oblast Soviet of People's Deputies). Interview with the author, Saratov, 27 April 1993.

King, Anthony. "Overload: Problems of Governing in the 1970s." *Political Studies* 23, nos. 2–3 (September 1975): 284–96.

Kommersant-Daily, no. 133, Moscow, 16 July 1993.

Kommunist. Saratov.

Komsomol'skaia pravda, Moscow, 14 March 1991.

Kopiilov, D. I., V. Y. Kniazev, and V. F. Retunskii. *Goroda nashego kraia: Tiumen'*. Sverdlovsk: Sredni-Ural'skoe Knizhnoe izdatel'stvo, 1986.

Kornai, Janos. *The Socialist System: The Political Economy of Communism*. Princeton, N.J.: Princeton University Press, 1992.

Kozlov, Vasilii (chair of Economic Prognosis Department, Nizhnii Novgorod Oblast Administration). Interview with the author, Nizhnii Novgorod, 10 May 1993.

Krestianinov, Evgenii (chairman of the Nizhnii Novogorod Oblast Soviet of People's Deputies). Interview with the author, Nizhnii Novgorod, 18 December 1992.

Krestianinov, Evgenii (chair of the Nizhnii Novgorod Oblast Soviet of People's Deputies). Interview with the author, Nizhnii Novgorod, 19 December 1992.

Kux, Stephen. *Soviet Federalism: A Comparative Perspective*. Boulder, Colo.: Westview, 1990.

Layard, Richard. "Stabilization versus Reform? Russia's First Year." In Olivier Blanchard, Maxim Boycko, et al., eds., *Post-Communist Reform: Pain and Progress*, 15–36. Cambridge, Mass.: MIT Press, 1993.

Lijphart, Arend. *The Politics of Accommodation: Pluralism and Democracy in the Netherlands*. Berkeley: University of California Press, 1968.

Lijphart, Arend, and Bernard Grofman. "Choosing an Electoral System." In Arend Lijphart and Bernard Grofman, eds., *Choosing an Electoral System: Issues and Alternatives*, 3–12. New York: Praeger, 1984.

Lincoln, W. Bruce. *The Conquest of a Continent: Siberia and the Russians*. New York: Random House, 1994.

Linz, Juan. "The Perils of Presidentialism." In Larry Diamond and Marc F. Plattner, eds., *The Global Resurgence of Democracy*, 108–26. Baltimore, Md.: The Johns Hopkins University Press, 1993. Also in *Journal of Democracy* 1 (Winter 1990).

Lipset, Seymour Martin. *Political Man: The Social Bases of Politics*. New York: Doubleday, 1950. Reprinted, 1963.

Lisitsyn, Anatolii (Head of Administration, Yaroslavl' oblast). Interview with the author, Yaroslavl', 15 April 1993.

Malia, Martin. "Russia's Democratic Future: Hope against Hope." *Problems of Post-Communism* (Fall 1994): 32–36.

March, James G., and Johan P. Olson. *Rediscovering Institutions: The Organizational Basis of Politics*. New York: Free Press, 1989.

Marnie, Sheila. "Warning Strike at Defense Industrial Plants." *RFE/RL*, 30 July 1993.

McAuley, Mary. "Politics, Economics, and Elite Realignment in Russia: A Regional Perspective." *Soviet Economy* 8, no. 1 (January–March 1992): 46–88.

McFaul, Michael. "Agency Problems in the Privatization of Large Enterprises in Russia." In Michael McFaul and Tova Perlmutter, eds., *Privatization, Conversion, and Enterprise Reform in Russia*, 39–56. Stanford, Calif.: Center for International Security and Arms Control, 1993.

Michels, Robert. *Political Parties: A Sociological Study of the Oligarchical Tendencies of Modern Democracy*. New York: Dover, 1911. Reprint, 1959.

Mills, C. Wright. *The Power Elite*. New York: Oxford University Press, 1956.

Milner, Helen V. *Resisting Protectionism: Global Industries and the Politics of International Trade*. Princeton, N.J.: Princeton University Press, 1988.

Moore, Barrington, Jr. *Social Origins of Dictatorship and Democracy: Lord and Peasant in the Making of the Modern World*. Boston: Beacon, 1967.

Mosca, Gaetano. *The Ruling Class*. Edited by Hannah D. Kahn. Translated by Arthur Livingstone. Westport, Conn.: Greenwood, 1939. Reprint, 1980.

Moses, Joel C. "Saratov and Volgograd, 1990–1992: A Tale of Two Russian Provinces." In Jeffry W. Hahn and Theodore Friedgut, eds., *Local Power and Post-Soviet Politics*, 96–137. Armonk, N.Y.: M. E. Sharpe, 1994.

Naishul, Vitali. "Institutional Development in the USSR." *Cato Journal* 11, no. 3 (Winter 1992): 489–96.

Narodnoe Khoziastvo RSFSR 1989. Goskomstat.

Naustdalslid, J. "A Multi-level Approach to the Study of Center-Periphery Systems and Socio-Economic Change." *Journal of Peace Studies* 14, no. 3, 203–22, as cited in Ronan Paddison, *The Fragmented State: The Political Geography of Power*. Oxford: Blackwell, 1983.

"Nemtsov Resigns as Yeltsin's Representative in Nizhnii Novgorod." *RFE/RL*, no. 75, 20 April 1994.

Nemtsov, Boris (governor, Nizhnii Novgorod Oblast Administration). Speech at Nizhnii Novgorod Conference on Regional Aspects of Economic Reform, 17 December 1992.

Nezavisimaia gazeta, 21 January 1994.

Nizhegorodskaia pravda, 25 January 1992, 5 March 1992.

North, Douglass C. *Institutions, Institutional Change and Economic Performance*. New York: Cambridge University Press, 1990.

Novoe vremia, no. 12 (March 1992).

O'Donnell, Guillermo, and Philippe Schmitter. *Transitions from Authoritarian Rule: Tentative Conclusions about Uncertain Democracies*. Baltimore, Md.: The Johns Hopkins University Press, 1986.

"O glavnykh zamechaniiakh k proektu. Interv'iu s professorom, rukovoditelem gruppoi ekspertov Konstitutsionnoi komissii RSFSR V. Zor'kinym." *Konstitutsionnyi vestnik*, no. 8 (oktiabr' 1991): 12–13. Moskva: Konstitutsionnaia komissiia RSFSR.

"Ob organizatsii pervoi ocheredi regional'noi informatsionno-kompiuternoi seti Tiumenskoi oblasti," no. 208 (25 November 1992).

Obriadina, Irina D. (head of the Protocol Section, Nizhnii Novgorod Oblast Soviet of People's Deputies). Interview with the author, Nizhnii Novgorod, 7 May 1993.

Olson, Mancur. *The Logic of Collective Action: Public Goods and the Theory of Groups*. Cambridge, Mass.: Harvard University Press, 1971.

Ordeshook, Peter C. "Institutions and Incentives: The Prospects for Russian Democracy." Typescript. California Institute of Technology, 1994.

Oseichuk, Vladimir (chair of the Tiumen' oblast soviet committee on the work of the soviet). Interview with the author, Tiumen', 19 July 1993.

Ostrom, Elinor. "Constituting Social Capital and Collective Action." Indiana University Workshop in Political Theory and Policy Analysis, Indiana, 1993.

———. *Governing the Commons: The Evolution of Institutions for Collective Action*. New York: Cambridge University Press, 1990.

Pappas, James L., and Mark Hirschey. *Managerial Economics*. 5th ed. New York: Dryden, 1987.

Petrov, Nikolai V. *FBIS*, 9 June 1995.

Pipes, Richard. *The Formation of the Soviet Union: Communism and Nationalism 1917–1923*. Rev. ed. New York: Atheneum, 1964; originally Cambridge, Mass.: Harvard University Press, 1954.

Plato. *The Republic*. Translated by G.M.A. Grube. Indianapolis, Ind.: Hackett, 1974.

Pokazateli sotsial'nogo razvitiia respublik, kraev i oblastei Rossiiskoi federatsii. Moskva: Respublikanskii informatsionno-izdatel'skii tsentr, 1992.

Pokazateli ekonomocheskogo razvitiia respublik, kraev i oblastei Rossiiskoi federatsii. Moskva: Respublikanskii informatsionno-izdatel'skii tsentr, 1992.

Polanyi, Karl. *The Great Transformation: The Political and Economic Origins of Our Time*. Boston, Mass.: Beacon Hill, 1957.

Powell, G. Bingham. *Contemporary Democracies: Participation, Stability, and Violence*. Cambridge, Mass.: Harvard University Press, 1982.

"Protokol namerenii o sotrudnichestve." Saratovskii oblastnoi sovet narodnykh deputatov, Spring 1993.

Puffer, Sheila, ed. *The Russian Management Revolution*. Armonk, N.Y.: M. E. Sharpe, 1992.

Putnam, Robert D. *The Comparative Study of Political Elites*. Englewood Cliffs, N.J.: Prentice-Hall, 1976.

Putnam, Robert D., with Robert Leonardi and Raffaella Nanetti. *Making Democracy Work: Civic Traditions in Modern Italy*. Princeton, N.J.: Princeton University Press, 1993.

Putnam, Robert D., Robert Leonardi, Raffaella Nanetti, and Franco Pavoncello. "Explaining Institutional Success: The Case of Italian Regional Government." *American Political Science Review* 77 (March 1983): 55–74.

Radkey, Oliver Henry. *The Election to the Russian Constituent Assembly of 1917*. Cambridge, Mass.: Harvard University Press, 1950.

Raleigh, Donald. *Revolution on the Volga: 1917 in Saratov*. Ithaca, N.Y.: Cornell University Press, 1986.

Regini, Mario. "The Conditions for Political Exchange: How Concertation Emerged and Collapsed in Italy and Great Britain." In John Goldethorpe, ed., *Order and Conflict in Contemporary Capitalism*, 124–42. New York: Oxford University Press, 1984.

"Regional Representatives Discussed." *FBIS*, 10 August 1991.

"Regional'naia ekonomika—zelenyi tsvet." *Sovetskaia Sibir'*, 3 July 1991.

Reisinger, William, and John Willerton. "Elite Mobility in the Locales: Toward a Modified Patronage Model." In David Lane, ed., *Elites and Political Power in the USSR*, 99–126. London: Edward Elger, 1988.

Resheniia malogo soveta Yaroslavskogo oblastnogo soveta narodnykh deputatov, March–November 1992. Yaroslavl' Oblast Department of Soviet Affairs (*spravochniki* [handbooks]).

Riasanovsky, Nicholas. *A History of Russia*. 4th ed. New York: Oxford University Press, 1984.

Robbins, Richard C. *The Tsar's Viceroys: Russian Provincial Government in the Last Years of the Empire*. Ithaca, N.Y.: Cornell University Press, 1987.

Roeder, Philip. *Red Sunset: The Failure of Soviet Politics*. Princeton, N.J.: Princeton University Press, 1993.

Rogowski, Ronald. *Commerce and Coalitions*. Princeton, N.J.: Princeton University Press, 1989.

Romanov, Vitali (People's Deputy, Tiumen' Oblast Soviet). Interview with the author, Tiumen', 22 July 1993.

Ruble, Blair A. "The Applicability of Corporatist Models to the Study of Soviet Politics: The Case of the Trade Unions." *The Carl Beck Papers in Russian and East European Studies*. Paper No. 303. Pittsburgh, Pa.: University of Pittsburgh Press, 1983.

———. *Money Sings: The Changing Politics of Urban Space in Post-Soviet Yaroslavl'*. Washington, D.C.: Woodrow Wilson Center Press with Cambridge University Press, 1995.

"Russian Federation Defense Conversion: Two Enterprises in Transition." Case studies prepared by the International Finance Corporation and Company Assistance, August 1992.

Rutland, Peter. *The Politics of Economic Stagnation in the Soviet Union: The Role of Local Party Organs in Economic Management*. New York: Cambridge University Press, 1993.

Samuels, Richard J. *The Business of the Japanese State: Energy Markets in Com-

parative Historical Perspective. Ithaca, N.Y.: Cornell University Press, 1987.

Saratovskie vesti. Saratov. 28 February, 1992.

———, 20 June 1992.

———, 24 June 1992.

———, 16–20 July 1992.

Saratovskii oblastnoi sovet narodnykh deputatov. Informatsionnyi biulleten' no. 6, "O trinadsatoi sessii Saratavskogo oblastnogo soveta narodnykh deputatov dvadtsat' pervogo sozyva," Saratov, 1993.

Schmitter, Philippe C. "Interest Intermediation and Regime Governability in Contemporary Western Europe and North America." In Suzanne Berger, ed., *Organizing Interests in Western Europe*, 285–327. New York: Cambridge University Press, 1981.

———. "Still the Century of Corporatism?" *The Review of Politics* 36 (1974): 85–131.

Sharlet, Robert. "Russian Constitutional Crisis: Law and Politics under Yeltsin." *Post-Soviet Affairs* 9, no. 4 (October–December 1993): 314–36.

Sheinis, Viktor (member of the Constitutional Commission, Russian Federation Supreme Soviet). Interview with the author, Moscow, 10 March 1992.

Shepsle, Kenneth, and Barry Weingast. "Structure-induced Equilibrium and Legislative Choice." *Public Choice* 37 (1981), as cited in Robert Bates, "Contra Contractarianism: Some Reflections on the New Institutionalism." *Politics and Society* 16, nos. 2–3 (1988): 387–401.

Shleifer, Andrei, and Maxim Boycko. "The Politics of Russian Privatization." In Olivier Blanchard, Maxim Boycko, et al., eds., *Post-Communist Reform: Pain and Progress*, 37–80. Cambridge, Mass.: MIT Press, 1993.

Shumakhanov, Yurii (Deputy of the Yaroslavl' oblast soviet). Interview with the author, Yaroslavl', April 1993.

"Siberians Push for Economic Autonomy." *CDPSP* 44, no. 13 (1992): 9–10.

Skilling, Gordon. "Interest Groups and Communist Politics Revisited." *World Politics* 36, no. 1 (1983): 1–27.

Skilling, Gordon, and Franklyn Griffiths, eds. *Interest Groups in Soviet Politics.* Princeton, N.J.: Princeton University Press, 1971.

Slider, Darrell. "Federalism, Discord, and Accommodation: Intergovernmental Relations in Post-Soviet Russia." In Jeffrey Hahn and Theodore Friedgut, eds., *Local Power and Post-Soviet Politics*, 239–69. Armonk, N.Y.: M. E. Sharpe, 1994.

Smith, Regina. "Political Strategy in the Transition: The Case of Saratov." In Timothy Colton and Jerry Hough, eds., *The Russian Elections of 1993.* Washington, D.C.: The Brookings Institution, forthcoming.

Solnick, Steven. "The Breakdown of Hierarchies in the Soviet Union and China: A Neo-Institutional Perspective." *World Politics* 48, no. 2 (January 1996): 209–38.

Spector, Paul E. *Summated Rating Scale Construction: An Introduction.* Newbury Park, Calif.: Sage, 1992.

"Spisok mezhregional'nykh assotsiatsii po RSFSR," 13 March 1991. Produced by the Supreme Soviet's Committee of Inter-republic Relations and Regional Policy provided to the author by the committee's staff in April 1992.

Starodubrovskaia, Irina. "Attitudes of Enterprise Managers toward Market Transitions." In Michael McFaul and Tova Perlmutter, eds., *Privatization, Conversion and Enterprise Reform in Russia*, 57–68. Stanford, Calif.: Center for International Security and Arms Control, 1993.

Starr, Frederick S. *Decentralization and Self-Government in Russia, 1830–1870*. Princeton, N.J.: Princeton University Press, 1972.

Stipak, Brian. "Citizen Satisfaction with Urban Services: Potential Misuses as a Performance Indicator." *Public Administration Review* 39 (January–February 1979): 46–52.

Stone, Randall. *Satellites and Commissars: Strategy and Conflict in the Politics of Soviet-Bloc Trade*. Princeton, N.J.: Princeton University Press, 1996.

Sukunin, Valerii (head of Foreign Trade Department, Saratov Oblast Administration). Interview with the author, Saratov, 15 April 1993.

Tarasov, Aleksei. "Krasnoiarsk Territory Wants to Become the Yenisei Republic." *Izvestiia*, 25 February 1992, 2, as summarized in *CDPSP* 44, no. 8 (25 March 1992): 4–5.

"The Russian Federation of Independent States." *Rossiiskaia gazeta*, 31 January 1992, 1.

Tiumenskaia pravda, Tiumen', 15 April 1990.

———, 16 May 1990.

———, 24 September 1991.

———, 1–9 October 1991.

Tiumenskie izvestiia, Tiumen', 6 October 1991.

———, 17 October 1991.

———, 29 November 1991.

Tocqueville, Alexis de. *Democracy in America*. Edited by J. P. Mayer. Translated by G. Lawrence. Garden City, N.Y.: Anchor, 1969.

Treisman, Daniel. "The Politics of Intergovernmental Transfers in Post-Soviet Russia," *British Journal of Political Science* 26 (1996): 299–335.

Ukaz prezidenta RSFSR. "O razvitii Tiumenskoi oblasti," no. 122, 19 September 1991.

Ukaz prezidenta RSFSR, no. 194 (November 1991).

Ukhaniov, Viktor (first deputy chair of the Saratov Oblast Soviet). Interview with the author, Saratov, 28 April 1993.

Urban, Michael E. *More Power to the Soviets: The Democratic Evolution in the USSR*. United Kingdom: Edward Elgar, 1990.

Varukhin, Vladimir (Presidential representative). Interview with the author, Yaroslavl', 5 January 1993.

Vasiliev, Vsevolod (former director of the Institute of Legislation and Comparative Law). Interview with the author, Moscow, 10 February 1992.

Vaskov, Sergei Timofeevich (head of Sector, Interregional Affairs Committee, Russian Federation Supreme Soviet). Interview with the author, March 1992.

Vedomosti verkhovnogo soveta RSFSR, September 1991–March 1992.

Veselov, Aleksandr (chair of the Yaroslavl' Oblast Soviet of People's Deputies). Interview with the author, Yaroslavl', 6 January 1993.

Vestnik oblastnogo soveta narodnykh deputatov 24, no. 15 (December 1992).

Vestnik oblastnogo soveta narodnykh deputatov. Tiumen': Tiumenskaia oblastnaia tipografiia, December 1991–November 1992.

Vneshneekonomicheskie sviazi RSFSR. Moskva: Goskomstat Respublikanskii informatsionno-izdatel'skii tsentr, 1991.

Wade, Robert. *Governing the Market: Economic Theory and the Role of Government in East Asian Industrialization*. Princeton, N.J.: Princeton University Press, 1990.

Wallich, Christine I. *Fiscal Decentralization: Intergovernmental Relations in Russia*. Studies of Economies in Transformation, Paper No. 6. Washington, D.C.: World Bank, 1992.

———, ed. *Russia and the Challenge of Fiscal Federalism*. Washington, D.C.: The World Bank, 1995.

Weaver, Kent R., and Bert A. Rockman. "Assessing the Effects of Institutions." In R. Kent Weaver and Bert A. Rockman, eds., *Do Institutions Matter?: Government Capabilities in the United States and Abroad*, 1–41. Washington, D.C.: The Brookings Institution, 1993.

Young, John F. "Institutions, Elites, and Local Politics in Russia: The Case of Omsk." In Jeffrey W. Hahn and Theodore Friedgut, eds., *Local Power and Post-Soviet Politics*, 138–61. Armonk, N.Y.: M. E. Sharpe, 1994.

"Zaiavlenie o sessii Tiumenskogo oblastnogo soveta narodnykh deputatov." *Tiumenskaia pravda*, 16 May 1990.

"Zakliuchitel'noe slovo general'nogo sekretaria Tsk KPSS, M.S. Gorbachev na plenume Tsk KPSS, 28 ianvaria, 1987 g." *Izvestia*, 30 January 1987.

Zharikov, Viktor (chair of the Department of Foreign Economic Activity, Yaroslavl' Oblast Administration). Interview with the author, Yaroslavl', 5 January 1993.

Zimmerman, William. "Mobilized Participation and Soviet Dictatorship." In James Millar, ed., *Politics, Work, and Daily Life in the USSR: A Survey of Former Soviet Citizens*, 332–53. New York: Cambridge University Press, 1987.

Zisk, Kimberly Marten. "The Foreign Policy Preferences of Russian Defense Industrialists: Integration or Isolation?" In Celeste A. Wallander, ed., *The Sources of Russian Conduct after the Cold War*, 95–120. Boulder, Colo.: Westview, 1996.

Zolotoe kol'tso, Yaroslavl'.

Zvonkova, Zoia (chief specialist, Committee on Education, Tiumen' Oblast Administration). Interview with the author, Tiumen', 27 July 1993.

* Index *

About the Author

KATHRYN STONER-WEISS is Assistant Professor of Politics
and International Affairs at Princeton University.